Henry Flagler

Visionary of the Gilded Age

by

Sidney Walter Martin

Tailored Tours Publications
Box 22861
Lake Buena Vista, Florida 32830

Acknowledgements

In developing *Henry Flagler, Visionary of the Gilded Age*, we are grateful to many people. First, of course, to Sidney Walter Martin for his thoughtful and masterful study of Henry Flagler's life and times. Mr. Martin had the opportunity to directly interview many of Flagler's relatives and contemporaries, as well as identifying a number of the key historic documents. The craftsmanship and skill with which he developed his study were exceptional. Working from the Martin work, which has been out of print for many years, key staff members at the Flagler Museum provided exceptional cooperation in the creation of *Henry Flagler, Visionary of the Gilded Age*.

We are particularly grateful to the entire staff of the Flagler Museum in Palm Beach, Florida, for their efforts to bring to life Henry Flagler and his era. Our special thanks to the Flagler Museum's Executive Director, John M. Blades. In his introduction to this book, he clearly places Henry Flagler in his role as a visionary of the Gilded Age. Four members of the Flagler Museum's staff also contributed greatly to the development of this book. Jessica Johnston, Public Affairs Director, worked tirelessly to ensure that current research and information enhanced, supported, confirmed, or corrected materials in the original study. No compliments are too great for her exceptional efforts. Sandra Barghini, Chief Curator, and Amy R. Shook, Education Director, were also key experts in the review and, where appropriate, revision to the work. And, importantly, thanks to Sharon A. Thomas, Flagler Museum Shop Manager, who strongly emphasized the need to bring this book to light.

The Martin study was partially sponsored by the University of Georgia Press and its Alumni Association. It was published in 1949 and in 1977 under the title *Florida's Flagler* (©copyright, University of Georgia Press, all rights reserved). We are grateful to several members of the Press, particularly Tom Payton, Assistant Marketing Manager, for working closely with us to ensure the rights leading to the development of *Henry Flagler, Visionary of the Gilded Age*.

Personal and professional thanks go to Sara Lee for her exceptional editing efforts; to Joan Morris and Joanna Norman of the Florida Photographic Archives; and to Mark Kellum of Success by Design for the cover graphics.

Cover Graphics include: Marble Hall (color) at Whitehall (inset);
Florida East Coast Railway train crossing the Florida Keys; and
two images of Henry Flagler, one in 1870 (l) and one in 1909 (r)

ISBN: 0-9631241-1-0

Introduction

Henry Flagler and the Gilded Age

When Sidney Walter Martin's biography of Henry Morrison Flagler was first published in 1949, there were still individuals living who had direct knowledge of Flagler's many impressive achievements. But, today, few seem to know much at all of Flagler, or of the time in which he lived. However, what we have gained in the last four and a half decades since this biography was first published is some perspective on a truly fascinating and important period in the development of American Culture, America's Gilded Age (1865 through 1929), and Flagler's role in it.

As the twentieth century draws to a close and the twenty-first is about to begin, it is clear now that through foresight and deliberate action, the titans of industry and commerce of America's Gilded Age, like Flagler, created a wholly new American Culture. The new American Culture has survived throughout the twentieth century and appears likely to be not only America's Culture in the twenty-first century, but very likely the dominant culture worldwide.

Enjoying the incredible wealth generated during the industrial age, Flagler and his contemporaries thought of themselves as the new Venetians, and like the Venetians of the Italian Renaissance, they were self-made businessmen *and* society leaders. They set out to meld America's prodigious technological abilities with the great heritage and tradition of nearly three millennia of Western Culture. Through their clear vision and certainty of purpose, America was transformed from an agrarian and rural society to a corporate and urban society.

Of the many forms corporations took in American Gilded Age Society, one is virtually unique to America even now: the nonprofit corporation. Using the wealth and know-how generated by American technology, Flagler and his contemporaries established public works systems, hospitals, universities, libraries, museums, and charities, in order to benefit society in general, and to enhance opportunities for individual Americans.

*S*o great and pervasive is the legacy of America's Gilded Age and its leaders, that it is virtually invisible and has certainly been taken for granted, especially in the last half of the twentieth century. But, the legacy of America's Gilded Age and its great figures, like Henry Morrison Flagler, is the essence of what we think of as truly American Culture. And, as we move into a new century and millennium, perhaps it is time we reacquaint ourselves with the key figures and events of America's Gilded Age, for their legacy will certainly continue well into the new millennium.

January, 1998

John M. Blades
Executive Director
Flagler Museum
Palm Beach, Florida

Table of Contents

Family Tree

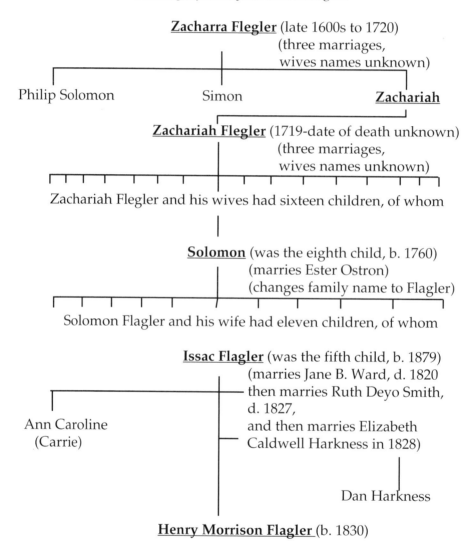

Zacharra Flegler (late 1600s to 1720)
(three marriages,
wives names unknown)

Philip Solomon   Simon   **Zachariah**

Zachariah Flegler (1719-date of death unknown)
(three marriages,
wives names unknown)

Zachariah Flegler and his wives had sixteen children, of whom

Solomon (was the eighth child, b. 1760)
(marries Ester Ostron)
(changes family name to Flagler)

Solomon Flagler and his wife had eleven children, of whom

Issac Flagler (was the fifth child, b. 1879)
(marries Jane B. Ward, d. 1820
then marries Ruth Deyo Smith,
d. 1827,
and then marries Elizabeth
Caldwell Harkness in 1828)

Ann Caroline
(Carrie)

Dan Harkness

Henry Morrison Flagler (b. 1830)

1. *Heritage and Youth*

*H*e was a lad of 14 years—tall and handsome. His eyes were gray, and his hair was light brown, blending perfectly with his ruddy complexion. There was a shy but determined look on his face. The boy was dressed in coarse homespun clothes. In his hand he held a bulging carpetbag which contained all of his possessions. Hidden in his safest pocket was a little money to be used for his travels. It was October, 1844, when Henry Morrison Flagler said farewell to his parents in western New York and began his journey to the edge of the Western Reserve in northern Ohio. It was a long distance for a boy to travel alone. Since there was not much this ambitious youth could find to do around his home, he had persuaded his parents to let him try to find his future in more promising surroundings.

*R*epublic, Ohio was his destination.[1] For several months he had urged his parents to let him go there to join his half brother, Daniel M. Harkness. The fact that Henry would not be entirely unknown in Ohio made his departure a little more bearable for his mother. Young Henry was eager to test himself in the game of life. His father, Isaac Flagler, a poorly paid preacher-farmer, ministered to a small Presbyterian congregation nine miles from Medina, New York. He had served several other churches in western New York and northern Ohio. Henry had become tired of moving from one poor congregation to another. It was always the same story: hard work and little remuneration. He disliked poverty and dreamed of the day when he might have some of the luxuries money could buy. Despite the wishes of his father that he remain on the farm, Henry gave little consideration to doing so. The farm had no attraction for him. He was too ambitious to live in such circumstances.[2]

*T*he frugal home Henry was leaving had been established from a long line of Flaglers. His ancestry was traced to an immigrant who came to America in the early part of the 18th century from Franconia in the German Palatinate. The Wars of Louis XIV, which devastated that region, caused a great number of people to lose their property and flee to England, among them one Zacharra Flegler (as the name was then

7

spelled). Zacharra Flegler spent several years in Walworth, England, with other Palatines working as a carpenter.[3] Their stay in England was temporary. They saved what money was possible and with some governmental aid from England, they crossed the Atlantic in several groups.

$\mathcal{F}$legler, with his wife, two small sons, and a baby daughter, left England for America in January, 1710. This company of Palatines, led by the Reverend John Tribbeko, filled 10 small ships. The horrors of the six month trip across the ocean were indescribable. Many of the voyagers died, one of the victims being the wife of Zacharra Flegler. The company finally reached New York in June, 1710, and proceeded up the Hudson River where they established settlements on both banks of the river in Columbia and Ulster counties. Only the river separated the newly created towns which were called East Camp and West Camp. Of the Palatines who settled in this area, the majority built homes and became permanently located. The more adventurous minority group drifted into Dutchess County to a territory owned by Henry Beekman, a German, who sold them land on favorable terms. Zacharra Flegler was attracted to Dutchess County, but did not leave until he had courted and married a second time. The wedding took place in August, 1710, less than six months after the death of the first Mrs. Flegler. His second wife died shortly and, in May, 1711, he married for the third time. Flegler died in March, 1720, having established firmly the roots of what was destined to become a prominent New York family. All of the American Flaglers are descended from one or the other of the three sons of Zacharra Flegler— Philip Solomon, Simon, and Zachariah.[4]

$\mathcal{Z}$achariah Flegler was the youngest son, having been born in 1719 to Zacharra's third wife. He lived most of his life in the town of Clinton, in Dutchess County, New York—probably in the portion of the county which was set off in 1821 as the town of Pleasant Valley. Zachariah Flegler married three times. To Zachariah Flegler and his three wives were born 16 children, most of whom grew up and settled in Dutchess County. Solomon Flegler, the eighth child, was born on May 8, 1760 and subsequently became the grandfather of Henry Morrison Flagler.

$\mathcal{S}$olomon made at least one contribution to the family. He changed the spelling of the name Flegler to Flagler. The revision was readily accepted by all the relatives. Solomon lived in Dutchess County all of his life with the gradually increasing Flagler clan. Though not as prolific as his father, Solomon and his wife, Ester Ostron, had 11 children. Their fifth child, Isaac Flagler, was born on April 22, 1787. He became the father of Henry, who would grow up to become an oil magnate and railroad builder.[5]

*I*saac Flagler spent his early life at home in the Pleasant Valley area. Although his formal education was scant, he was a widely read man. Isaac heeded the call to preach. He was ordained as a Presbyterian minister in 1810. On October 7, 1813, he married his childhood sweetheart, Jane B. Ward. Isaac, an able minister and a good farmer, continued to live in Dutchess County until after his wife's death on October 1, 1820. There were no children from the marriage, and since there were no responsibilities which tied him to his home in Dutchess County, Isaac decided to go to a different section of the state and start over. He accepted a call to Milton, New York, and began his ministry there in 1821. He soon became attracted to one of his parishioners, Ruth Deyo Smith, and married her on May 10, 1824. They spent three happy years together, and one child, named Ann Caroline but called Carrie, resulted from the union. Mrs. Flagler died on September 25, 1827. For the second time in his life, Isaac Flagler was left a widower. This time he also had the responsibility of raising a young daughter. Within a few months he met a young widow, Elizabeth Caldwell Harkness. Their acquaintance led to a short courtship and they married in the fall of 1828.[6]

*E*lizabeth Flagler , too, had been married twice before. Her first husband was Hugh Morrison of Washington County, New York. Her second husband was David Harkness, a physician, of Bellevue, Ohio who died in 1825. The Harkness family was large and prominent, and would later play an important part in the life of Henry Flagler. After the death of her second husband, Elizabeth took her only child, a young son, Daniel M. Harkness, to Salem, New York, where she made her home with relatives. It was while she was living in Salem that she met Isaac Flagler, who at the time was serving a pastorate in Seneca County. They started life together with a ready-made family, consisting of young Dan Harkness and little Carrie Flagler. From all indications, they were extremely happy. Shortly after their marriage, they moved to Hopewell, New York, a small town not far from Canandaigua. It was in Hopewell that Henry Morrison Flagler was born on January 2, 1830.[7] At the time, Carrie was five and Dan was eight. A new baby in the family was a novelty for them both. The rural congregation at Hopewell rejoiced with the parents, and many gifts were brought to the minister's home when the baby arrived. The child was named for Henry Flagler, an uncle, and for Hugh Morrison, Mrs. Flagler's first husband.

*B*aby Henry's father was proud of his new son. He planned to interest the boy in remaining on the farm and following in his footsteps as a minister. However, as Henry grew older he showed other inclinations. Henry and his half brother, Daniel Harkness, liked each other. They became very companionable, despite the eight year difference in their ages. As Dan reached his early teens he became restless at home. He often talked with his mother about returning to his birthplace in northern Ohio. There were Harkness relatives in both Bellevue and Republic, Ohio. His mother had no particular objection other than the fact that she thought that her son was too young to be so far from parental influence. After much discussion she persuaded him to defer his plans until he was a little older.

*F*inally in 1837 the opportunity for which young Harkness had wished arrived. Isaac Flagler was called to the ministry of a rural church not far from Toledo, Ohio, and he accepted.[8] Dan was 15 years old. Instead of going to Toledo with the family he was allowed to proceed to Bellevue where he was given a job with a relative in the firm of Chapman and Harkness. Several years later he went to Republic, Ohio, where he was employed as a salesman in the store of L. G. Harkness and Company.[9] The boy liked his work in Republic. He never went back to live with his mother and stepfather.[10]

*T*he Flaglers' sojourn in Ohio was short. Within two years, they decided to return to New York. Isaac accepted a call as pastor of a rural church nine miles from Medina. Carrie and Henry were enrolled in the country school, but the latter followed closely the success of his half brother in Republic. Occasionally a letter came from Dan telling how well he was doing. It was not long before Mrs. Flagler realized that young Henry wanted to follow her other son, Dan, and make his way alone. The pinch of poverty at home spurred Henry on in his determination. He became restless and dissatisfied. Although he neglected his school work, he did finish eighth grade before dropping out. Henry worked at several odd jobs, but he did not seem particularly suited for any of them. For a time he worked as a deck hand on one of the Erie Canal boats running out of Medina; but that, too, was far from what he liked. He decided that he would not be denied a chance in life.

*H*enry was eager to satisfy a desire he had had since he was old enough to realize the economic situation in which he and his family were living. Henry had the desire to make money. His immature mind had long pondered the thought. Young Henry was confident and he was not concerned about failure. Henry knew he could succeed if given the opportunity. He also knew that an opportunity would not present itself as long as he remained at home. In some respects the boy hated to leave. He was genuinely fond of his sister and his parents. Henry knew little about northern Ohio other than that Dan Harkness had written that Henry would like it. Dan had also written that there were opportunities in which Henry would be interested. Mrs. Flagler had lived in Bellevue and Milan, Ohio. Although she knew little about Republic, she realized that her older son, Dan, would take a brotherly interest in young Henry.

*I*t was a chilly fall day when Henry received his last-minute instructions as he stood at the gate of the fence encircling his father's modest home. Signs of a cold winter were beginning to appear. He assured his parents that he was thoroughly familiar with the route he was to take. He would walk nine miles to Medina. He did not mind walking,[11] as there was no other means of getting there. He knew the route and had walked it many times before. Henry gave his parents a fond farewell, then turned slowly and started down the little path leading from the house. Of all his qualities, Henry's ambition and energy were among the most outstanding. Despite a tinge of sadness over leaving his parents, his heart must certainly have been full on that October day when he tramped onto a dirt road and into his adventurous future. Whether this day or a day 68 years later when he completed his life's greatest achievement gave him the biggest thrill was never known.

Henry Flagler's
Early Business Career

1844   Deckhand on an Erie Canal boats
Medina, New York
age 14

1845   Clerk in the L. G. Harkness and Company store
Republic, Ohio
age 15

1848   Manager, Chapman, Harkness and Company
Republic, Ohio
age 18

1849   Grain dealer for Chapman, Harkness and Company
Bellevue, Ohio
age 19

1852   Partner, Harkness and Company (grain and liquor)
Bellevue, Ohio
age 22

2. *Early Career*

*A*lthough Medina, New York, was an interesting little canal town, Henry Flagler lingered only long enough to make plans for his journey to Buffalo, some 40 or 50 miles down the Erie Canal. All kinds of boats traveled from Medina to Buffalo, ranging from the larger and more luxurious types to small freight boats. Within a few hours Henry found a small boat headed for Buffalo. An extra crew member was needed to help handle the large amount of freight being carried. It was not difficult for young Henry to talk the skipper into allowing him to make the trip free of charge in return for his services while on board. Arriving in Buffalo late at night, the boy helped unload the boat as part payment of his fare. It was early morning before the task was finished. He was tired, hungry, and sleepy. As Buffalo was an enterprising lake town, the docks were always busy with shipping activities. Flagler easily found a boat for the next part of his journey. His fare on the lake boat took almost all the money he had saved. Early on the morning of his second day away from home, a boat pulled away from the dock at Buffalo with young Flagler on board. The northern shore of Ohio lay in the distance. Sandusky was his next stop.[1]

*T*he journey across the lake, which took three days and nights, was not pleasant. During the first day the weather was extremely rough. The little boat was tossed and tumbled about by the waves. Most of the passengers, including Henry, got seasick. He was as miserable as he had ever been. He wished many times during the three days and nights that he had never left home. To the discomforts of seasickness were added those of homesickness. Henry declared to himself that, if he ever saw shore again, he would head in the nearest direction toward home—on land. However, as the weather finally got better, his spirits rose. He ate a little of the four-day-old lunch his mother had prepared and put in his carpetbag when he left home. The little vessel finally reached Sandusky. Weak from the lack of enough nourishing food, he was a bit dizzy and groggy from the rough trip. As he left the boat, he staggered along the wharf. Henry was fearful that someone might see him and believe that he was drunk. Then, and throughout his life, he detested liquor. After eating a hot breakfast he felt much better. The dizziness left him and he regained his strength quickly.[2] Henry took the time to walk around Sandusky for a portion of the day and to enjoy being on land once more. Sandusky, which had been settled in 1817, was a thriving town with a population of about 3,000. The ice, fish, and lumber trades had grown with the town. Sandusky Bay, on which the town was situated, was an important place on Lake Erie, offering excellent shipping facilities. Four large harbors were indicative of the volume of commerce the town attracted from the lake.[3]

*H*enry was not attracted to Sandusky, but he spent a day and a night there before starting the last lap of his journey. It is not known exactly how he travelled the 30-odd miles from Sandusky to Republic, but in all probability he walked most of the way. At any rate, the trip took several days. Along the way, he stopped for a day or so to visit friends of his mother in Bellevue which was about halfway between Sandusky and Republic. He liked the town and this short visit may have influenced him to return there later to live. He then pushed on to Republic, a town of a little less than 1,000 persons where he was met by Dan Harkness. Dan, more than anyone else, was responsible for his coming to Ohio. It was fortunate that he had someone in Republic whom he knew, for Henry arrived there with only a French coin, a nickel, and four pennies in his pocket. In 1844, that was his entire fortune.[4]

*T*he newcomer to Republic began work the next day with L. G. Harkness and Company. The founder of the company, Lamon G. Harkness, an uncle of Dan Harkness, was a prominent physician and a native of Salem, New York. After taking his medical degree at Union College in New York, he moved westward to northern Ohio in 1823. He first practiced in Lynne and then for a short time lived in Republic, but he finally settled in Bellevue in 1833, where he had a reputation of being a good doctor, but a much better businessman. Soon after settling in Bellevue, Harkness married Julia Follett, a native Ohioan. They had seven children; namely: Isabella, Follett, Mary, Lamon, Julia, Tryphene, and Louisa.[5] Mary Harkness, their third child, later became Henry Flagler's wife.

*A*fter moving to Bellevue, Lamon Harkness still kept in close touch with his business at Republic, but relied considerably on Dan for its management. Dan's father, David, was Lamon's brother. After David Harkness's death, Dan's mother married Isaac Flagler.[6] Dan, already an exceptionally good businessman, gave young Henry a sound background in the business world.

*H*enry worked hard. He was eager to make a positive impression on Dan and Lamon Harkness, who visited the store frequently from nearby Bellevue. He never asked for time off and labored uncomplainingly six days a week. His pay was $5 a month, plus room and board. Henry and Dan lived in a room at the rear of the store. It was not very comfortable. There was a large wood-burning stove in the store where they cooked most of their meals, a feature of bachelor life to which Henry never became accustomed. On cold nights they abandoned their unheated room and slept in a warmer place under a counter near the stove. Sometimes their thin blankets would be supplemented with coarse brown wrapping paper from the table in the front of the store. There may have been easier jobs he could have found, but young Henry believed that there might be a future with the Harknesses. Even so, he was still not satisfied. Henry was ambitious to advance and never seemed to be thoroughly content. Speaking later about his first job, Henry Flagler said he had wanted to do things, not especially to become rich, but that he "might be useful and take a part in the work of the world."[7]

*A*t first his advancement was very slow, or so it seemed to him. Ten months after he began work with L. G. Harkness and Company his pay was increased to $7 a month. Now 15, Henry saved a good portion of each monthly pay envelope. He was never a spendthrift. Often when other boys his age insisted that he accompany them for an evening or a Sunday of fun, he remained behind because of the expense which the outing involved. Dan Harkness watched with interest the boy's ambition and ability. Through methods of his own Flagler boosted the business of L. G. Harkness and Company. The business community soon took notice of his untiring efforts and his keen mind.

*I*n nearby Rome (the town's name was later changed to Fostoria) another young man was making a name for himself in the field of salesmanship.[8] He was Charley Foster, who at that time was working for his father in a general store. He and Flagler, who became fast friends, were said to be the best salesmen in Seneca County. Occasionally the boys visited each other. The elder Foster tried several times to convince Henry to come to Rome and take a job with him. He thought seriously of going, but decided that Mr. Foster would have been an extremely hard taskmaster. Foster took young apprentices into his store to learn the art and trade of merchandising, and would not let them "gamble, mingle with women, nor marry, nor could they frequent taverns. They were to learn to read and cipher and to know the 'rule of three.'" It was not that Henry wanted to indulge in the vices prohibited by Foster, but he did want a little more freedom than he could have found in this village of less than 300 people. Consequently, he decided to remain with his kinsman in Republic. It was a wise decision, perhaps one that meant the difference between ultimate success and failure. The futures of young Henry and young Charley Foster turned out differently. Both later made great fortunes. Foster entered politics and became governor of Ohio. Later he was appointed Secretary of the Treasury in President Benjamin Harrison's administration. Business and politics are often unlike, however, and he died a poor man.[9] Later, when Henry Flagler saw how Foster's money was so easily lost, he profited by his friend's example. He resolved never to become deeply involved in politics.

$\mathcal{H}$enry learned many things during his three year stay at the general store in Republic. Besides salesmanship, he had much training in the exercise of thrift, ingenuity, and good judgment. Dan and Lamon Harkness were pleased with their discovery of such a person. Perhaps, at times, Henry may have thought the tangible compensations for selling candles, weighing coffee, measuring calico, and cranking molasses faucets were not enough, but on reflection he realized that his experiences behind the counter gave him the foundation for a business education. While there he acquired a sense of commercial values and learned the rudiments of good and profitable business.[10]

$\mathcal{M}$any were the lessons the boy learned, one being to inquire closely into the merits of what was offered for sale. There were some things in stock that he had to sell which he knew were not worth the price. For example, in the cellar of the store there was a keg filled with brandy from a large vessel. At the time, there were three economic classes of people living in separate communities around Republic—English, German, and American Indians. The price of brandy was different for each of the three groups. Out of the same keg, Henry was instructed to sell one kind of brandy to the English at $4 a gallon, another kind to the Germans at $1.50 a gallon, and still another kind to the American Indians for what he could get.[11]

*I*n the meantime, while Henry was gaining a reputation as a teenage businessman, his half brother, Dan Harkness, continued to grow in the estimation of his Uncle Lamon. In 1845, Dan, then in his early 20s, was asked to come to Bellevue and join the partnership of F. A. Chapman and L. G. Harkness, dealers in general merchandise. The partnership was reorganized. Dan Harkness became a member of the new firm which took the name of Chapman, Harkness and Company.[12] For the next few years Henry continued in Republic, taking Dan's place as manager of the store there. The reputation which he won soon after his arrival continued to flourish. Given the chance, he proved to his employers that he was a mature business man though only in his late teens.

*I*n 1849, after five years in Republic, 19 year old Henry Flagler was given a job in Bellevue with Chapman, Harkness and Company.[13] This was a deserved promotion. His salary was increased to nearly $400 a year. Bellevue, which offered many more opportunities than Republic, was the place in which he laid the foundation for the great fortune which he later made. The town was situated about 12 or 15 miles northwest of Republic. Although Bellevue was then about the same size as Republic, it was a much faster growing place. About half of Bellevue was in Huron County and half in Sandusky County. It had slow growth before 1840, but in 1839 the Mad River Railroad was completed to the village from Sandusky, an outlet to Lake Erie, and people began to move in. F. A. Chapman, T. F. Amsden, and L. G. Harkness bought all the land in Bellevue on the Huron County side. They began to encourage outsiders to settle there. These men sold their land at high prices to the newcomers, and subsequently became the town's most wealthy and influential citizens when Bellevue was incorporated in 1851. In 1852, a branch line of the Toledo, Norwalk, and Cleveland Railroad was built to Bellevue, greatly increasing the commercial advantages of the town.[14]

*Y*oung Flagler was happy to be with Dan Harkness again. Henry accepted the challenge which business opportunities in Bellevue offered. He roomed with Dan and often accompanied him to the home of Lamon Harkness. Dan and Isabella, oldest daughter in the Harkness

Isabella Harkness, 1853

home, were involved in a gradually deepening courtship, which, despite their being first cousins, led to their marriage on August 23, 1849.[15] The entire Harkness family liked young Henry. After all, he was part of the Harkness clan, though no blood relation. The fact that his mother had at one time been married to David Harkness, Lamon's brother, made him feel like one of the group. The two younger Harkness sisters. Mary, 15, and Julia, nine, enjoyed keeping Henry company while Dan courted Isabella. He made quite an impression on the two girls and his visits became regular. After Dan and Isabella were married, Henry continued to visit in the evenings with Mary and Julia. It was perhaps at first through sheer habit, but as time passed something kept drawing him back to the Harkness home. The attention he gave the Harkness girls did not interrupt his work; instead, it seemed to stimulate him. Mary at first thought that he visited there to gain the good will of her father, but he already had that. Henry was just slow about getting to the point and declaring his intentions. Everyone in Bellevue knew that Henry Flagler was in love before he realized it himself.

*B*efore long Julia began to get in the way. She wanted to play children's games. Henry preferred to be entertained by Miss Mary, a lovely young woman with considerable charm and talent. In due time he knew that his actions toward Mary were prompted by love. Visits to the Harkness home became more frequent and more formal. Julia was withdrawn from the picture by the thoughtful parents, and every encouragement was given the young man of Mary's choice. After a short engagement they were married on November 9, 1853.[16] The only unhappy member of the family was 13 year old Julia. In her childish way, she, too, claimed Henry, who was always fond of her.

Mary Harkness Flagler, 1853

*J*ulia later became interested in a newcomer to Bellevue, young Barney York, who showed nearly as much business ability as Henry Flagler. Julia and Barney York were married on January 8, 1863,[17] thus bringing the third son-in-law into the Lamon Harkness family. All three men became prominent businessmen in Bellevue; their father-in-law had set a good example for them.

*P*erhaps the most successful member of the Harkness clan was Stephen V. Harkness. He was the only son of David Harkness by his first wife. Dan and Stephen were half brothers; Henry and Dan were half brothers; yet Stephen and Henry were not kin. Until about 1850 Henry had never seen Stephen and Dan had been with him very little. Stephen was born in Seneca County, New York, on November 18, 1818, and spent most of his early years in that state with his mother's people. He worked hard as a boy, having been apprenticed in the trade of harness making at the age of 15. Stephen applied himself to the task with determination. He become its master and made of it a stepping stone to the success he was determined to achieve. In 1839, at the age of 21, he moved to Bellevue, Ohio to be with his uncle, Lamon Harkness. There he ran a general store for a number of years in connection with an eating establishment. In the early 1850s, he settled in Monroeville, a small town not far away. His stay there was of short duration, as the urge to find greener pastures got the better of him. He tried several northern Ohio towns, but finally went back to Monroeville where he became established in business as a grain dealer and distillery operator. He soon had good business connections in Bellevue and Cleveland, Ohio.

*I*n Bellevue, Flagler watched Stephen closely and noted with interest the progress he continued to make in Monroeville. No doubt, Stephen was admired by the younger man for his ability to get ahead. The admiration was mutual because Stephen Harkness observed the progress young Flagler made, too. Flagler had opportunity to prove his ability because Chapman, Harkness and Company expanded into the distillery and liquor field.
Henry Flagler, 1853

They also began to deal in grain. Ohio, then the center of the grain belt, was particularly suited for the raising of corn. Its production laid the foundation for other related crops and industries. The grain business was new to Flagler, but he learned it. When Chapman, Harkness and Company doubled their volume of business through Flagler's efforts, they began paying him a commission as well as a salary.

*B*y 1852, Flagler had saved several thousand dollars from commissions he made shipping grain. He was highly thought of by his business associates and was invited to join the firm. Chapman, who had saved enough to retire, decided that it might be well if he withdrew. Lamon Harkness was also ready to retire, but was persuaded by the two younger men to remain with them. Henry Flagler bought the Chapman interest and the firm was renamed Harkness and Company.[19] It is not known exactly how much Flagler paid for his one-third interest in the business. Perhaps he had saved enough, but if he had not done so, either Dan or Lamon Harkness would have lent him the money. They were anxious for him to become associated in the business and neither of them underrated his abilities.

*F*rom Bellevue, Harkness and Company shipped large quantities of wheat during the 1850s to Cleveland for market. One commission merchant in Cleveland, John D. Rockefeller, handled most of their shipments. In the course of time, Flagler came to know his agent there.[20] Little did either of the men realize that someday they would become associated in a business known around the world for its great concentration of wealth. Rockefeller's dealings with Flagler made it possible for the two men to know each other fairly well. They had much in common, one characteristic being their great desire to get ahead in life.

*T*he distillery business in the 1850s was eminently respectable, and Harkness and Company found it very profitable. Most companies dealing in grain found it easy to establish a distillery in connection with their other interests because the manufacture of liquor gave them an outlet for considerable grain. Flagler had scruples about dealing in liquor; his strict Puritan training would not have permitted anything else, but the paramount thing in his life was making money.[21] Since the liquor business was profitable, Flagler tucked his convictions in his pocket and hurried on in the making of a small fortune.

While Dan Harkness and Henry Flagler were increasing their holdings in Bellevue by shipping grain and making liquor, Stephen V. Harkness was doing the same in nearby Monroeville. They worked separately as two organizations, but cooperated to their mutual benefit. In fact, Monroeville claimed Flagler as a resident. Though he never moved from Bellevue, he spent much time with Stephen learning more about the distillery business. In addition to wines and liquors, Stephen dealt in grain, livestock, and banking. He was accustomed to big money deals and always traded on a larger scale than did the two liquor makers in Bellevue. After Flagler had spent several years in the business, those scruples which he had from the beginning began to worry him. He sold out, but not before making a sizeable fortune. Dan Harkness, who took over Flagler's liquor interest, did not sell the Bellevue distillery, which was part of Harkness and Company, until 1868.[22]

Stephen Harkness also held on to his Monroeville distillery. If he had any scruples concerning making whiskey, they were never detected. Stephen's big money haul in this business came with the first comprehensive Internal Revenue Act of July 1, 1862.[23] Among other things, the law included a tax upon malt and distilled liquors. Prior to the passing of the law, Senator John Sherman, a prominent Ohio politician, warned Harkness of its significance and what its results might be. Sherman, who was on the Senate Finance Committee, had inside information. He foresaw a tax of $2 on each gallon of spirits. Harkness immediately set forth to accumulate an abundant stock before the law went into effect. He used all his reserve to buy up supplies of whiskey so that he could sell it at the higher price when the tax was enacted.

The local bank in Monroeville, which he owned, felt the strain of Harkness's determination to buy up all the whiskey he could find. The bank's funds were almost exhausted. Farmers who had funds on deposit became alarmed when they heard of the Harkness scheme, especially those who had difficulty cashing their corn receipts. Business in the town was tied up for days, but Harkness was never at a loss to keep the people fooled. He employed Hiram Latham to stand on the street and assure the anxious farmers that "old Steve Harkness" was all right, and that his intentions were sound and good. Latham did not get very far in trying to persuade the farmers that Harkness was not building his own fortune at their expense. The tension was fierce. One story was told of a man who entered the bank and demanded the cash for a couple of loads of corn. Harkness, who appeared on the scene just in time, talked to the irritated farmer about the prospect for rain while the cashier disappeared through the back door to borrow the sum of money from a nearby druggist in order to meet the demand. He was also shipping grain constantly at this time in order to raise further capital.

*H*arkness was blunt and frank at all times. In the midst of the excitement, he became irked at John D. Rockefeller, in Cleveland, who acted as commission merchant for him as well as for his acquaintances in Bellevue. It seems that Rockefeller, whom he knew well, had delayed payment for a shipment of grain. His tardiness prompted Harkness to dispatch the following pointed message: "Why … don't you remit for the last car of corn I shipped you? Unless I get it soon I will bust." His frantic efforts proved lucrative. The law was passed, as he had been advised. Harkness's business was stocked from cellar to ceiling with all sorts of whiskey and wines. He sold out his stock at the advanced price without having to pay the tax and made over $300,000 clear profit.[24] Not every liquor dealer could have succeeded so well. Steve Harkness impressed the best businessmen in northern Ohio. In 1866, he sold his property in Monroeville and moved to Cleveland, where he continued in various business interests for a number of years.[25]

3. *Success and Failure*

$\mathcal{T}$he years in Bellevue were happy ones for Mary and Henry Flagler. From 1853 until 1862 they lived there among their friends and relatives and became a part of an expanding community. During this time, Henry Flagler was growing his business. It was a trying period in American history. The argument between the North and the South over slavery was rapidly reaching a breaking point. Flagler, a keen student of national affairs, watched with much interest the situation in Kansas following the passage of the Kansas-Nebraska Act in 1854. Being a Republican, he probably disagreed strongly with the decision in the Dred Scott Case in 1857 and may have cheered Lincoln's rapid rise to prominence just prior to the election of 1860. Flagler was aware of the significance of the Republican victory in 1860, and was not surprised when the Southern states began to secede from the Union soon after the election.

$\mathcal{T}$he Civil War followed as did four years of bitter struggle. Flagler remained calm. He shared the views of most fellow Ohioans on the slavery issue, but he was not a radical. To him, war meant waste and destruction. It was not a profitable business in an economic sense. He strongly favored a compromise with the South, and saw no reason why some workable plan could not be adopted. When Lincoln issued his call for volunteers in 1861, Dan Harkness was one of the first to offer his services to the Union Army, but Flagler did not do so.[1] There was no moral obligation on his part to become engaged in the hostilities. After all, John D. Rockefeller, Philip Armour, and John Wannamaker did not enlist.[2]

$\mathcal{T}$his period in American history was one of profit and gain for Flagler. The war increased the volume of his grain business many times over. With Dan Harkness in the Union Army, his work in Bellevue was made very heavy, but as long as Flagler could count substantial gains each month he did not mind. He routed grain purchased by the United States government to the federal troops, a transaction which meant great financial returns for him.[3] While his fortune was growing in Bellevue, his

Mary and Baby Harry Harkness Flagler, ca. 1870

family, to which he gave much attention, was also increasing. He was fond of children, and was exceedingly happy when his first child, Jennie Louise, arrived on March 18, 1855.[4] His home life became more interesting as the baby became the center of his attention. A second child was born on June 18, 1858, and was named Carrie for his half sister. Sadly, little Carrie was never well and died when she was only three years old. Their youngest child, Harry Harkness Flagler, was born a number of years later.[5] Mary was never robust and many of the home responsibilities were undertaken by Henry.

*F*rom childhood, Mary's health had to be safeguarded. Henry derived great pleasure from making her comfortable and economically secure. They usually spent their evenings at home and very seldom did either seek entertainment in other places. Despite Mary's infirmities, they lived a fairly normal life. She was naturally happy and cheerful and the rest of the family was influenced by her actions.[6]

*I*n Bellevue, most of their friends were members of the Congregational Church. The Flaglers also held memberships since there was no Presbyterian Church in the community.[7] Both Mary and Henry were religiously inclined and participated as frequently as her health would permit in all activities of the church. Their closest associates were Isabella and Dan Harkness; Isabella had always been Mary's favorite sister and the relations between Dan and Henry were warm. In fact, the four seemed like one family since Isabella and Mary were sisters, Dan and Henry were half brothers, and Isabella and Dan were first cousins. Mary's parents were frequent visitors at the Flagler's modest home. In 1855, Henry's parents retired and moved to Bellevue to spend their last years. With them came Carrie Flagler, the half sister who had always been a favorite.[8] Another couple who liked the company of the Flaglers was Julia and Barney York. Julia was Mary Flagler's younger sister and though young York was a newcomer to Bellevue, he immediately won his way into the affections of the entire family. He, too, was associated with his father-in-law in business. L. G. Harkness prided himself upon his business associates, his three sons-in-law, Dan Harkness, Henry Flagler, and Barney York. The three young men remained fast friends all of their lives.

The Bellevue years brought sorrows and joys alike to the Harkness and Flagler clans. Isabella and Dan Harkness had five children; all but one, however, died in early infancy.[9] When Dan went into the Union Army in 1861, he left a despondent wife who never fully recovered from the loss of her babies. Mary and Henry Flagler lost their second baby during their residence in Bellevue and Mary had one or two serious illnesses which kept her husband disturbed for a long time. Henry's mother died in 1861. His father's health was bad until his death a number of years later. There were happier times, however; so life was anything but drab. Dan, Henry, and Barney always had a good time when they got together. Instead of relaxing at a game of tennis or a few holes of golf as young men of a later day may have done, those of the 1850s and 1860s found much sport in playing tenpins. Henry and Dan were frequently found at the tenpin alley at lunch time, but after an hour or so they were back at their desks at the office of Harkness and Company.[10] Business always came first.

By 1862, Henry Flagler had accumulated $50,000. Although he was happily settled in Bellevue, he was once again becoming restless. He could not help feeling that he might get ahead faster if he went to some other place. After he reached the top in Bellevue, his interest in the grain business seemed to wane. There was more money to be made if he stuck with it, but the business had lost its charm. Consequently, he decided to push on to something more speculative and more adventurous. Perhaps it would be something that might make him a bigger fortune in a shorter time. No one tried to persuade him against the course he set out to follow. His family and friends knew him too well. Henry Flagler was a man of much determination.

In 1860, abundant deposits of salt were discovered around Saginaw, Michigan and the first salt made in that section was put on the market in May of that year. Earlier the Michigan legislature had passed an act paying 10¢ a bushel for salt produced in the state. The law also made salt-producing property tax exempt, a decided inducement.[11] Excitement ran high, and many capitalists, or would-be salt producers, moved in hoping to make a fortune. The little town of Saginaw felt the effects of the boom. People went wild. The get-rich-quick feeling spread rapidly. Flagler was not the only person to get caught in the wave of enthusiasm.

*E*ncouraged by the act giving a bounty on each bushel of salt, a group of Michigan businessmen quickly organized the East Saginaw Salt Manufacturing Company with capital stock of $50,000, consisting of 2,000 shares of $25 each. The whole amount was subscribed in two days. The company at once proceeded to the erection of works for the manufacture of salt, consisting of two kettle blocks after the manner of those which were in use in other salt-producing areas. Production the first year was 10,722 barrels of salt consisting of five bushels each. In the second year, the production of this company alone was 32,250 barrels.[12]

*F*lagler's father-in-law, L. G. Harkness, was the first person from Bellevue to be attracted by the salt strike. He already had extensive interests in the lumber business in Michigan. As soon as the boom began, he immediately realized the possibility in producing salt and bought a large block of shares in the East Saginaw Salt Manufacturing Company. For the first two years Harkness was pleased with the profits he made from the venture. His enthusiasm no doubt influenced his son-in-law's thinking. It was at this time, in 1862, that Henry M. Flagler yielded to the temptation of casting his fortune with this new and uncertain industry. He pulled stakes in Bellevue and moved his family to Saginaw in the hope of becoming a wealthy man in record time. His brother-in-law, Barney York, was persuaded to go to Saginaw also. York did not have as much money to put into the business as Flagler did, but borrowed an equal amount from his father-in-law. Flagler sank his savings of $50,000 into a new firm named the Flagler and York Salt Company. Many other speculators had the same idea and several new salt-producing companies were formed in Saginaw in 1862 and 1863.

*F*lagler, who entered his new work with all the energy that characterized his previous business ventures, received encouragement from everyone who knew him. He made an impressive beginning. From the start he liked Saginaw, and was happy to be part of so progressive a community. Mary Flagler continued in poor health, but the presence of her sister, Julia York, kept her from becoming despondent among so many strangers. The Flaglers took an active interest in the community, especially in religious activities. For several generations the Flaglers had been Presbyterians, but in Saginaw, as in Bellevue, the Presbyterian Church had recently become united with the Congregational Church due to the rapid growth of the latter group. The Flaglers affiliated with the Congregational Church. Before many months had passed, Flagler was made superintendent of the Sunday School, a position for which he was well qualified. Until his departure from Saginaw in 1865 he continued his work, not only in the Sunday School, but also as a member of the board of trustees.[13]

*F*or about two years Flagler and York made money in the salt business; however, the process was not as easy as they had expected. There was much to be learned in producing salt. Those manufacturers with previous experience had the advantage over those just beginning. The many processes of manufacture were never completely mastered by the get-rich-quick fellows. Sad to say, many did not discover, until they had invested their money, that skill was required to make good salt. Henry Flagler was one who soon learned this fact. One thing which drove Flagler out of salt production was the keen competition in Michigan and Ohio which cut down drastically on the desired profits. Perhaps the thing that finally forced him out of the business was the collapse of salt prices at the close of the Civil War. After several years of overproduction, the salt market went to pieces. Flagler was left with nothing.[14] By late 1865 Flagler had not only lost the $50,000 that he had sunk in the venture, but in addition was $50,000 in debt. It was his first and last financial failure. It was one failure that he never forgot and one which he profited by many times later when the urge to try something new arose. The loss made him cautious about speculating on anything until he had thoroughly investigated its merits and possibilities.[15] Flagler's financial failure came the same year the Civil War ended. Although the nation was crippled and bruised from four years of bitter fighting, it had made remarkable progress during the first 60 years of the 19th century. The four years of Civil War marked only a temporary halt in its advancement. So it was with Flagler: his reverses of the 1860s were of a temporary nature. After the war, America started through a slow process of recuperation. Flagler's comeback was much quicker.

*E*merging from the financial debacle with much determination, Flagler looked about for a new start in the business world. He went to Bellevue and talked the matter over with his father-in-law and Dan Harkness, who were still engaged in the grain business. From them he borrowed $50,000 at 10% interest and paid off his debts in Saginaw. He was not bitter over his failure; however, he was disgusted with himself. His greatest desire was still to make money. In fact, this desire became more persistent than ever, for he had a sizeable debt hanging over his head. His back was against the wall.[16]

*H*enry Flagler was 35 years old when he left Saginaw. No doubt it was a temptation for him to go back to Bellevue and enter his father-in-law's business. The Harknesses encouraged him to do so. Mary had little to say about it. She relied wholly on Henry's judgment. The easiest thing would have been to take up in Bellevue where he had left off in 1862, but the enterprising Flagler chose Cleveland as the place where he would try to remake his fortune.[17] In 1865, Cleveland was one of the leading towns in Ohio and offered many opportunities. It was a city of about 45,000 people at the time and was strategically located on Lake Erie. Its founder, General Moses Cleaveland, an agent and director of the first Connecticut Land Company, had settled there in the 1790s. When Flagler arrived, the city had transportation facilities that were almost unrivaled. Situated on Lake Erie, Cleveland had access to the other Great Lakes and the Erie Canal. It was served by five railroads: the Cleveland, Columbus and Cincinnati; the Cleveland and Pittsburgh; the Lake Shore Railroad, which connected with the Erie and the New York Central; the Cleveland and Toledo; and the Cleveland and Mahoning. The Atlantic and Great Western was added a few years later. In 1860 there were no more than 30,600 miles of railroad in the United States, but that was great progress over the 2,818 miles in 1840.[18] Flagler was fortunate to have chosen Cleveland as his home, and Cleveland was fortunate to have attracted a citizen as enterprising as Flagler.

*H*is family accompanied him to Cleveland, refusing to remain in Bellevue until he was settled. Mary went against the wishes of her family. She chose to be near her husband. They rented a modest home and with only a few hundred dollars, which his father-in-law forwarded to him, Flagler set himself up in the grain business. His knowledge of the business was good. Since he had made money in it before, he had hopes of doing so again. It was a slow start for Flagler, who was impatient and anxious to begin to pay back his debts. He got little business at first; so on the side he became associated with a concern which made barrels, a venture that proved a failure, too. In another effort to make money quickly, he tried to market a specially-built horseshoe which was his own creation, but this scheme fell through. For the first time in his career, Henry Flagler was discouraged and about ready to quit. Everything seemed to be against him. Bellevue, with all that the Harknesses had to offer there, seemed more inviting than ever before. He remarked to a friend one day that if he ever paid off his debts and was $10,000 ahead, he would retire from business.[19] Fortunately, this loss of enthusiasm and desire to make a fortune did not last long.

*I*n 1866, Maurice B. Clark, grain commission merchant in Cleveland, heard that Flagler was having a hard time getting started. Clark offered him a job with his firm, Clark and Sanford. Maurice Clark was a likable young Englishman who was about the same age as Flagler. Before the formation of Clark and Sanford he had been associated with Otis, Brownell and Company, probably the oldest grain dealers in Cleveland. For a while he was associated with John D. Rockefeller in the same kind of business and it was then that Clark and Rockefeller became acquainted with Flagler. In 1865 the Clark and Rockefeller partnership dissolved. Rockefeller followed his oil interests. Clark remained in the grain business.

*C*lark was looking for an experienced dealer in grain. When a financially exhausted Henry Flagler arrived on the scene, the search was over. Flagler cheerfully took the job Clark offered, but did not invest any money in the partnership. He enjoyed his association with Clark and ably filled the place left by Rockefeller. This marked a turning point in Henry Flagler's life. Clark gave him considerable authority in the business. He had freedom to act as if he were an investor in the partnership. Flagler met with success from the start and Clark and Sanford liked his work. Within a few months the firm began to show a noticeable increase in its volume of business. Flagler's commissions increased each month, and he began to think in terms of large sums again. By 1867, he owed less than $30,000 on the $50,000 he had borrowed two years before from the Harknesses.

The Flaglers moved into a larger home on Euclid Avenue. There were nine rooms in their two-story house, some of which were often occupied by relatives. Flagler's mother had died a number of years earlier; so his father spent some time with them before his death in July, 1876.[20] In 1870 his father-in-law, L. G. Harkness, came to live with them after retiring from his business in Bellevue. In that same year, Mary Flagler gave birth to their third child, a son, Harry Harkness Flagler.[21] Henry Flagler had long anticipated the boy's arrival. Like his own father, he started making early plans for the baby's future.

Flagler's friends in Cleveland were influential and some of them were exceedingly wealthy. Stephen V. Harkness, who moved to Cleveland in 1866 after selling his liquor business in Monroeville, was an intimate associate. His fortune, one of the largest in the city, continued to increase through his efforts in real estate.[22] Mary Flagler, Stephen's first cousin, was his favorite relative. As her physical infirmities grew worse with the years, Stephen shared Henry's growing concern over her condition. He was a regular visitor in the Flagler home and enjoyed their hospitality on many a winter evening.

Flagler's business again brought him into contact with John D. Rockefeller, whom he had known since the days he had worked as a grain dealer in Bellevue. Their acquaintance grew into a friendship. The early years of the two men were quite different. Rockefeller, born in Richford, New York on July 8, 1839, was nine years younger than Flagler.[23] His father was in the business of peddling medicine throughout Western New York. The elder Rockefeller had many other pursuits in life, some of which he never followed too closely. However, his large family was never poverty stricken. They always had enough to eat and wear and usually saved a little on the side. One brother, William Avery, Jr., born in 1841, was also among Flagler's acquaintances. William later became associated with his brother and Henry Flagler in what would become the Standard Oil Company.

John's mother, Eliza, perhaps had more influence over the child than did his father largely because of the latter's frequent absences from home. Eliza Rockefeller was stern with her children in their guidance and discipline. The boy grew to be more like his mother than any of the other children. The resemblance pleased her, for he had been named for her father, John Davison. John D. became more serious and conscientious as he grew older. He was considered more outstanding than William who, like his father, was carefree and restless. William gave evidence of becoming a good salesman, which he later proved to be. He had an attractive personality and was a good mixer with people.

*A*s a boy, John D. Rockefeller was thorough in everything he did. This instinct was deeply embedded. The story is told about how cautiously he played checkers. He would ponder a move at great length, and never let anyone hurry him in making a decision. When urged by an opponent to move more rapidly, he always let it be known that he was playing the game to win and not to lose; therefore, to him time was of minor consequence in the game. Certainly that instinct, so early seen in his character, stayed with him throughout his life.

*I*n 1850, the Rockefeller family moved to Owego, New York, which was not far from their previous home. There were financial reverses from time to time in the family, but John and William were given the advantages of what educational training they could get in the village. Not only did the children attend school, but they all were required to attend Sunday school and church. Religion was a passion with Eliza Rockefeller. Her husband merely respected it. They were members of the Baptist Church and John always leaned strongly in its favor. The children were taught to contribute regularly to their church, a habit which young John never forgot. This training perhaps had a great deal to do with his later program of philanthropy.

*I*n 1853, the elder Rockefeller sought greener pastures and turned his attention westward. Selling medicine flourished in frontier places where trained physicians were few in number. He moved to the fringe of the Western Reserve and settled in Cleveland, Ohio.

*A*s a lad of 14, John, accompanied by his younger brother William, entered Cleveland schools that fall. Among his associates in Cleveland was Mark Hanna, son of a prosperous grocer, Leonard Hanna, with whom he became good friends. Hanna was to become a leading politician: first in Ohio and then in national politics. It was quite by accident that another of Rockefeller's boyhood chums was Tom Platt who later became a major figure in New York politics. At first, John's chief interest in girls centered around Lucy Spelman, whom he respected and admired for her scholastic attainments. However, Rockefeller later married Lucy's younger sister, Laura Spelman.

*J*ohn D. Rockefeller graduated from high school in 1855, but did not go to college. His mother had hoped he could go to Western Reserve or possibly Oberlin, but his father felt that practical experience would be of more value to him in later life. For three months, John attended a commercial college in Cleveland. He then began to look for employment. Business was bad in Cleveland in 1855. Getting a job was no easy matter. Finally he was given employment by Hewitt and Tuttle, commission merchants and produce shippers. This was the beginning of his steady rise to the top. The 16 year old lad did well and the way soon opened for further opportunities. In 1858, he and Maurice Clark organized the Clark and Rockefeller Company grain commissioners. Each man invested $2,000 in the business. Rockefeller was happy to be independent, and to know that his advancement depended entirely on himself. The firm prospered during the war. Clark and Rockefeller came out of the Civil War period well-to-do businessmen.[24] Their next venture was in the oil business, but Clark retired shortly and resumed the selling of grain. At this point Samuel Andrews joined Rockefeller in the steadily expanding oil industry. Like Clark, Andrews was an Englishman, and had come to Cleveland in 1857. He was an energetic young man with a special liking for chemistry. He fitted into the petroleum picture perfectly. He first found employment in a lard-oil refinery where he gained much knowledge about oil, tallows, and candle-making. He made many practical experiments which added to the knowledge of petroleum and its uses.[25] Andrews was bound to go far in his field. All he needed was financial backing and some energetic partners. He soon got both.

4. *Flagler Strikes Black Gold*

*D*uring the time that Henry Flagler was dealing in grain and salt, the petroleum industry in America was making rapid strides. The natural resources of this country were virtually untouched before 1800, but soon after that time considerable attention was centered on petroleum. In the states of Pennsylvania, Ohio, Kentucky, and what was later West Virginia, traces of petroleum were discovered on the surface of springs and streams. Some time later, speculators drilling for salt found the dark green, evil-smelling substance. Since oil and salt do not mix, some salt wells were abandoned because of the abundance of crude petroleum. Later, the abandoned salt wells became productive oil wells.[1]

*A*s more and more crude oil appeared, speculators wondered if some real value might be derived from it. In Burkesville, Kentucky, where oil was found in abundance, it was first used for medicinal purposes. "American Medicinal Oil," used as a liniment or rubbing oil, was bottled and sold in the area where it was found, in the East, and even in Europe. The fluid was also used as fuel for lamps in shops, factories, and later in homes. Crude oil was found to give good light and before long, streets were illuminated by it.[2] More and more uses were made of petroleum and the demand for it increased. In western Pennsylvania, where petroleum was found in great abundance, the substance was called "Seneca Oil." It may have been named for the Seneca Indians who inhabited the region.[3] It was in this section where most of the oil was discovered prior to 1845. The exact location was on a little stream known as Oil Creek which emptied into the Allegheny River. In this area boom towns like Titusville and Oil City sprang up.

*C*hemists were busy during the 1840s and 1850s working with petroleum. Its value was partially known, but its real worth had not been fully discovered. Until this time, tallow candles, beeswax, and whale oil had been used for lighting purposes. Their place in the American home would soon end. With the decline of whale fisheries, the price for whale oil was exceedingly high by 1850. Lard oil was found only in small quantities; in fact, there was an increasing shortage of oil not only in the

United States but all over the world. In the face of this shortage there was increasing demand for more oil. Many new machines were in use which required oil. Factories appeared in various sections. Railroads were constructed with much rapidity and steamboats were plying more and more of the country's rivers. All these facilities made demands on the small supply of oil in America.[4]

*P*rior to 1860 there were many advances in the field of petroleum. Samuel M. Kier, who owned salt wells in western Pennsylvania, near Pittsburgh, in the late 1840s, was one of the earliest leaders. Like many other salt men he grew tired of the smelly green substance which came in such abundance from his salt well. It was such a nuisance that he sought some way of using it. In 1849, he thought of selling it as medicine. His wife, a consumptive, had used several bottles of an oil sent from Kentucky. Kier compared the bottled medicine with the substance he was getting from his salt wells. It seemed to be identical. He asked his wife to use the local product rather than the Kentucky oil which her doctor had prescribed. It had the same results and Kier opened a business in nearby Pittsburgh where the curative spirit was bottled and sold. These eight ounce bottles of "Kier's Petroleum" were selling widely by 1850. They were used chiefly as a liniment, but were also recommended for a number of other things including consumption, bronchitis, liver complaints, and cholera morbus. Kier also distilled small quantities of petroleum to use as an illuminant. However, none of his experiments sought to use the substance for its own quality. He worked only on the by-products of petroleum. There is little doubt that Samuel M. Kier was the first man to test the possibility of refining oil. He hit upon this process in 1849 after consultation with a chemist in Philadelphia.[5]

*A*nother person to become actively engaged in the development of raw petroleum was George H. Bissell. A graduate of Dartmouth College, he was practicing law in New York. By chance, Bissell visited Hanover, New Hampshire in the fall of 1853. While there, he saw a small bottle of petroleum in the office of Doctor Dixi Crosby of the Dartmouth Medical School. Dr. Francis Beattie Brewer, a graduate of Dartmouth Medical School and at that time a practicing physician in Titusville, Pennsylvania, had brought the sample to his professor at Hanover for inspection and study. Bissell became interested in petroleum after talking with Professor Crosby about its possibilities.[6]

$\mathcal{A}$n enterprising young man, George Bissell was determined to find out more about the strange substance. He arranged for Professor Crosby's son, Albert H. Crosby, to visit Titusville and bring back further evidence of petroleum in that section. Young Crosby made the investigation and returned with a favorable report. In the fall of 1854, Bissell and his law partner bought about 105 acres of oil lands in the Titusville area. On December 30 of that year they organized the Pennsylvania Rock Oil Company, the first company of its kind in America.[7]

$\mathcal{T}$he newly organized oil company sent a small quantity of surface petroleum to a noted Yale chemist, Benjamin Silliman, Jr., for analysis. Silliman's father, Benjamin Silliman, Sr., also a noted Yale professor, had made a chemical analysis of some petroleum secured from the springs at Cuba, New York, as early as 1833. Young Silliman had been interested in the strange oily substance since the time of his father's experiment. The tests were made. In the spring of 1855 his report was ready for delivery, but he refused to send the report to Bissell until a bill of $426.08 was paid. After a short time, that first important scientific analysis of petroleum was delivered. The report was significant in that it was a prime factor in the beginning of the oil industry.[8]

$\mathcal{S}$illiman's report listed petroleum as a promising commodity. It emphasized the usefulness of oil as an illuminant and a lubricant. The findings further stated that many valuable products could be manufactured from it and mentioned many uses for the refined substance. The report also explained how oil was to be refined. For some time general attention focused on the report. Many activities dealing with petroleum were vigorously undertaken. Bissell thought of drilling extensively for oil on the land he had bought near Titusville, but because of the Depression of 1857 his plans never materialized.

$\mathcal{B}$efore Bissell could get financial backing and make preparations to drill for oil, that feat was accomplished by Edwin L. Drake, a 38 year old jack-of-all-trades. Drake went to Titusville in 1857 with the financial support of

Edwin Drake (in top hat) at site of the world's first commercial oil well in Titusville, Pennsylvania. August 27, 1859

James M. Townshend, an Eastern banker. After studying the situation, he became enthusiastic over the possibilities. With no practical experience in drilling, Drake hired several men and began work. The task was long and tedious. In August, 1859, they struck oil. Drake became famous. He had tapped the subterranean supply of petroleum in a section that was already known for its surface oil. The opening of this well meant that petroleum could now be secured in large quantities. There was no longer any doubt about the supply being exhausted. With the value of petroleum already well known, the United States stood on the threshold of an era marked by a rich new industry. Few men knew much about oil and the refining process, but there were many who were anxious to learn. The second well was drilled by William Barnsdall, a Titusville tanner, in 1860. In only five months the owner sold over $16,000 worth of oil.[9] Many new wells were opened along Oil Creek and the Allegheny River in western Pennsylvania during the early 1860s. An even greater expansion of the industry was soon under way. Fortune hunters poured forth in streams.

The oil regions of western Pennsylvania became a center of bustle and activity. Oil men and persons connected indirectly with the industry made money fast. Manufacturers of wooden tanks for oil receptacles made fortunes. Teamsters who drove the wagons carrying barrels of oil out of the oil regions became rich. Traffic on the Allegheny River grew so rapidly that it could hardly take care of the accelerated activity. By 1863, a railroad was extended into Titusville. By 1865, Oil City was supplied with rail service.[10]

Other places also rapidly felt the impact of the oil boom. Pithole, Pennsylvania, was engulfed in the tide of prosperity by 1865. In 10 months, a field there was producing over 10,000 barrels of petroleum a day. The Civil War had just ended. Many soldiers were anxious for a chance to find some of the "black gold." Persistent rumors about its value had reached the Union soldiers as the war was drawing to a close. Hundreds of them joined other oil enthusiasts in Pithole. Within a year, the place had grown from a village to a town of 6,000 inhabitants. The region suffered and profited simultaneously. Pine shanties and oil derricks silhouetted the sky. Among the newcomers were whiskey sellers, horse traders, and dead beats. Everyone was there for only one purpose—to get rich quick. Of course, not everyone who rushed into the oil regions retired with a fortune. Many hardships awaited the newcomers—fluctuation of prices, speculation, and discrimination by the railroads gradually helped to bring order and sobriety to Pithole and other boom towns.[11]

*P*rosperity soon spilled across the neighboring borders of New York and Ohio, especially into Cleveland, Ohio, where people became oil conscious. Because of Cleveland's good transportation facilities, oil was soon being shipped there for refinement and then on to other places for sale. By 1865, Cleveland had about 30 refineries and more were being built. Located on the southern shore of Lake Erie, and connected with other important points by rail, Cleveland was destined to become an outstanding petroleum center. By 1864, pipe lines were used to send oil out of the oil regions to nearby refining and marketing points.

*S*amuel Van Syckel laid the first successful pipe line. It carried about 80 barrels of oil per hour. This was a great improvement in the transporting of oil. The teamsters, who had carried large portions of the petroleum to the refineries before 1864, were through. They resented the coming of the pipe lines, but there was nothing they could do. Railroads and pipelines soon became the chief mediums of transportation for unrefined oil.[12]

*D*uring the 1860s the fabulous story of oil was discussed throughout New York, Ohio, and Pennsylvania. The news soon seeped into other sections of the country as well. Henry M. Flagler, working hard first at his grain business and later in his salt venture, did not have much time to think about oil and its possibilities. It no doubt aroused his curiosity, as it did that of John D. Rockefeller and other get-rich-quick seekers. The first connection Rockefeller had with oil was in 1862, the year in which Flagler went to Saginaw to invest in a salt mine.

*I*n 1862, Rockefeller and his partner in the grain business, Maurice B. Clark, backed Samuel Andrews, an Englishman, in starting a refinery in Cleveland. The move was a gamble for Rockefeller because he knew very little about either Samuel Andrews or the oil game. The first loan was for $4,000. Andrews soon proved his ability. A genius in mechanics, Andrews devised a new process for refining oil. As a result, Rockefeller and Clark poured more capital into the refinery.[13] Rockefeller continued to invest more heavily in the oil business. Since business differences had come between Rockefeller and Clark, he decided to pull out of the grain partnership. Since Maurice Clark was a partner with Andrews in the oil business, Rockefeller gave his half in the grain business, plus $72,500 in cash, for Clark's share in the refining company.[14]

The new oil firm of Rockefeller and Andrews was the largest of its kind in Cleveland, and one of the largest in the United States. Both men were extremely capable. Andrews knew the mechanics of the refining business and Rockefeller had a flair for buying and selling. Together they worked well. While 25 year old John D. Rockefeller was teaming up with Samuel Andrews in the oil refining business in Cleveland, Henry Flagler was moving to the same town with hopes of remaking his fortune after the Saginaw salt debacle.

It was an amazing era for American business. Speculation, expansion, and competition were all the order of the day. Rapid growth would continue until the Panic of 1873. Many great fortunes were in the making. There was seemingly no limit to the amount of money a person might acquire. Rockefeller was caught in the rising tide of prosperity and it was not long before Flagler was to share this success. By January, 1866, Rockefeller and Andrews had a business worth $1,200,000. It led the field of refineries in Cleveland. Second came Hussey, McBride and Company and then the Pioneer Oil Works, both with much smaller capitalization. Rockefeller and Andrews hired 37 workers and had a capacity of 505 barrels a day. This was more than twice the output of any of their Cleveland competitors.[15]

In 1866, Rockefeller and Flagler had a chance to renew their acquaintance. They both officed in Cleveland's Sexton Building and often talked of the days when Flagler had shipped grain from Bellevue to Rockefeller in Cleveland. Over time, their association became more friendly. They each enjoyed each other's company. Since they lived on the same street, they frequently walked home together, sharing stories of the day's happenings in their respective offices. Grain did not have much of an attraction for Rockefeller, although Flagler thought well of the business because he was in the process of making money from it. At 36, Flagler was not a handsome man, but was distinguished. He had black hair and a closely cropped mustache. His eyes were dark and he possessed a magnetic personality. His passion for wealth was equal to that of Rockefeller. In business, both men were determined and untiring in their efforts. Neither would be denied success.[16]

Henry Flagler, December 1870

$\mathcal{R}$ockefeller and Andrews began to think of expansion. Early in 1866, William Rockefeller was taken into the partnership to handle sales. He was sent to New York to establish an office there. Andrews superintended the refinery while John D. Rockefeller directed the organization. In the second year of their business it is believed that they sold more than $2,000,000 worth of oil. There was still room for expansion. With more capital, there could be a much larger output. Rockefeller had great faith in the future of the industry. He believed the business would make money as long as it was given attention. By 1866, rapid development was being made in the field of petroleum. The invention of a more efficient refining-still, the use of torpedoes in drilling, replacement of the clumsy flat car with its wooden tubs by the tank-car, and regular use of pipe lines to transport petroleum from the wells to the railroads helped refiners turn out their product at a greatly accelerated rate. But not all refiners could afford these economies. Small concerns either had to increase their capital to about $500,000 or combine with some larger unit. Rockefeller, who was among the first to realize the situation, began to look for additional capital. Rockefeller wanted Henry Flagler, but Flagler did not have the capital which Rockefeller needed to feed the growing business. In fact, Flagler still owed several thousand dollars in 1866; however, within a year he had paid back all his debts.

$\mathcal{R}$ockefeller did not dismiss the possibility of working with Flagler. After trying unsuccessfully to persuade John Gardiner of Norwalk, Ohio, to join him in the firm, he approached Flagler on the matter. Flagler told him about Stephen V. Harkness, his wife's first cousin, who had made a fortune in the liquor business and who had a flair for speculation and uncertainty. Rockefeller immediately went to see Harkness. Within an hour, Harkness agreed to put $100,000 in the business with the understanding that Flagler should have complete control of the Harkness investment.[17] As far as Rockefeller was concerned, it was a perfect arrangement. He was thoroughly familiar with Flagler's ability as a businessman and had already talked with him about joining the firm. Flagler was doing well in the grain business, but at his cousin's insistence was delighted to enter the oil company with Rockefeller. Harkness and Rockefeller both had complete faith in him. With Flagler in the business, Rockefeller tapped the Harkness treasury chest several times later. He never failed to get the money he wanted.[18]

*I*n 1867, the partnership of Rockefeller, Andrews and Flagler was formed. It marked the beginning of a petroleum oligarchy which lasted for several years. Stephen Harkness remained a silent partner in the new firm, leaving all interests in the hands of his kinsman. Flagler worked well with Rockefeller in the organizing and handling of the business. William Rockefeller, who was in New York, did little of the partnership's planning. Samuel Andrews remained busy superintending the refinery.[19] On March 4 and 5, 1867, the new firm advertised its product in the *Cleveland Leader*. The new firm also announced its offices in Cleveland at the Case Building and in New York at 181 Pearl Street. The *Leader* commented on the new partnership as follows:

> *Our readers will notice by the advertisement in another column, that the old and reliable firm of Rockefeller and Andrews has undergone a change, and now appears under the new title of Rockefeller, Andrews and Flagler.*
>
> *This firm is one of the oldest in the refining business and their trade already a mammoth one, is still further enlarged by the recent change; so that with their New York House, their establishment is one of the largest in the United States. Among the many oil refining enterprises, this seems to be one of the most successful; its heavy capital and consummate management, having kept it clear of the many shoals upon which oil refining houses have so often stranded.[20]*

*F*or the next 10 or 15 years Flagler was Rockefeller's strongest and closest associate. In his *Random Reminiscences*, Rockefeller frankly discusses his warm friendship with Flagler. As Flagler once remarked, it was a "friendship founded on business rather than a business founded on friendship."[21] For years the two men worked together in the same office, their desks being only a few feet apart. They always walked home together in the evening and back to the office in the morning. If there was ever any time off from the office, they usually got together and did their planning for days to come.[22] Rockefeller knew he could team with Flagler to make a great organization. His observations had not deceived him. Though Flagler was nine years older than Rockefeller, there seemed to be perfect understanding between them. Flagler's imagination and bold temperament lighted the way.[23]

$\mathcal{T}$he Flaglers and Rockefellers lived on Euclid Avenue in Cleveland. At that time, it was one of the most beautiful streets in any American city. By the 1860s, what was once a muddy trail and later a road had become a fashionable avenue. Most of Cleveland's wealthiest citizens lived there in spacious homes surrounded by beautiful lawns and well-kept flower beds. In view of the waters of Lake Erie, it was home to railroad builder Amasa Stone, the banker Stillman Witt, the politician Henry B. Payne, and industrialists John D. Rockefeller, Samuel Andrews, and Henry Flagler. Rockefeller's home was one of the most pretentious on the avenue. It was a two-story brick structure surrounded by beautiful lawns. In 1880, Samuel Andrews built his new home on Euclid Avenue. It outshone all his neighbors. Andrews had a flair for doing the unreasonable and the five-story brick structure, with 33 rooms, was no exception. A hundred servants were required to maintain the house and grounds. Andrews soon abandoned the mansion because of lack of adequate help to run it.[24]

$\mathcal{F}$lagler took an active part in the business life of the city, but engaged in none of the social activities.[25] His religious activities, which he always enjoyed, were limited because of his wife's increasingly poor health. It was said that for the last 17 years of Mary's life, from 1864 to 1881, Henry Flagler spent only two evenings away from home. He found diversion from business in reading aloud to his wife. His children also claimed much of his time. Occasionally he would take part of an afternoon away from his office to take the two little Flaglers on a picnic in the country. He was an ardent member of the Cleveland Board of Trade and the Manufacturers Association of Cleveland, but neither took much time away from his family or his business. Two years after the Civil

War was over he urged the Board of Trade to donate money to help destitute people of the South, especially those in Georgia, where the horrors of war were so forcibly seen. At the urging of J. J. Jones of Harrison County, Georgia, Flagler contributed to the cause, his sum being equalled by four other Cleveland citizens.[26] On December 2, 1867, he was elected one of the 73 delegates from Cleveland to attend the National Manufacturers Convention to be held in the same city. He felt that such activities were a part of his business.[27]

The new firm of Rockefeller, Andrews and Flagler was a thriving business from the start. Its growth was never in doubt. Among Flagler's duties was the drawing up of contracts. He always did this well despite the fact that he had no legal training. The intent and purpose of the contract was always stated accurately and clearly. Rockefeller, a fair judge of men, always insisted that Flagler had more common sense than almost anyone else.[29] Another of his activities included the construction of new refineries. Flagler insisted on putting up sound structures. He would not allow a flimsy shack to be built. As John D. Rockefeller later stated,

> *Everyone was so afraid that the oil would disappear and that the money expended in building would be a loss that the meanest and cheapest buildings were erected for use as refineries. This was the sort of thing Mr. Flagler objected to. While he had to admit that it was possible the oil supply might fail and that the risks of the trade were great, he always believed that if we went into the oil business at all, we should do the work as well as we knew how; that everything should be solid and substantial; and that nothing should be left undone to produce the finest results.*[29]

The new firm expanded its business widely. William Rockefeller opened up European markets and sold a large amount of oil abroad. Flagler and Rockefeller were elated over the increase in the volume of business. Rockefeller later spoke of the fun they had as young men watching their business grow.[30] When Flagler went into the business they were refining about 500 barrels each day. Two years later they were shipping 1,500 barrels of refined oil and 3,000 barrels of crude oil a day.[31] The partnership did not fail to make use of the by-products of petroleum. For instance, no market had yet developed for gasoline. While most refiners were trying to find a place to dispose of it, Rockefeller and Flagler used it as fuel. Flagler had added to the partnership energy, aggressiveness and drive, along with the combination of qualities already contributed by Rockefeller. Together they formed a smoothly functioning unit. Flagler's most important contribution to the business was perhaps in the field of freight-rate negotiations. He took over that task as soon as he joined Rockefeller, realizing that transportation continued to be one of the biggest obstacles facing refiners. Any refiner who had the advantage in the transportation business usually had the advantage in the petroleum industry; so he put himself to the task of outmaneuvering the other refiners. Pipe lines were used and so was water transportation, but not as extensively as railroads because the railroads had early learned what profits might result from the petroleum industry.

*I*n the late 1860s, there were three different railroad systems serving as an outlet from the oil regions. The Atlantic and Great Western, which in 1868 was absorbed by Jay Gould into his Erie System, shuttled into the oil regions at Titusville and Franklin. The second railroad, the Lake Shore and Michigan Southern, which later became a part of the New York Central, tapped the regions at Oil City. The Pennsylvania was the third road reaching into the petroleum-producing area. It controlled the Allegheny Valley Railroad, terminating at Franklin, and the Philadelphia and Erie which served Franklin and Titusville. All three of these railroad systems made great profits from oil traffic and competition among them was spirited.[32]

*J*ay Gould's Erie System was possibly the first railroad to favor Rockefeller, Andrews and Flagler with special rates and rebates. This was done because Gould wanted to divert all the crude oil shipments to the Cleveland market.[33] Gould also favored two other Cleveland refineries at this time. As chief negotiator, Flagler also began to bargain very early with the Lake Shore and Michigan Southern Railroad. This was one of the few roads which brought crude petroleum from the oil regions to Cleveland where it was refined. From Cleveland the refined product could easily be routed on to New York by the Lake Shore-New York Central route. J. H. Devereux became vice-president and general manager of the Lake Shore in 1868 and Flagler very soon found favor with the former Civil War general. Both Flagler and Devereux were just beginning in their respective fields and each was determined to make good. Flagler approached Devereux on the proposition that Lake Shore give him a rate of 35¢ a barrel on crude oil from the oil regions to Cleveland and $1.30 on refined oil from Cleveland to New York. In return for this consideration, Rockefeller, Andrews and Flagler would guarantee to ship 60 carloads each day. In addition, the firm would assume any risk due to fire. It is not known exactly what the refund or rebate amounted to, but it was probably not less than 15¢ on each barrel of oil shipped. At any rate, the agreement was made which put the partnership in a fair position to outdistance its competitors.[34] Flagler was jubilant over the agreement because he had won a great victory.

*F*lagler was, without doubt, one of the pioneers in the practice of rebates although he later maintained that Thomas Scott, of the Pennsylvania Railroad, was the instigator of the practice.[35] Much concerning these early rebates was held in secrecy. However, it was pretty generally known that many refiners were being favored by rebates. Because of Flagler's efforts, his firm began to receive greater concessions from the Lake Shore. One railroad was played against the other by shrewd Henry Flagler and his associates until they became the favored refiners in Cleveland, as far as railroad rates were concerned. As their volume of shipping increased, their rebates grew. When other refiners complained, as they often did, and petitioned for equal treatment, their requests were usually denied. The railroads told them if they would ship as much oil as Rockefeller, Andrews and Flagler, they would be given the same rebates.[36] To the refiners, then, it was a simple case of the survival of the fittest. The era of ruthless competitive warfare began. Each refiner realized that his days were numbered unless he could outdo his competitors. Flagler had put his firm far out in front. He and Rockefeller were destined to win the race.

*R*ockefeller and Flagler realized the importance of expansion. The possibility of merging or combining with weaker refineries had been considered by the two men. Their business was foremost in their thinking and their planning was constant. These well matched partners carefully studied the methods which Western Union Telegraph Company had used in forming its combination. They also watched the methods used by the railroads in the process of combining and forming large systems. The idea of the formation of the Standard Oil Company began in the following way. Flagler first mentioned to Rockefeller the possibility of combining with smaller refineries one morning as they were walking to work.

> *Rockefeller thought about the idea and replied, "Yes, Henry, I'd like to combine some of these refineries with ours. The business would be much more simple. But how are you going to determine the unit of valuation? How are you going to find a yardstick to measure the value?"*
>
> *In a few minutes Flagler answered, "John, I'll find a yardstick."*[37]

That afternoon Flagler went hunting for refineries. He found an operator on the lake front who was about ready to quit. The man said that oil was not his game. After a little while with Flagler, he was convinced he would never make any money at it. Flagler bought him out for $4,700. This was the first move toward combination—perhaps the first step toward the creation of what would later become the Standard Oil Company. By 1869 Rockefeller, Andrews and Flagler had outdistanced all the other refineries in Cleveland.[38] In all of their early purchases, Flagler used his "yardstick." He determined the value of the refinery and set the price which he and Rockefeller would pay for it. His aggressiveness often caught the seller off guard and the "bargains" he obtained on his purchases were outstanding. In addition, Flagler was adept at meeting people and this trait served well to enrich himself and his partners.

Rockefeller later stated that Flagler was always on the active side of every question, and that his energy was responsible for the rapid growth and progress of the partnership, and later for the Standard Oil Company; Flagler's faith in the future of oil production often boosted his partner's spirits. Said Rockefeller, "His courage in acting up to his beliefs laid strong foundations for later years."[39]

In those early years of the partnership, Samuel Andrews did only technical work. Rockefeller commented later that "He had nothing whatever to do with the office affairs, or the oil freighting business, and would not have had as much knowledge about these questions as the clerks in our office."[40] But chubby, friendly Samuel Andrews made a definite contribution to the partnership which bore his name.

*I*n the opinion of scholars who have studied the men connected with the rise of the petroleum industry, Flagler stands tall.

• Allan Nevins commented that "next to John D. Rockefeller," Flagler counted for most in industry in Cleveland.[41]

• John T. Flynn maintained that Flagler did a great deal of Rockefeller's thinking, and that the "two men were admirably suited to each other," and that Flagler, "a bold, unscrupulous self-seeker . . . could be relied upon to propose the needful course . . . "[42]

• John Winkler believed that Flagler was "fully as capable an organizer" as Rockefeller and did most for the rapidly expanding monopoly.[43]

• Ida M. Tarbell declared that when the Standard Oil Company was formed Flagler, next to Rockefeller, was the strongest man in the firm. He was untiring in his efforts to increase the business. Miss Tarbell believed that he "had no scruples to make him hesitate over the ethical quality of a contract which was advantageous." She continued, "He was not a secretive man, like John D. Rockefeller, not a dreamer, but he could keep his mouth shut when necessary and he knew the worth of a financial dream when it was laid before him." [44]

*T*here can be no doubt that Henry Flagler was an important figure in the infant petroleum industry. As the industry expanded, he became much more important and much, much wealthier. However, his vision remained clearly fixed on the future.

5. The Standard Oil Company

The petroleum industry was booming by 1870. The center of most of the activity dealing with oil was in northwestern Pennsylvania around Titusville and Oil City. This section, popularly known as the oil regions, was not more than 50 miles in length. Not only were the oil wells located there, but it was also where some of the petroleum was refined. Earlier the oil regions were unimportant, but after 1860 no other section of the country was more famous.

Cleveland, Ohio was nearby. It soon became prominent in the petroleum industry as a refining center. Pittsburgh and Philadelphia gave promise as refining towns, but the Ohio city soon took the edge over other refining towns because of its location on the shore of Lake Erie. More and more crude oil was shipped from the oil regions to Cleveland for the refining process because of its excellent transportation facilities and its aggressive refiners. It was largely due to the efforts of Henry Flagler and John D. Rockefeller that the city became so prominently known for its refining activities.[1]

Rockefeller and Flagler had been successful in their efforts to take over or combine most of the small refineries in Cleveland and their own organization grew considerably during the years between 1867 and 1870. By 1870, they were on the threshold of further expansion by means of the combining and unifying process. The late 1860s and 1870s were a period in which a great deal of unifying was being done in other industries in the business community. Rockefeller said later that there was always the possibility of making more money with a larger organization.[2] And Rockefeller and Flagler were bent on making money—it was the motive behind most of their actions.

Rockefeller, Andrews and Flagler decided to incorporate their partnership in 1869 because they needed more capital. It is safe to say that Henry Flagler conceived the plan for incorporation. Later when John D. Rockefeller was asked if the Standard Oil Company was the result of his thinking, he answered,

> *No, sir, I wish I'd had the brains to think of it. It was Henry M. Flagler.*[3]

*A*t first, Rockefeller thought the idea of incorporation was farfetched. He thought it would not work. Flagler proved him wrong. Many times over the years, Flagler's imagination and ingenuity were responsible for the continued growth and expansion of the business.[4]

*T*he Standard Oil Company became a reality on January 11, 1870. The partnership was incorporated as a joint stock company.[5] The *Cleveland Leader*, which became very friendly to the Standard Oil Company, had this comment to make several days after the incorporation:

> *On the 11th inst., one of the most flourishing oil companies of this city, commencing business with a full paid capital of $1,000,000, was incorporated under the name of the 'Standard Oil Company.' The corporators are John D. Rockefeller, Henry M. Flagler, Samuel Andrews, Stephen V. Harkness and William Rockefeller. The company has purchased of Rockefeller, Andrews and Flagler all their real estate, factories, offices, etc., in Cleveland, Oil City and New York. Their real estate in Cleveland amounts to about 50 acres in the heart of the city. The offices and factories possess all the requisites found in business establishments of the highest order.*
>
> *A meeting of the directors of the company was held on the 13th inst., and the following officers were elected: President, John D. Rockefeller; vice-president, William Rockefeller; secretary and treasurer, H. M. Flagler; superintendent, Samuel Andrews.*
>
> *The general offices are in the Cushing block, and are connected with the refinery by telegraph. The branch office is at 181 Pearl Street, and the warehouse is at Hunter's Point, New York.*[6]

*T*he act of incorporation under the laws of Ohio was signed by Rockefeller, Flagler, Andrews, and Stephen V. Harkness, all of Cleveland, and by William Rockefeller, of New York. The capitalization of the new corporation was $1,000,000, divided into 10,000 shares. Each share was valued at $100. The largest stockholder was John D. Rockefeller who took 2,667 shares. This amount represented his new investments in the corporation as well as his old holdings in the partnership of Rockefeller, Andrews and Flagler. The second largest stockholder was Stephen V. Harkness, the silent partner in the old firm, who subscribed for 1,334 shares. Flagler, along with Samuel Andrews and William Rockefeller, each took 1,333 shares. The old partnership of Rockefeller, Andrews and Flagler bought 1,000 shares as a unit and the last 1,000 shares were subscribed by a newcomer, O. B. Jennings, brother-in-law of William Rockefeller, from New York. Although the Standard Oil Company was a new corporation, nine-tenths of the stock was owned by the people who had invested in the partnership in 1867. Jennings, the only new person in the group, was there because of William Rockefeller's influence.

*S*tandard Oil Company was born as a big enterprise ready to plunge forward into a period of expansion and development. The company was soon was doing one-tenth of all the petroleum business in the United States. Besides two refineries and a barrel plant in Cleveland, it possessed a fleet of tank cars and warehouses in the oil regions as well as warehouses and tanks in New York.[7] The new organization gave Rockefeller and Flagler better opportunities for flexibility. The structure made the entrance of new capital into the business easier. Flagler and Rockefeller had no intention of relinquishing leadership in the new firm. The two Rockefellers, Flagler, and Harkness owned nearly seven-tenths of the corporation. There was no question about Rockefeller and Flagler continuing as the leading figures in the new organization.

*I*n order to have complete control of the production in Cleveland, Rockefeller and Flagler made no secret of their plans to buy or force out of existence all refiners there with whom they had not already combined. Their chief competitors were Clarke, Payne and Company; Alexander, Scofield and Company; Hanna, Bashington and Company; Westlake, Hutchins and Company; Cleveland Petroleum Refining Company; and Critchley, Fawcett and Company. In addition to these, there were a number of small plants—a total of 25 in Cleveland in 1870. Some of them were producing only a barrel or two of oil a day. Most of them were inefficiently operated. Flagler and Rockefeller studied the situation as if playing chess or checkers. The next step was important because of their determination to control all the refinery interests in Cleveland. Shrewdly, they moved forward.[8]

Several owners of smaller refineries anticipated what was coming. They closed their businesses. Other refiners talked among themselves about their future, often expressing feelings of terror and despair. There was nothing to be done against the strength that opposed them. Within a few months after the Standard Oil Company was incorporated, 20 of the 25 refiners were in the hands of Rockefeller and Flagler.[9] The public was getting a first idea of the corporation which would become vastly more powerful in the years to come. There was some small amount of criticism, but people were too stunned by the suddenness of the Standard's actions to fully appreciate what had happened.

Flagler always denied that the "freezing-out" process was Standard Oil's only method. When a competitor was approached on the subject of combining with the corporation, he was given his choice of accepting cash or stock in the firm. Most of the small oil men, realizing they could not stay in competition with Standard Oil in Cleveland, sold out for cash. They often retired from the business in disgust and became violent critics of the rising corporation.[10] No matter how they wanted to justify their actions, Rockefeller and Flagler could not convince the public that they were right. Opposition to the corporation mounted. Rockefeller and Flagler contended that any "killing" of a competitor's business was always done in a cheerful way. Flagler tells about one victim of Standard Oil who was considered a "freeze-out" case:

> *When I was selling flour and grain in Cleveland, I had a certain German for a customer. He owned a bakery in the suburbs, and I often trusted him for a barrel of flour when collections were slow and money was scarce. One day I met him on the street and he surprised me by saying that he had sold his bakery and was running a little oil refinery. Usually Mr. Rockefeller and I walked downtown in the morning to talk over private matters. Next day I told him about the little German baker who had gone into the oil business without my knowledge. We bought the refinery for $5,200. The German owed $5,000. At my suggestion he took $2,700 in money, with which he pacified his creditors for the time being, and $2,500 in Standard stock. We made him superintendent of our stove department and sent him into the woods, where he arose to a salary of $8,000 a year. I was pleased later to ask him for his $2,500 in stock and to issue in its stead $50,000 of stock in the larger corporation. Still later he received $10,000 more in a stock dividend.[11]*

On another occasion Frank Arter, a small Cleveland refiner, was being threatened by Standard Oil. Flagler offered him $4,000 in stock for his business, but Arter held out for $25,000 in cash. The trade was deadlocked for some time. Finally, the small refiner realized he could not buck the larger corporation. He yielded and let his refinery become absorbed by Standard Oil. Frank Arter died a rich man a number of years later.[12] Perhaps these cases were exceptional ones. Other smaller refiners were not so lucky. There can be no question of Standard Oil's ruthlessness. To Flagler their methods were just good business; Rockefeller agreed. By 1872 Standard Oil had bought out most of the larger and smaller refiners in Cleveland. Many new stockholders appeared in the Company, among them Amasa Stone, Benjamin Brewster, J. A. Bostwick, P. H. Watson, and O. H. Payne.[13]

This process of concentration among stronger concerns and extermination of weaker ones continued for several years. No refinery could stand up under the savage competition of such organizations as the Standard Oil unless it had capital of at least $500,000. Through its process of concentration and its superior efficiency, the Standard Oil Company became larger than all its competitors in Titusville, Pittsburgh, Oil City, and New York. The first round in the battle for the survival of the fittest was over. From this time on instead of each refiner being primarily interested in the efficiency of production, the new primary issue became cheaper transportation in order to survive competition and stay in business. The advantage each sought was in favorable rebates.[14]

Flagler's experience in securing rebates since 1867 gave him an advantage over most of the refiners. He played the game shrewdly. The Standard Oil Company's first concession in the field of rebates came from the Lake Shore Railroad when Flagler secured a better freight contract than the one previously granted to the old partnership. At this time the Company was shipping some of its oil to New York and other eastern points by water, which was a slow method. Since one bad feature about water transportation was the inability to use it year round, Flagler agreed to ship oil by Lake Shore Railroad all through the year. He guaranteed a volume of 60 carloads of oil each day, whether business was good or bad. Of course, a heavy rebate was asked for this consideration on the part of Standard Oil. Competitors of Standard Oil also asked Lake Shore for the same favors granted Standard Oil. They were told that they would receive the same consideration when they shipped as much oil as did the Standard Oil Company.[15] Standard Oil managed to stay out front. They had established their advantage and did not mean to relinquish it.

Other railroads began to lower their rates. A real freight war was developed for traffic to points both East and West of Cleveland. The New York Central, the Erie, and the Pennsylvania Railroad had completed connections to Chicago. They fought each other bitterly for traffic. Even though the roads met once a year and agreed on certain freight rates, they regularly broke their agreement in order to get a larger volume of business. This reckless competition extended into the oil regions. The Pennsylvania Railroad hauled oil to Pittsburgh and to Philadelphia. The Erie Railroad, which entered the oil fields by a connection with the Atlantic and Great Western road, hauled oil to New York, as did the New York Central, which bought out the Lake Shore Railroad. The Standard Oil Company's traffic affairs were managed so well by Flagler that he could ship oil 740 miles to New York by New York Central at precisely the same rate the Pittsburgh refiners were charged for a haulage of 400 miles.[16]

In 1872, Rockefeller and Flagler became involved in a scheme known as the South Improvement Company. The scheme created much opposition and criticism, especially in the oil regions. It is not known if Rockefeller or Flagler actually had anything to do with creating the South Improvement Company. Flagler said later that neither he nor Rockefeller believed in the idea at first, but they were forced to join under pressure. He said in testifying before a House Committee investigating trusts that it originated with Peter H. Watson and W. G. Warden. This may or may not be true. John Flynn, however, states that the scheme had all the earmarks of Flagler's mind and experience, despite the fact that he denied any responsibility for its origination.[17] Other scholars in the field have also accused Flagler of conceiving the idea.[18] The one thing that looked suspicious was the fact that no one admitted having begun the South Improvement plan and all blamed different people.

The name of the scheme was a misnomer. In fact, the South (or Southern as it was correctly written) Improvement Company had no significance at all. The gist of the whole plan was to bring together secretly all the refiners and shippers and to force the railroads to give special rebates and drawbacks. In other words, the South Improvement Company was set up to do throughout Ohio, Pennsylvania, and New York what the Standard Oil Company had done in Cleveland. It was set up to exterminate all opposition and competition that would not yield to the large corporation. Because of overproduction and the falling off of the foreign market, the price of oil had decreased over a period of several years. Producers felt that a larger combination would tend to force prices up at least 50% and by controlling the refining interest they could also fix their own price on crude oil shipped from the oil regions. Since they would be the only buyers and sellers, the speculative aspect of the business would not exist. The plans looked perfect on paper—the scheme would put the entire petroleum industry in the hands of a few persons. The combination was projected on January 2, 1872, in Philadelphia. However, no new charter was secured from the state for the organization. By an earlier act of the Pennsylvania legislature on May 1, 1871, the South Improvement Company had been created and had been vested with all the powers given by a previous act of April 7, 1870. The secondhand charter with which the oil men formed the new combination had power "to construct and operate any work or works, public or private, designed to include, increase, facilitate, or develop trade, travel, or the transportation of freight, livestock, passengers, or any traffic by land or water, from or to any part of the United States."[19] This very indefinite charter had no connection with what the oil men were trying to do. The name was so misleading that the officers talked of changing it to the American Cooperative Refining Company, but they never got around to doing it.[20] By no means were they as vague about their business as was the charter. There were 2,000 shares created in the South Improvement Company; of that number, 900 were owned by Henry M. Flagler, John D. and William Rockefeller, O. H. Payne, and H. Bostwick. The fact that all these men were prominent in the Standard Oil Company gave rise to speculation as to the part the corporation played in the newly created enterprise.

The South Improvement Company lost no time in making preliminary plans for its operations. It completed contracts on January 18, 1872, with the Pennsylvania, the New York Central, and the Erie Railroad. The contracts stated that the South Improvement Company was to ship 45% of all its oil by Pennsylvania and to divide equally the rest of its shipments between the Erie Railroad and the New York Central Railroad. The company also agreed to furnish adequate storage facilities for the oil both en route and at its destination. The company would also keep an accurate check of all the petroleum shipped over the railroads both by itself and other parties. The three railroads in return were to allow the South Improvement Company rebates on all shipments carried by them. They agreed to charge all other refiners, those who were not affiliated with the South Improvement Company, not less than full rates. The roads further agreed to protect the South Improvement Company from any loss or injury by competition. The spider was in the process of winding its web a little tighter around the helpless independent refiner.

The agreement between the South Improvement Company and the railroads supposedly went into effect on February 26. Up to this time much secrecy had shrouded the developments. Not much was known about the new company, but word got around among the producers in the oil regions as to the purpose of the organization. On February 27 the refiners in the oil regions, and especially Titusville, became thoroughly aroused. At first the producers did not believe what they heard, but they were soon seeing for themselves. Oil drillers in the regions realized what the South Improvement Company would mean for them. They did not intend to fall in line with any such proposition. An impromptu mass meeting was held in the Titusville opera house to throw up some sort of defense against the newly organized combination. Producers from all over the oil regions were there ready to take action. They were not rough or rowdy. They were angry and determined not to yield to the refiners, headed by Rockefeller and Flagler.

The meeting resulted in the formation of the Petroleum Producers Union. Its sole purpose was to fight the South Improvement Company. That was the most important thing accomplished; however, several other actions were taken. A committee was chosen to ask the legislature of Pennsylvania to revoke the charter of the South Improvement Company, and another committee was appointed to ask the Congress of the United States to investigate the whole situation. It also ordered that a review of the conspiracy against them be written and that a list of names of the persons involved be made ready. A lengthy report was prepared and 30,000 copies were distributed. The review told an ugly tale about Rockefeller, Flagler, and their associates. They were dubbed traitors to the industry. For weeks producers in the oil regions abandoned regular business and surged from place to place speaking and holding demonstrations. The whole section was awakened to action. They were intent on destroying the "Monster" or the "Great Anaconda," as the South Improvement Company was called and its "Forty Thieves" the name by which Rockefeller, Flagler, and the other refiners were known. The producers had expected nothing but robbery from the railroads. They were accustomed to that. But they refused to be robbed by men in their own business like the refiners. In other words, they would not sit idly by while the railroads and refiners teamed up against them. The leader in this movement against the South Improvement Company was John D. Archbold, who, strangely enough, later became vice-president of the Standard Oil Trust.[21]

*I*t was open warfare for some time between the Petroleum Producers Union and the South Improvement Company. The controversy lasted for about 40 days before anything was actually accomplished. The Producers Union, headed by William Hasson, refused to let oil supplies leave the wells. This action antedated the modern strike. The industry was at a standstill. As long as there was no oil from the wells, the refiners and the railroads might as well not have been in business. In most refining cities plants were closed. In Cleveland mass meetings for the relief of workmen were held. There was much excitement. Strangely enough, though, little vandalism was committed. Cooler heads prevailed. On April 15, 1872, the refiners gave in and promised to dissolve their scheme of combination. The South Improvement Company failed, but its actual origin remained in darkness.[22]

*T*hroughout the conflict, public sympathy lay with the Petroleum Producers Union. Most of the newspapers helped out the fight against the combination of refiners and railroads. The *New York Tribune* insisted that the combination was trying to choke the life from producers. The *Derrick* of Oil City went so far as to publish a black list of all the refiners involved in the conspiracy. Fortunately for Henry Flagler, his name was omitted from the first list. But Flagler was just as deeply involved as any on the list which included Watson, Rockefeller, Bostwick, Warden, and others.[23] The *Cleveland Herald* opposed the combination but knew little about what it was. The editor assured the refiners that he doubted the organization was for their benefit.[24] The *Cleveland Leader*, the

Herald's competitor, took an opposing view. The *Leader* tried to make Cleveland refiners think the new company would solve their problems. It was as vague in trying to do so as was the charter of the combination.[25] On April 11, 1872, the *Leader* published a lengthy statement signed by the Standard Oil Company and four other refineries in which they tried to justify the existence of the South Improvement Company. Their attempt to make the producers like it was feeble. They failed miserably.[26]

During the heat of battle between the producers and the refiners, the House of Representatives started an investigation of the giant scheme, as the producers had requested. President Ulysses S. Grant, well known for the scandals in his administration about this time, was interested in the conspiracy in Pennsylvania. He urged that some official action be taken. Nothing immediate came of the investigation. However, in an indirect way it may have helped influence the refiners to yield. At any rate, the South Improvement Company never did a dollar's worth of business. Because of the opposition it never got started and soon died.[27]

Instead of losing from the South Improvement scheme, the railroads gained. General George B. McClellan, president of the Atlantic and Great Western Railroad, started the ball rolling. He made overtures to the producers while the oil war was in process. He told producers that he was not interested in becoming allied with the refiners. It was not long before the railroads revoked their contracts with the South Improvement Company. One by one the railroads made contracts with producers. But the victory for the producers was not to last. Some refiners still had plans to alter the situation.

Rockefeller and Flagler were impressed with the possibilities of such an organization as the South Improvement Company. They did not mean to let the scheme die. They planned to create another combination similar to the former one and had faith in their ability to get the railroads on their side. Flagler knew if he could give the railroads enough traffic they would sign any contract he offered them. Consequently, their next move was to carry their idea to other refiners. They went to Pittsburgh and discussed their plan with several men they thought would be interested. They then journeyed to Titusville where they hoped to sell it to other refiners. The scheme became known as the Pittsburgh Plan, since it originated in that city.

*I*n early May, 1872, Flagler and Rockefeller appeared in Titusville. They talked with Jacob J. Vandergrift, one of the oil region refiners. Then they went calling on other refiners in the region. They convinced John D. Archbold, the leading refiner of the oil regions, of their plan. They argued that their new scheme was void of any of the objectionable features of the old one, in that it was not clouded by secrecy and suspicion. A public meeting was called on May 15 and 16, at which time the new Pittsburgh Plan was explained. Henry Flagler acted as spokesman for the visiting refiners. He did a creditable job of explaining the new scheme to the local refiners and later in trying to defend it. The organization, called the Central Association of Refiners, would cater to all refiners. Flagler explained that it was a scheme to save the oil industry rather than destroy it. There was to be an organization to manage the oil business throughout the United States. All refiners were allowed to become stockholders. There would be a board of directors which would handle the buying of crude oil and all arrangements for transportation. It was assumed that the parent organization would be the Standard Oil Company.

*T*he audience, which was filled with hundreds of producers as well as refiners, listened attentively to Flagler's speech. They had not forgotten that he was connected with the South Improvement scheme and the producers greatly distrusted him. After Flagler finished, both John D. Archbold and J. J. Vandergrift, oil regions' refiners, tried to speak in favor of the new scheme, but the patience of most of the audience had been worn threadbare. Neither Archbold nor Vandergrift was allowed to speak. They were howled down by all sorts of uncomplimentary remarks and were dubbed traitors because of their current affiliation with Flagler and Rockefeller. Several producers made impromptu speeches. They denounced the Pittsburgh Plan as "rotten" and "overbearing." Flagler, Rockefeller, and their associates were greatly embarrassed. The meeting was adjourned in an uproar. Flagler and Rockefeller went back to Cleveland. They had walked into an open trap which had been set for them by their enemies in Titusville and the oil regions.[28]

*N*either Rockefeller nor Flagler was discouraged by the setback. They were convinced that a large-scale combination could be perfected. They were determined to carry their point. The next attempt was to organize the National Refiners Association. It was a scheme similar to the Pittsburgh Plan, but it, too, failed before long.

*A*nother attempt to organize the refiners came in the summer of 1874. It was the result of a well-planned scheme. Two of the biggest refiners outside of Cleveland were Charles Lockhart and W. G. Warden. The new plan was to include them both. Lockhart and Warden were asked to be the guests of Rockefeller and Flagler at a fashionable hotel in Saratoga, New York. The gathering of the four men involved a few social activities. However, the main purpose of their short stay in Saratoga was to sell their two guests on the idea of consolidating with the Standard Oil Company. The plan for wholesale consolidation was certain to work this time. As the four men dined and talked together, Rockefeller and Flagler revealed to their guests the success they had achieved in bringing all the refiners in Cleveland together under their direction. They explained that the Standard Oil Company at that time had such a monopoly in Cleveland that their profit in 1873 was over $1,000,000—the result of combination in one city. The hosts went ahead to emphasize that they could do nothing by an open association. It had to be a closed affair. Lockhart and Warden were impressed by Standard's record of achievement in Cleveland. They had visions of a larger combination in which they might figure prominently. Rockefeller and Flagler made it plain that in any new arrangement Standard Oil Company would continue to take the lead. They also emphasized that the four men present—Rockefeller, Flagler, Lockhart, and Warden—would become the nucleus of the new company which would gradually acquire control of all refiners everywhere. Their scheme also included a mastery of the railroads in the matter of freight rates.[29]

*T*he conference lasted for six hours. At the conclusion of the meeting, Warden and Lockhart were thoroughly sold on the plan. They agreed to transfer their refineries, located in Philadelphia and Pittsburgh, to the Standard Oil Company in Cleveland. In exchange they took stock in the organization and continued to operate their respective plants as if no change had taken place. Rockefeller and Flagler were probably elated that evening as they returned to their rooms in the United States Hotel. These two canny, money-lustful, yet pious, men must have been happy. They were on the right road to the control of a vast industry which would lead to enormous wealth. The transaction was done in secrecy, because of popular disapproval for such action and since public opinion had been partially responsible for the defeat of the previous plans. Lockhart and Warden also agreed to help in the process of absorption of smaller refineries. They were to start a campaign of persuasion as soon as they reached their respective homes. They did this most effectively.

*F*urther consolidation soon took place. On October 15, 1874, in secret purchase, the Standard Oil Company engulfed Charles Pratt and Company of New York. This brought into the fold Charles Pratt and H. H. Rogers, two of the shrewdest oil men in the business. Pratt and Company continued to operate under its own name, ostensibly the chief rival of the Standard Oil Company in New York. With Warden, Lockhart and Pratt now in the company, Rockefeller and Flagler had as their allies the most successful men in the business. Added to this advantage was the fact that the new associates in the business were located in three of the best refining centers in the country outside of Cleveland—Philadelphia, Pittsburgh, and New York.[30]

*T*heir next move was to invade the oil regions and become entrenched in such towns as Titusville and Oil City. Accordingly, Flagler and Rockefeller approached John D. Archbold and J. J. Vandergrift. Both men had at first violently opposed any such action with the Standard Oil Company. By now, they realized that no progress in the future could be made without some connection with the firm. They, too, agreed to absorb the small oil companies in that region. The Standard Oil Company increased its stock on March 10, 1875, to $3,500,000 in order to take care of these new purchases. Ten thousand shares were added and Warden and Lockhart secured 6,250 of them. Charles Pratt received 3,125, and the remaining 625 were subscribed by Stephen V. Harkness.[31]

*I*n addition to this monstrous growth, the Standard Oil Company also had a monopoly with the railroads and pipe lines. Pipe lines, which were increasingly being used for the transportation of oil, were falling under the control of one or the other of the great systems being created. The battle, which Standard Oil finally won, was centered against the Empire Transportation Company. By 1878, Standard Oil Company controlled most of the pipe lines carrying petroleum from the oil regions.[32] Rockefeller and Flagler were also dictating the rates they were to receive from the railroads. The New York Central, the Erie, and the Pennsylvania railroads were not hard to convince. This practice of fixing rates continued despite rising opposition from the public against discrimination on the part of the railroads.

*T*he story of how Standard Oil Company and its affiliates drove the other refineries out of business is an interesting one. There was no stopping the rampaging organization. Among the many new subsidiaries of the Standard Oil Company in the late 1870s were the following:

— Standard Oil Company of Pittsburgh,
— Atlantic Refining Company of Philadelphia,
— Acme Oil Company,
— Imperial Oil Company,
— Charles Pratt and Company,
— J. A. Bostwick and Company,
— Sonce and Fleming Company,
— Camden Company, and the
— Baltimore United Oil Company.

*A*ll these companies worked faithfully in their respective communities, which extended from New York to Cleveland, to bring smaller refineries into the fold. Their connection with the parent organization, the Standard Oil Company located in Cleveland, was never mentioned. The affiliation with Standard Oil was supposed to be a secret at first. Rockefeller and Flagler soon realized that the true nature of such a powerful organization could not be kept from the public for any great length of time. By 1879 the above corporations, which became known as the Standard Alliance, controlled 95% of the country's petroleum industry. They had made almost a clean sweep of the field.

*R*ockefeller and Flagler had accomplished in about four years what no other oil concern had ever done. They had used outright coercion by underselling the smaller concerns which balked at their offers. So well did they control the field that they could force the railroads to raise freight rates on the smaller refiners who would not yield. Throughout the oil regions, where Rockefeller and Flagler were despised most, an especially thorough job had been done. John D. Archbold and J. J. Vandergrift were exacting and hard on the small refiners there. It was not unusual to observe closed refinery doors with such signs as, "Sold Out," "Dismantled," and "Shut Down." By 1879 practically nothing was left in the oil regions but the Imperial Oil Company of Oil City and the Acme Oil Company of Titusville, both subsidiaries of Standard Alliance. The Standard Alliance was nothing more than an informal substitute for the trust which was to come a few years later.[33]

*H*enry Flagler's part in the combination process which formed the Standard Alliance was important. His official position was that of secretary of the parent organization. He was also considered the "lawyer" of the company. Flagler had a keen legal mind despite the fact that he had not been trained for this work. Cold and remorseless, he was a shrewd analyst of delicate matters. His decisions were invaluable. Rockefeller depended upon Flagler's judgment as much as he did his own. One of the greatest achievements of the late 1870s was Flagler's work bringing the James N. Camden Oil Company into the Standard Oil fold.

*A*t that time, the Camden Company faced an uncertain future, a point on which Flagler capitalized. When the Camden Company was consolidated with Standard, the output of its refineries at Parkersburg, West Virginia, was reduced and a large refining plant was established at Baltimore.[34] James N. Camden was one of the few men connected with the Standard Alliance who sought public office. He was elected to Congress for several terms. As was to be expected, he favored the growth of big business. After he went to Washington, D.C., Camden kept Flagler posted on matters in Congress pertaining to their business. He reported in December, 1878, about an antidiscrimination bill, "I have the ear of some half dozen Senators that I will see. I can't think there is the least probable danger of such a bill getting through the Senate. . . ."[35] Many of the messages between Camden and Flagler were written in code. Their transactions were in deepest secrecy. For example, for some time in 1878 Camden had been trying to buy out a small refinery belonging to a Mrs. Hunt in Maryland. His first report to Flagler concerning this deal was unfavorable. It looked as if the owner would not give in to pressure.[36] Several days later a telegram from Camden to Flagler no doubt bore good news, if the reader could crack the code. The telegram read: "Mix with Taint. Saved has Macron Saxon and Meat to—Nailer put in force Kingdome over Sirup Maze. St. Louis Rail Road Meduse to have it Martyr. Rivers frozen up tight."[37] Another telegram from Camden addressed to Flagler bore this message: "Macar Kiss, but no Malted Marshal Maslin will be Spring King evening if you advise."[38]

*I*n the late 1870s there were a number of investigations concerning the workings and operations of the Standard Oil Alliance. There was a growing feeling on the part of the public that this ever-expanding monster should be curbed. More and more demands were being made of Congress to do something. State legislatures were also being aroused to action. James N. Camden was brought before a Senate committee in the West Virginia legislature in January, 1879. Nothing resulted from the investigation whose queries were mostly about rebates and special favors which the corporation was receiving from the railroads. Camden was noncommittal and replied, "We have had no rebates . . . for a long time, and we are having none at this time."[39] Also about this time, the Pennsylvania legislature was bringing suit against several members of the Alliance and the Hepburn Investigation was taking place in New York. The Ohio legislature also instituted an investigation where Flagler gave interesting testimony concerning rebates; however, none of his answers were found satisfactory. Other Standard associates also testified. Their statements were vague and proved to be truculent and unsatisfactory. The investigation in Pennsylvania was as unsuccessful as the one in Ohio. The two Rockefellers, Bostwick, Warden, Lockhart, Vandergrift, Camden, and Flagler were all under fire.[40]

*T*he public knew that the Standard Oil Alliance was simply a revival of the old South Improvement Company, which was considered a conspiracy in every respect. The public was not to be denied. A rocky road lay ahead for the leaders of the Standard Alliance in their battle. A short message from Camden to Flagler in 1879 indicates the end of the first round of investigations. He wrote that "The legislative investigations of the Alliance have fizzled out in West Virginia. How are you getting along with the legislative investigation in Pennsylvania?"[41]

6. *Retirement from Oil*

*N*ew York was selected as the site of the Standard Oil Company and would become the home of its secretary, Henry M. Flagler. By the 1870s, it had become America's largest city with a population of nearly 2,000,000 people. Visitors came from all over the world to see the sights. Sober Philadelphians and puritanical Bostonians were sometimes shocked at the goings-on when they visited. From Manhattan to Coney Island one could find entertainment of various sorts.[1] The city was rapidly becoming the center of much of the nation's industrial and banking interests. Many capitalists chose New York for their companies and their homes. Cornelius Vanderbilt, who ranked high among the railroad builders, William B. Astor, of fur fame, and Alexander T. Stewart, department store mogul, all made New York their home.[2] Flagler's fortune, as yet, did not compare with the largest in New York, but he soon established himself as one of the city's promising citizens. The Flaglers looked forward to the move to New York. Although Flagler had visited on several occasions, the family first saw the city in the winter of 1877 when Henry, Mary, and their children, Jennie Louise and young Harry, moved into the Buckingham Hotel. They lived at that hotel for a time.[3]

*D*uring 1877, the same year that the Flaglers moved to New York, much history was being written in America. Rutherford B. Hayes assumed the duties of President of the United States. The 1876 election had been hotly disputed when Republicans outmaneuvered the Democratic candidate, Samuel J. Tilden. The last of the federal troops were removed from the South and home rule was once again enjoyed by the onetime Confederate states. The new South had been conceived, but it had by no means matured. The smoldering embers of the Civil War had not completely died out. Reconstruction would take some time. As early as 1873, the period had been given a name—the Gilded Age. The road to reunion of the North and the South was underway. People believed better days lay ahead. The Panic of 1873 which caused a halt in the economic progress of America was over, and the Republican party was trying to live down the misconduct of several persons in the Ulysses S. Grant administration.[4]

*A*lthough Mary continued in poor health, the Flaglers liked living in New York. Her physician suggested that she should spend part of the next winter in Florida and they decided to go south for the coldest part of the next winter. Despite business pressures, Flagler accompanied Mary and the children on the trip. They went no farther than Jacksonville, Florida because of the lack of adequate transportation south of that point. Flagler noticed with concern the great need for better hotel facilities and travel accommodations in a state which boasted of its magic curative qualities for invalids. Mrs. Flagler rested well in Jacksonville, but after a few weeks Henry felt that he had to return to business in New York. Mary and the children returned north with him since she refused to remain without her husband. The responsibility of the children in a strange place would have been a burden for a person who was not well.

*T*he Flaglers changed their New York residence to the Windsor Hotel and with the exception of several long visits to their home in Cleveland, remained at that hotel until Flagler purchased a house at the corner of 54th Street and Fifth Avenue.[5] Mrs. Flagler's bronchial trouble grew steadily worse. The cold weather seemed to aggravate her condition. Her husband insisted that she go alone to Florida each winter, but she refused. It was a long, wearisome trip to Jacksonville and, besides, she did not want to be away from her husband and children. Flagler was in the midst of a busy life creating a fortune. He felt he could not spare the time to take her to Florida. Sometime during the winter of 1880 he realized the inevitable. Mary's condition became critical. By this time not even the warm Florida sunshine could make her better. Flagler insisted that she be allowed to go, but the doctor advised against the trip. For the first time, wealthy Henry Flagler realized that money was not the key to one's happiness.

*O*n May 18, 1881, Mary Harkness Flagler died.[6] Her death had a profound influence on Flagler. He determined to direct some of his attention toward himself and their children. These sobering effects began slowly to make a new man of him. He was sad and lonely. He tried not to give in to his feelings for the children's sake. Harry, who was 11 at the time, needed more than his father's influence. Flagler persuaded Carrie, his devoted half sister, to come to New York and preside over the home at 54th Street and Fifth Avenue. She soon won young Harry's confidence and did all she could to fill the vacancy left by the death of

Harry's mother. Jennie Louise, the Flagler's daughter, had been married for several years to John Arthur Hinckley. Her frequent visits to the Fifth Avenue home were a source of pleasure for her father as well as for Harry, who was devoted to his sister.[7]

*I*n the summer of 1881, Flagler realized the need for a change in their surroundings. He rented Satanstoe, a large house at Mamaroneck, New York, on Long Island Sound. It was accessible by both water and rail from New York City. Situated on a narrow extension of land, the beautiful 40-room frame home was surrounded by 32 acres of land. Frequent guests, mostly relatives, shared in the pleasures of the summer home. Flagler visited his office in the city regularly, but spent most of his time during the summer with Harry, Jennie Louise, and "Aunt Carrie" at Mamaroneck.

*T*hey liked Satanstoe so well that Flagler decided to buy it from the owner, Leonard Jacob. The transaction took place on June 1, 1882, and the property became Flagler's for the sum of $125,000. During the next few years he made many improvements. By January 2, 1885, Flagler had spent $330,992.51 on the Mamaroneck property.[8] The house was completely renovated inside and out. New fixtures were installed throughout the dwelling and attractive furniture was purchased. Even the chandeliers were according to Flagler's own ideas. One chandelier, designed of solid brass with crystal hangings, weighed more than 1,000 pounds. The new owner constructed a sea wall around most of his property and created a private breakwater which extended 200 yards into Long Island Sound. Sand was brought from the New Jersey coast for the transformation of the rocky muddy shore into a smooth bathing beach.[9] Flagler enjoyed his role as a creator of this place of beauty. Satanstoe became one of the most attractive vacation places on the Sound. Its wide verandas and large halls became the scene of many social functions. Satanstoe did its part in creating within Flagler a desire for more leisure time. It helped him set aside some of the pressing duties of the Standard Oil Company.

*F*lagler's influence in the Standard Oil Company and with John D. Rockefeller steadily diminished after 1882. Although he remained a vice-president of the company until June, 1908, John Dustin Archbold, a younger man, gradually took Flagler's place in the upper ranks of the business. In many respects Archbold was a much more aggressive man than Flagler. He had attracted John D. Rockefeller's attention from the start. Archbold was born July 26, 1848, in Leesburg, Ohio, the son of a Methodist preacher. He had a hard time during his early life, but after a steady climb became a petroleum producer in the oil regions. He organized the Acme Oil Company which expanded later into the Standard Alliance. A real genius in the new firm, Archbold became one of the vice-presidents. No task was too great for him to undertake. He frequently called upon men in high government positions to do favors for him and for his company. They responded favorably. From 1882 until he died in 1916, Archbold helped dominate the policy and counsels of the Standard Oil Company.[10]

*A*lthough Archbold took Henry Flagler's place in the inner circle of the Standard Oil magnates, Flagler did not withdraw completely from the great organization. There was no break between Rockefeller and Flagler. Henry Flagler had merely decided to retire slowly from the business. He maintained an office at 140 Pearl Street in New York. However, by 1888 not more than half of his time was spent there.

*F*lagler seemed to find a new zest in life after he became interested in his developments in Florida. By 1895 he was spending more time in Florida than in New York. By 1908 he was virtually inactive as far as the Standard Oil Company was concerned. It was in that year that he resigned the vice-presidency; however, it was not until 1911 that he gave up his membership on the Board of Directors.[11] He always maintained an interest in the Standard Oil Company and was one of the largest stockholders in the company until his death. Flagler's wealth multiplied more rapidly in the two decades between 1880-1900 than during all the other years in his life because of his large holdings in Standard Oil. The Company experienced a period of great development. From 1870 to 1882 its capital increased from $1,000,000 to $55,000,000. In seven years it paid some $11,000,000 in dividends, and at the same time it had laid by $45,000,000 in new assets.[12]

*T*o keep pace with the growing company, a new organization was formed on January 2, 1882. It was known as the Standard Oil Trust.[13] Standard Oil Trust brought in all the existing stockholders in the various enterprises taken over by the old Standard Oil Company. These included refining, piping, buying, and selling oil. Thirty-seven stockholders were involved in Standard and all the subsidiary and allied corporations. The 37 merely conveyed their shares in the various companies into the hands of nine trustees. The nine men had all been prominently connected with the old concern.[14] They were John D. Rockefeller, William Rockefeller, Henry M. Flagler, O. H. Payne, Charles Pratt, John Archbold, W. G. Warden, Jabez Bostwick, and Benjamin Brewster. The trustees controlled two-thirds of the shares and became the direct stockholders in the various companies connected by the system. The other stockholders controlled one-third of the shares. They received trust certificates in $100 denominations in return for the shares they had deposited in the newly created trust.[15] The trustees were to receive salaries of $25,000 each, with the exception of the president, who was voted a salary of $30,000. The principal office of the trust was to be located in New York.[16]

*W*ith capital of $55,000,000 and properties valued at $75,000,000, the Standard Oil Trust was the biggest business concern in America. It soon became notorious. Public sentiment began to form against the monstrous organization. Wave after wave of criticism broke over the heads of Rockefeller, Flagler, and their associates. The public demanded that governmental action be taken which would curb the growth of the Trust. As early as December, 1882, Flagler, Rockefeller, and Benjamin Brewster were summoned to appear before a United States Senate Committee which was inquiring into certain practices of the new business. The inquiry was held at the Metropolitan Hotel in New York, but all efforts to extract from the witnesses any information as to the exact workings and nature of the Trust failed. The committee also was determined to find out the reasons for its formation and the size of the dividends that were paid. The witnesses said virtually nothing that would throw light on the new organization. Flagler remained adamant. He became furious at the committee's attorney who kept reminding the group about the rising tide of public sentiment against the organization. At one point he demanded that Flagler answer a certain question.

*R*efusing, Flagler shouted, "It suits me to go elsewhere for advice, particularly as I am not paying you for it." The government attorney quickly rejoined by saying, "I am not paying you to rob the community, I am trying to expose your robbery."[17] Needless to say, the hearing ended in failure.

*A*s monopolies began to be formed in other areas, definite plans were soon made to curb the consolidation of big business. The public was disturbed over consolidation and was thoroughly aroused at the methods of dishonesty in competition. These methods were often responsible for the success of the corporation.

*H*enry George's *Progress and Poverty* (1879), Edward Bellamy's *Looking Backward* (1887), and Henry Demarest Lloyd's *Wealth Against Commonwealth* (1894) were all directed against the growth of monopolies. In politics, too, there was considerable opposition. Both the Republicans and Democrats opposed railroad corporations and monopolies as early as 1872. In 1880 the Greenback party condemned monopolies and in 1884 an Anti-Monopolistic Party was created for the purpose of preventing further gains by the corporation. In 1888, the platforms of the Republican, Democratic, Prohibition, and Union Labor parties all opposed the growth of monopolies. Many states had definitely banned monopolies by this time, but the federal government had not taken any effective action.[18]

*T*he committee on manufacturing of the United States House of Representatives began an investigation in 1888. In the same year the Senate of the state of New York began a similar inquiry. The inquiry made by the House committee was the most important since the investigation made by the Hepburn Committee. The Standard Oil Trust and the Sugar Trust were both under fire. The chairman of the committee, Henry Bacon, started the hearings on April 6, 1888. Franklin B. Gowen, the attorney, was the chief questioner.

*G*owen was a fiery, energetic person who more than once drew anger from his witnesses. Among the Standard executives he questioned were Flagler, John D. Rockefeller, and Archbold. Flagler came to the stand on April 27. He explained his early connections with the Standard Oil Company as its secretary. He let it be known that he had ceased to serve in that capacity when the Trust was formed in 1882 and that since that time he had served as one of the nine trustees.[19]

*F*lagler was deliberate and calm with his answers, but at times he was evasive. He was asked several questions pertaining to the history of the Standard Oil Company. He answered these with brevity. Gowen queried him about the South Improvement Company, but Flagler appeared to know little about it. He disclaimed any part in the organization of the South Improvement Company; however, his critics placed a good bit of the responsibility for that organization on his shoulders. Flagler insisted that neither he nor Rockefeller had any confidence in or respect for the South Improvement Company. He said:

> *We did not believe in it, but the view presented by other gentlemen was pressed upon us to such an extent that we acquiesced in it to the extent of subscribing our names to a certain amount of the stock, which was never paid for. The company never did a dollar's worth of business and never had any existence other than its corporative existence, which it obtained through the charter. Through its president it negotiated certain railroad contracts, which, as I remember now, were signed by the company and by the officers of the railroad. Those contracts were held in escrow a few weeks and were destroyed or canceled by mutual consent."*[20]

Many of Flagler's answers concerning the South Improvement Company were made in short terse remarks, such as, "No, sir," "Yes, sir," or "I do not remember."

*F*lagler was questioned thoroughly on the makeup and workings of the Trust Company. He argued that the Trust was not a corporation, saying that it derived its existence by virtue of a contract "entered into by and between the individuals who created" the Trust. He admitted that the Trust was a combination of the Standard Oil Company of Ohio, the Standard Oil Company of New York, the Standard Oil Company of New Jersey, the Standard Oil Company of Pennsylvania, the Standard Oil Company of Minnesota, the Standard Oil Company of Iowa, and the Standard Oil Company of Kentucky. Since each of these companies was chartered in a different state, persons who were stockholders of these several companies were parties to the agreement. Flagler's contention was that the Trust simply became the custodian of the stock. The state corporations remained intact as independent combinations.[21] He also admitted that the National Transit Company was part of the Standard Oil Trust and that the Trust owned the company which possessed pipe lines.

$\mathcal{A}$s to the control of railroad rates and pipe lines, Flagler defended the combination saying that it was a necessity to get control of the medium of transportation. He admitted that the Standard Oil Company went all out to kill the Empire Transportation Company because it was in competition with the Standard Oil Company. However, as a witness, Flagler was not consistent with remarks he had made earlier. For example, in 1880, Flagler admitted that the Standard Oil Company owned properties in Ohio and New Jersey and swore that the company did not own, operate, or control any other refineries in the United States. On the witness stand on April 27, 1888, he reversed his earlier statement when he declared that the Standard Oil Company owned refineries in Pittsburgh as early as 1874.[22]

$\mathcal{G}$owen kept hammering on the subject of railroads. He was trying to draw from Flagler some fact concerning the Trust's interest in that field. When answering the questions Flagler insisted that the Standard Oil Trust was not interested in railroads. He did admit that, personally, he was connected with three different railroads. He said that he was a director of the Chicago, Rock Island, and Pacific Railway and was president of the Jacksonville, St. Augustine, and Halifax River Railway. He also explained that he was a large stockholder in the Tampa, Jacksonville, and Key West Railway.[23]

$\mathcal{F}$lagler's testimony revealed that the Standard Oil Trust had increased its capital to about $90,000,000 by 1888. The market value of all the shares was estimated at about $154,000,000. Annual dividends of 7% had been paid the stockholders since 1882. This was indeed a very good showing for any concern.[24] The hearings lasted for several months. A mass of facts and information was gathered from all the executives. Flagler was called back to the stand in Washington on July 20, 1888, at which time the query was limited to railroad rates and rebates.[25] Little substance was gained by the committee from either of Flagler's appearances, and perhaps less from his associates' testimony. The Standard Oil Trust was a hard nut to crack.

$\mathcal{P}$rior to the hearings held by the committee from the House of Representatives, the New York State Senate investigated trusts. Those hearings took place in February, 1888, with the Standard Oil Trust as its principal target. The hearing process generated a report of 1,500 pages, 1,000 of which were devoted to the creation and early history of the company. Flagler was in Florida during most of the investigation. He returned to New York on February 28 to serve as a witness. His remarks included an explanation of the early history of the company, information about the South Improvement Company, the 10¢ rebate Standard received from all the railroads in 1875, and the purchase of the Empire Transportation Company.[26] The investigation led to nothing definite or specific; in fact, it proved a disappointment to the people of New York. Public hatred for the continued growth of these combinations intensified. One indirect result of the hearings was the passage of the Sherman Anti-Trust Act in 1890, but, like the Interstate Commerce Act of 1887, it was far from effective during the first few years of its existence.

The first effective and energetic effort to dissolve the Standard Oil Trust came from Ohio in 1890. David K. Watson, attorney general of that state, filed a proceeding in *quo warranto* on May 8 in the Ohio Supreme Court against the Standard Oil Company of Ohio. The court rendered a decision depriving the company of the right to remain a part of the Trust.[27] The case was followed by critics of the Trust all over America. Politicians who leaned toward the large combinations tried to discourage Watson in his fight, but he would not be stopped. Mark Hanna, who had approved the tactics of the Standard Oil Company, wrote to the attorney general as follows: "You have been in politics long enough to know that no man in public life owes the public anything."[28]

The movement started by Watson led to vigorous action by the United States Supreme Court. The Standard Oil Trust was dissolved on March 2, 1892. Henry Flagler, who was still the secretary, though mainly in name, called a meeting of the holders of Standard Oil Trust certificates for March 21, 1892. The meeting was held at the central office, 26 Broadway, New York, for purposes of liquidation. The Trust was apparently dissolved into 20 constituent companies with a capital of $102,233,700, and an evaluation of $121,631,312. However, the trustees continued to exist under the new name of "liquidating trustees." The dissolution process was not actually carried out at this time. In fact, the unity of action among the several companies was changed very little. It did not take long for the public to realize that the monopolistic power of the Standard Oil Trust had yet to be broken.[29]

$\mathcal{B}$y now, the old guard in the firm had, to a large extent, passed from the scene. Flagler retired. Samuel Andrews, one of the original partners, sold his shares in 1880. Charles Pratt died in 1891 and Jabez Bostwick passed away in 1892. O. H. Payne and William B. Warden withdrew from the combination in the 1880s. H. H. Rogers and William Rockefeller found other interests, as Flagler had done.

$\mathcal{T}$he changed lineup in Standard Oil saw some interesting new faces. One of them was John D. Rockefeller, Jr., who arrived at 26 Broadway just after his graduation from Brown University in 1897. He carried much of the burden for his father, to say nothing of John D. Archbold, who by this time had become an old hand at the business. There was complete revamping of the company in 1899, but it had no effect upon the management. Actually there had been very little change in the continuity of the Standard's management since the early 1870s. John D. Rockefeller continued as the president of the Standard Oil of New Jersey and John D. Archbold as the vice-president. The stockholders numbered 3,500.[30] The board of directors had considerable power. It was fairly well known that the board collected the dividends of all the other constituent companies. They then divided them among the stockholders, just as the dividends had been divided by the trustees after 1882, and by the liquidating trustees after 1892.[31]

$\mathcal{I}$n 1911, the Standard Oil Company of New Jersey, the parent organization, was finally dissolved into 35 units.[32] This was what had been attempted since the Trust was formed in 1882. All those who held the old Standard Oil Company stock were issued the same percentage of stock in all the new corporations. The dissolution of Standard Oil Company brought about many changes, and an entirely different organization.

$\mathcal{B}$y the time of Standard Oil's dissolution, Henry Flagler was merely an interested spectator on the side lines. His Florida interests had long since overshadowed completely any attachments that he might have had for the Standard Oil Company.

7. *A Florida Honeymoon*

*W*edding bells rang for Henry Flagler and his new bride in 1883. On June 5th of that year he was married to Ida Alice Shourds at the Madison Avenue Methodist Church in New York City.[1] The marriage was not entirely pleasing to the Flagler and Harkness clans, but there was nothing that could be done about it. The fact that Ida Alice was 18 years younger seemed to make no difference to the newlyweds. At the time of their marriage, she was 35 and he was 53. The friendship which grew into courtship began in the Flagler home where Miss Shourds had been an attendant to his first wife, Mary, during her years of declining health. Prior to becoming a practical nurse Ida Alice had aspired to be an actress. Unfortunately, her dramatic ability was not sufficient for her to gain a secure place in that field.[2]

*T*he second Mrs. Flagler's background was greatly different from that of her husband, despite the fact they were both reared in the homes of clergymen. She was born in Philadelphia on July 4, 1848. Her father, who was an Episcopal minister, died when Ida Alice was very young. Her mother, Margaret B. Shourds, moved to New York where her two brothers, Charles and Stephen, were em-

ployed. Mattie, an older sister, soon married and moved away. Ida Alice's formal education was limited. She was not inclined to follow intellectual pursuits. Henry was a self-educated man and reflected a certain amount of culture and refinement which she seemed not to appreciate. Flagler was a habitual reader. His wife's tastes ran much to the contrary.[3]

*N*evertheless, there was no doubt about Flagler's love for his new wife. His deep love for her apparently gave them a basis of understanding. He thought she was an exceptionally beautiful woman, and never hesitated to let her know that. *Ida Alice Shourds Flagler*

73

*I*da Alice Flagler was an attractive woman. She was small in stature and possessed a profusion of red hair which she usually rolled up on top of her head. Her eyes were bright blue and her complexion was fair. She had a small face and delicate features. She also had a violent temper which was virtually uncontrollable at times.[4]

*T*here was not much enthusiasm when the new Mrs. Flagler was welcomed to the family home in New York. Flagler was engrossed in a business deal that would not permit him to leave town at the time of the wedding and it was decided to postpone their honeymoon until fall. A few trunks containing Ida Alice's personal belongings were delivered to the Flagler home the day after the wedding. The newlyweds arrived soon after. Carrie Flagler, Henry's half sister who had mothered young Harry and looked after the home for two years, returned to Cleveland to live. Although she was asked to stay, she felt that her duty to her brother's family was finished. Ida Alice tried to fill the vacant place in the home. As far as Harry was concerned she never succeeded.[5]

*F*rom the outset, Ida Alice Flagler was impressed with her husband's wealth. His fortune, as far as she was concerned, was one of his engaging features. With an almost unlimited bank account, she launched a spending spree that would have astonished a man of modest means. Within a few months after she married, her wardrobe contained some of the most beautiful and elaborate clothes the fashion shops in New York could provide. She tried to bridge the gap between herself and her husband with his money. She worked hard at being the wife of a wealthy man, realizing all the while that she was living in a world different from anything she had ever experienced. She wanted New York society to recognize her, but no matter how hard she tried, that goal was never reached.

*T*he Flagler's belated honeymoon began in December, 1883. Flagler disliked cold weather. For months he and Ida Alice had been planning a trip to Florida. Aside from the trip to Florida in 1878, he had never been far away from his work.[6] Now, at the age of 53, he was worth between $10,000,000 and $20,000,000. He was ready to retire from his strenuous labors. Flagler made no definite plans about when they would return to New York. Their trip from New York to Jacksonville required 90 hours of traveling. It involved many changes and delays because of the different gauges of railroad tracks along the way. The Flaglers could have gone via boat from New York to Savannah and from there to Jacksonville. Instead they chose the overland route by rail. At that time, Savannah was probably the most important of the southern seaport towns. Railroad lines concentrated there from all parts of the country.[7]

*A*rriving in Savannah, they paused for only a short time before making the remainder of the trip. Jacksonville was not far away, but that part of the trip was more uncomfortable than the journey from New York to Savannah had been. One contemporary traveler expressed it in these words:

> *There are two ways of getting to Jacksonville [from Savannah], and whichever you choose you will be sorry to have not taken the other. There is the night train by railroad, which brings you to Jacksonville in about 16 hours; and there is the steamboat line, which goes inland nearly all the way, and which may land you in a day, or you may run aground, and remain on board for a week.*[8]

*M*ost people chose the journey by steamboat, despite the chance they took of being stranded before they reached their destination. It is more than likely, however, that the Flaglers continued their journey by rail. The route did not run directly to Jacksonville. The unlucky traveler would be routed from Savannah to a junction not far from Valdosta, Georgia, called Dupont. From Dupont, one took a bumpy little road to Live Oak and from there the route went to Jacksonville. It was perhaps three or four times the direct distance from Savannah to Jacksonville.[9] Whichever mode of travel the Flaglers decided upon, rail or steamboat, there can be one thing certain: it would not have been a comfortable journey.

*J*acksonville was already a thriving little resort town. Its history dated back to 1822 when it was surveyed, laid out, and named for Andrew Jackson, the first governor of the Florida territory. Its early growth was slow partially because of the Seminole Indian Wars which lasted from 1836 to 1842. There were fewer than 1,000 inhabitants living there by 1847.[10] All this changed after the Civil War when Jacksonville became a commercial center and an outlet for the transportation of lumber and cotton. Located a few miles inland on the St. Johns River,

Jacksonville gave promise of becoming an important seaport and rail-road terminus. Several hotels were constructed. They were designed especially for winter visitors who came from the North seeking winter warmth, pleasure, or improved health. Among the finest of the hotels built was the St. James and this is where the Flaglers stayed. At the time of their visit, the building was only about four years old. Constructed of brick and wood, it was considered one of the most famous hotels in the South. There were many amusements for its guests including bowling alleys, billiard rooms, and sun parlors.[11]

*F*lagler and his bride stayed for only a few days in Jacksonville. They had decided to go on to St. Augustine by way of the St. Johns River. At that time, many winter visitors in Jacksonville took a river trip on the St. Johns. A historic water highway to inland Florida, newcomers were charmed with the beautiful scenery. Orange groves and small settle-ments were located along both banks of the lazily flowing river. Flagler was impressed with the entire area.[12] At Tocoi, about 30 miles up river, the honeymooners left their steamer. It was there that they boarded the St. Johns River Railroad, a short line of 15 miles. Until 1870 the line had been horse drawn. After that time it operated with a little "coffee mill" engine. The road was built in 1858 by John Westcott who sold it to William Astor. Astor then rebuilt the line and operated it more effi-ciently. The fare from Tocoi to St. Augustine was $2 per person and the trip took several hours.[13]

*T*he Flaglers were eager to reach their destination. It is not known where they stayed on their first trip to St. Augustine. There were no large hotels. Henry and Ida Alice were charmed with the ancient city, despite the fact that it was so rundown. Nearly 2,000 persons lived in the town. They seemed to think in terms of the past, seldom speaking of the future. Flagler was astonished at the lack of development, but he was delighted with the weather and the numerous orange groves which were in and around the town. Their stay in St. Augustine was an enjoyable one and they remained longer than they had planned. A cold wave gripped the North around the first of the year while flowers bloomed in profusion in St. Augustine. On January 4, the thermometer dropped to 27° below zero in several places in the East; in St. Louis it was 23° below zero; in Cleveland 14° below.[14] The prolonged cold spell lasted until late in February. As the editor of the *New York Herald-Tribune* stated, it was a "phenomenal winter."[15] The Flaglers were glad to be away and remained in the Florida sunshine until about the beginning of March, 1884.

*T*his trip did something for Flagler. It convinced him that St. Augustine was an ideal place for them to retire. He was determined to come back often to the land where the thermometer seldom reached as low as the 30s, where flowers bloomed the year round.

*D*efinite plans to return to St. Augustine were made before they left for New York.[16] One thing about his decision to retire there worried him. Why didn't St. Augustine have better facilities for winter visitors? Why didn't someone build an attractive hotel to entice winter-weary, wealthy Easterners? To say that Flagler had any intention of playing the role of a developer this early would be a mistake. His thoughts, however, were soon to turn in that direction. He began to have visions of what St. Augustine might be if only a little money were lavished on the community. His vision and destiny soon set in to shape a new career for the former oil magnate.

*F*lorida was long overdue in the realm of development and expansion. She seemed to be waiting for the vision of a great benefactor like Flagler. There were dormant possibilities which were not obvious to the average eye, yet to the keen perception of men like Flagler much could be seen.

*T*he southernmost state had been the site of the first permanent settlement in the United States.[17] From the days of Pedro Menéndez in 1565 until 1763 the Spanish had dominated, although development had been negligible during much of the period.[18] More progress had been made in English colonies to the North. At the close of the French and Indian War in 1763 Spain was forced to cede Florida to the English and from 1763 until 1783 Florida was part of the British Empire. At the close of the American Revolution, Britain lost Florida along with the other American colonies. The colonies received their independence, but Florida was given back to Spain as a part of her settlement in the American Revolution. Accordingly, Spain took up where she had left off in 1763. Spanish Florida was a thorn in the side to the southern American states. There were border troubles involving Seminole Indians and slaves. To make matters more complicated there was a growing feeling among many Americans that their country should acquire the Spanish territory, thereby settling all controversies. That sentiment persisted for some time. Finally as a result of the Onis-Adams Treaty, ratified in 1821, Florida finally became an American territory.[19] The period from 1821 until 1845 was one of adjustment and preparation for statehood. American customs, habits, and ways of life slowly displaced those which had been brought in earlier by the Spanish. After a time the territory became a political unit and was finally admitted to the Union on March 3, 1845.[20]

*H*owever, Florida shared with her sister Southern states the bitter dregs of the Civil War and Reconstruction. Up to the time of the War, little advancement had taken place in Florida. The population remained small. It was still primarily a land of swamps, rivers, and marshes. The Reconstruction years, despite hardships and adversities, produced some rather decided material gains. The population grew rapidly from 1860 to 1880; in the latter year the state claimed 269,493 persons, a 90% increase over the 20 year period.[21]

*T*here were several reasons for the rise in population, most of which was in the northern part of the state. In the first place, many of the soldiers who had been sent to Florida during the Civil War found the state a surprisingly livable place. Some of them liked it so much, especially during the wintertime, that they returned to build homes and raise their families. At the time there were essentially no factories in the state; though there were a few saw mills and perhaps several small banks. Orange growing as an investment had just started in the northern and central sections. A small amount of northern capital was used in the infant citrus industry.[22]

*A*s early as 1880 Florida was known in various parts of the country for her warm sunshine, her mild winters, her long winding rivers, her virgin forests, and her desirability as a place for invalids, especially consumptives. The modern American tourist was unknown, but some few stout hearts made the long journey from the North to enjoy the pleasures that Florida had to offer. Edward King, in his series of articles on the South soon after the Civil War, called Florida "Our American Italy," and became very enthusiastic over the possibilities of the southernmost state. He stated that many northerners went to Florida each year as early as 1874. He continued,

> *It is not invalids who crowd Florida nowadays, but the wealthy and the well. One-fourth of the annual visitors are in pursuit of health; the others are crusading to find the phantom 'pleasure.' Fully one-half of the resident population of Jacksonville is northern, and has settled there since the [Civil] War.*[23]

*O*ther contemporaries put more emphasis on Florida as a health resort. *Harper's* Magazine maintained that by 1870 Florida had become the winter home of many thousands of persons having "pulmonary complaints." Most doctors advised their patients to go to St. Augustine. Others settled in Jacksonville or along the St. Johns River.[24]

*T*he St. Johns River flowed through one of the most attractive areas in Florida and people found ideal places to settle along its banks. Towns and villages grew up. They were served by picturesque river steamers. The St. Johns River was the chief highway for transportation for northeastern Florida. As early as the 1860s several steamers made weekly trips from Charleston and Savannah down the coast to Jacksonville, only a few miles inland from the mouth of the river. From Jacksonville, the boats proceeded up river to Tocoi, Palatka, Federal Point, and Enterprise. The steamers used fat pine which could be bought at various places up and down the river.[25] Since the steamboat era in Florida preceded the railroad era by many years passengers, as well as freight, were transported by boat. The importance of the waterways, especially the St. Johns River, cannot be overemphasized.

Steamboating on the River

*M*ost of the population in Florida during the 1870s and 1880s was situated in the northern part of the state, between Jacksonville and St. Augustine on the East and Pensacola on the West. Of the 269,493 people in Florida in 1880, the counties touching the East Coast, including the St. Johns River area, had 39,935. The gross valuation for taxes for these counties in 1884 was $12,166,134, whereas the gross valuation for taxes for the whole state of Florida at the same time was $60,042,655. Jacksonville's population was about 15,000, but there was no bridge across the sprawling St. Johns connecting the city with points to the South.

*D*aytona, a settlement of about 200 people, was 40 miles south of St. Augustine on the Atlantic Ocean.[26] It was on the fringe of the frontier; however, its ideal location gave it many possibilities. A Florida newspaper in 1877 noticed with interest the attention the region around Daytona was receiving and said that a considerable amount of land was being sold in the New Smyrna area. During the winter months stage coaches were put into operation between Enterprise on the St. Johns River and New Smyrna on the Atlantic Coast. The small villages of Port Orange, Volusia, and New Britain were also stops along the route.[27] The rich Indian River section just south of New Smyrna was virtually untouched. Melbourne was in existence, but that was about all. Around the shores of Biscayne Bay there were a few more scattered families. The little village of Key West was completely isolated from the mainland. Dade County, which extended in 1888 from the St. Lucie River to Key West, had a population of only 257 people. Ten years later the county would more than triple to 861 inhabitants.[28]

*L*ife along Florida's East Coast was simple. There were few luxuries and conveniences and people lived by fishing, hunting, and perhaps raising some fruits and vegetables. The products they raised or produced were mainly for home consumption. A market for perishables was limited. For example, livestock, especially cows, were almost unknown. It was virtually impossible for a person to get milk. Fresh protein, except for fish and eggs, was a rarity.[29]

*T*ransportation in Florida in 1880 was limited. Only a few railroads had been built before that time. Perhaps the first road in Florida was a short line from Tallahassee to St. Marks built in 1834. This road, completing a distance of 23 miles, was not only the first railroad in the state but also was one of the earliest in the United States. The road, which was crude, served as an important factor in the growth of the North Central section of Florida. It carried cotton from the plantations in northern Florida and southern Georgia to the Gulf of Mexico for transport to the mills. In 1834 several other companies were incorporated for the purpose of building railroads. The beginning of the Seminole Indian Wars in 1836 and the Panic of 1837 put an abrupt end to most of these ventures.[30]

*D*uring the next 25 years several hundred miles of railroad tracks were constructed in Florida. By the time the Civil War broke out, the following roads, comprising 414 miles, were in operation:

Florida Railroad	
Fernandina to Cedar Key	155 miles
Pensacola and Georgia Railroad	
Lake City to Tallahassee	114 miles
Florida, Atlantic and Gulf Central	
Jacksonville to Lake City	60 miles
Florida and Alabama Railroad	
Pensacola to the Alabama line	47 miles
St. Johns River Railroad	15 miles
Tallahassee Railroad	23 miles[31]

During the Civil War railroad mileage in Florida increased by 61 miles to 475 miles, but from 1866 until 1880 only two additional miles of railroad track were laid in the state. Railroad mileage in Florida increased rapidly in the early 1880s with a considerable portion of this construction taking place in East Florida.[32]

*E*conomic growth in Florida would not be dormant much longer. The early 1880s witnessed some development in the fields of transportation, industry, and agriculture. This was true of the entire south as Flagler must have noticed. A new spirit was beginning to pervade most of the southern states. They were thinking in terms of the future. Henry Grady, an Atlanta newspaper editor, was gaining fame as a prophet of the New South. To Grady and others, the term the "New South" meant industrialization and development. In 1881 Atlanta held an exposition for the purpose of showing the nation her advantages. At that time, cities of the New South included Atlanta, Birmingham, Chattanooga, and Knoxville. Older towns which received a new impetus from industrialization and development were Charleston, Columbia, New Orleans, Richmond, and Savannah.

*A*t the same time, the spirit of development also prevailed strongly in Florida. In 1880, William D. Bloxham was elected governor promising to help develop Florida by draining much of the swamp lands and making them inviting to settlers. Hamilton Disston, a saw manufacturer from Philadelphia, was given large acreage of reclaimed land in central and south Florida. He also bought 4,000,000 acres of swamp land at 25¢ an acre and began to make it fit for settlers. About the same time other builders came to Florida. H. H. De Land, a New Yorker, settled in central Florida and laid out a town which bears his name. Henry B. Plant, a Connecticut Yankee, contributed much to the growth of the state through his railroad construction and development on the West Coast. The discovery of phosphate deposits near Tampa and the cultivation of citrus fruit through central Florida brought many new people into these regions.[33] By 1885, Florida was on the way toward an era of progress and development. Economic advancement was definitely on the way.

*F*lagler pondered over the economic changes beginning to occur in Florida. Long after the warmth of the sunshine from his first winter in Florida was gone, his thoughts returned to the business opportunities and challenges he had identified.

8. *Permanent Stakes in Florida*

*T*he Flaglers did not forget Florida. Thoughts of their pleasant stay in Jacksonville and St. Augustine in 1883-1884 gave rise to plans for another trip the next winter. Flagler had pleasure and perhaps a little business in mind. He had hoped to spend part of the fall of 1884 in St. Augustine, but business obligations kept him in New York until after Christmas. In fact, Henry and Ida Alice did not leave the city until February 17, 1885. New York was experiencing its coldest weather of the year. It was a good time for them to be going south. Traveling in the private railroad car which Flagler had purchased the year before, they arrived in Jacksonville two days after their departure. Travel between New York and Jacksonville had improved during the year. The trip was not so long and tiresome as it had been in the past.[1]

*T*he Flaglers renewed many acquaintances at the St. James Hotel in Jacksonville, but remained there only a week. Flagler heard that a new hotel had been built in St. Augustine. He learned that many Jacksonville visitors were going on to the old town of St. Augustine and they were staying there for long periods of time since accommodations there were much better. Flagler was eager to see the hotel. On February 25, the couple left Jacksonville on the newly constructed Jacksonville, St. Augustine, and Halifax River Railway.[2] They left their private railroad car in Jacksonville, and were ferried across the St. Johns River from Jacksonville to South Jacksonville to the beginning point of the new railroad.[3] The trip to St. Augustine required the greater portion of one day and only a hearty soul made it without loss of spirit or appetite. The Flaglers were happy to reach their destination. He was happier still to see the new San Marco Hotel and to talk with its manager.[4] Flagler had visualized such a venture. He predicted it would do a good business.

*W*ith a luxury hotel in operation, St. Augustine had changed considerably in the 12 months the Flaglers had been away. The San Marco, though not extremely large, was up-to-date. It had been completed to the point of taking guests, but more work was yet to be done. A group of New Englanders had put up the money for the construction of the building. They had hired Osborn D. Seavey, with whom Flagler became friendly, to manage it. The same group of men had built the Magnolia Springs Hotel in Green Cove Springs on the St. Johns River halfway between Jacksonville and Palatka. Seavey, an experienced New England hotel man, had managed the Magnolia Springs before coming to St. Augustine. It was through his efforts that more Easterners spent the winter of 1885 in St. Augustine than ever before.[5]

Villa Zorayda, ca. early 1900s

There were several other building projects in St. Augustine which claimed Flagler's attention. One of the most pretentious was the Villa Zorayda, the handsome residence of Franklin W. Smith. Smith, who had been in St. Augustine for some time became interested in a building scheme for the town. The Villa Zorayda was constructed with the use of a new kind of material made from a mixture of cement, shells, and water. Considered the loveliest private dwelling in St. Augustine, it was a miniature reproduction of one of the palaces of the Alhambra in Spain. The Oriental palace in St. Augustine was square with a court in the center onto which opened several balconies. Around the building was a flower garden. At night the palace was lighted by colored lamps which were placed on the outside. The windows were of stained glass so that the light on the inside blended beautifully with the lamps outside.[6] Franklin W. Smith was also interested in building a resort hotel not far from his home and told Flagler of his plans. However, he did not build the Casa Monica, the name of his new hotel venture, until 1886. It was not completed until January, 1888.[7]

Flagler was impressed with St. Augustine's accessibility, particularly when compared with travel conditions several years earlier. Much was said and written concerning the new road from South Jacksonville to St. Augustine and even more advertisement was given the extension which William Astor was building from Tocoi Junction, just West of St. Augustine, to East Palatka on the St. Johns. Astor, who owned the little line from Tocoi to St. Augustine, completed his new extension in 1886. He named it the St. Augustine and Palatka Railroad.[8]

Other railroad construction in the St. Augustine area was taking place in the middle 1880s. U. J. White built a short logging road from the St. Johns River at East Palatka to San Mateo, a distance of only about four miles. With the financial aid of S. V. White, a Wall Street operator, the road was extended slowly across the deserted area from the St. Johns River to Ormond and Daytona on the Atlantic Coast, about 51 miles in distance. Before the road reached Daytona, the construction was delayed many times because of marshy land. In other spots it was necessary to cut through coquina rock, since it was not subject to blasting, in order to lay the road bed. Since there was no machinery available for cutting the rock, the work was done by hand. A bridge across the Halifax River was necessary, but building it was relatively easy compared to many of the other construction obstacles.[9]

All of these short railroads around St. Augustine were unrelated. To some extent they were unimportant except for the fact that they were an indication of better transportation facilities which were soon to come if ample hotel accommodations could be provided. Flagler realized the importance of St. Augustine as a resort center. He began to do a little figuring and a little talking. His friends said he had always wanted to own a hotel; some said he had been fascinated by the duties of a hotel manager. Be that as it may, he was becoming more interested every day in the future of St. Augustine. He postponed their planned return to New York in March. To build a hotel or not to build a hotel seemed to be the burning issue in his mind.

One thing that helped hasten his decision and activate his interests in St. Augustine was the celebration of the landing of Ponce de León in March, 1885. The celebration was an elaborate one, put on especially for the winter visitors. It impressed Flagler deeply. The name Ponce de León kept playing back and forth in his mind.[10] It would be the name for his first structure—a hotel, the Ponce de Leon. Another thing which helped Flagler decide to declare his commitment was a new acquaintance. Dr. Andrew Anderson was a prominent and influential St. Augustine citizen. He and Flagler had met soon after Flagler's arrival in February, 1885. Anderson, a practicing physician, had been born in St. Augustine on March 13, 1839—when Florida was still a territory of the United States. His parents had moved there several years earlier from New England. Anderson graduated from Princeton in 1861 and from the

College of Physicians and Surgeons, New York City, in 1865. Upon completing his medical training, Anderson returned to St. Augustine to practice his profession.[11]

$\mathcal{D}$r. Anderson owned a considerable amount of property in the St. Augustine area. As soon as he learned that Flagler was interested in making some investments in the city, he went to see him. They talked at great length.[12] Their discussions continued for several days. It can be safely assumed that Anderson's influence was largely responsible for the first of Flagler's investments in St. Augustine. A decision was reached and Flagler hastened his return to New York. He left on April 1, 1885, but not until he had purchased several acres of land from Dr. Anderson on which Flagler planned to build a magnificent hotel. As he bade his newly-made friend good-bye, he promised to return within six weeks to get his plans under way.[13] Flagler kept that promise. On May 15, he returned to St. Augustine with more definite ideas about what he wanted to do. Mrs. Flagler did not join him on this trip. In her stead was a business associate, Benjamin Brewster, known especially for his ability to evaluate men, property, and materials. Flagler needed his advice on many matters concerning his proposed plans. Also accompanying Flagler was Thomas Hastings, a young and promising architect from New York.

$\mathcal{T}$he New Yorkers were the guests of the Andrew Andersons. The doctor worked tirelessly with them on plans for the new hotel.[14] These plans and details, finished early one morning after an all-night session, were worked out in the Andersons' parlor. Hastings, who had sketched off a rough drawing of the building, returned to New York to make further studies of Spanish architecture before the blueprints were made. Flagler and Brewster followed on May 22, leaving Dr. Anderson highly enthusiastic over the proposed building program. No one knew more than he what added capital could mean to St. Augustine. His untiring efforts were crowned with success. However, Anderson's job was not finished. In fact, it had barely begun. Anderson promised to act as Flagler's agent in St. Augustine when Flagler was not there.[15]

$\mathcal{T}$he news of Flagler's decision to build the Ponce de Leon Hotel in St. Augustine spread rapidly. People began to speculate in land. Flagler was deluged with all sorts of offers of property, some good and some bad. People also tried to sell property to Dr. Anderson. When he would not buy, they sent their letters directly to Flagler in New York. A small land boom began. Flagler wrote to one prospect, "I have no desire to speculate in St. Augustine property. I only want to buy certain property which will be needed for the new hotel."[16]

*T*he enthusiasm over Flagler's coming to Florida was not confined to St. Augustine. People in Palatka, 28 miles away, also tried to interest him in purchasing their land. Dr. Anderson assured the Palatka people that Flagler was interested only in building a hotel in St. Augustine. He emphasized that it was not his purpose to set off a wave of land speculation. Becoming somewhat indignant over what they called his lack of attention, the Palatkans decided to send a delegation to New York for the purpose of calling on Flagler concerning their interests. Anderson warned Flagler of their proposed trip. He answered, "I note what you say about the Palatka people. If I can only be advised about their coming to New York, I will take pains to be out of town when they arrive."[17] Hearing of Flagler's attitude, the Palatka delegation cancelled plans for the trip.

*T*he summer of 1885 was a busy one for Flagler. He remained in New York, spending much of his time at his summer home, Satanstoe. He was in constant contact with Dr. Anderson and there was almost daily correspondence between them. Anderson spent most of the summer getting detailed matters cleared up in preparation for the actual building of the hotel. In the first place, a large portion of the land on which the hotel was to be built was low and marshy. It had to be filled in with sand and dirt. This was a long, hard job, but Dr. Anderson organized its completion well. Another rather tedious task which Flagler turned over to his representative in St. Augustine was the securing of permission from the government authorities to quarry coquina from certain areas in that region. They planned to use coquina rock to build the proposed structure. A third task which Anderson undertook for Flagler concerned moving the tiny railroad depot from the grounds of the San Marco Hotel. Naturally, Flagler wanted the depot to be situated at some central point in St. Augustine. There was another reason, too, why he wanted it moved: he believed that St. Augustine was destined to become a railroad center. Therefore, he decided, the town deserved a better depot. Henry Flagler, the new St. Augustine enthusiast, promised to give land for a new depot if it should be moved. His offer of land was accepted and he provided the town with better facilities.[18]

$\mathcal{F}$lagler gave Dr. Anderson free access to his funds. To Flagler, no task was too great or too expensive. If Anderson thought something should be done, Flagler saw to it that the task was accomplished. In one letter in June, 1885, the doctor suggested to his friend in New York that between them they were spending a lot of money. Anderson ended by saying that if he did not stop, they would both soon be in the poor house. Flagler answered jocularly, "If I crowd you too rapidly on improvements, you must lean back; I guess, between us, we can manage it."[19] There was one thing certain: after this, the St. Augustine doctor never worried about how much he spent.

$\mathcal{O}$nly once during this period of preparation did Flagler become pessimistic and think of giving up the program. The occasion was in July, 1885, when he learned that much more work would be needed in building up a fill or low portion of the grounds on which the Ponce de Leon was to be constructed. The land was an ideal location for the proposed structure, but there was a creek running across it. The Sebastian River was dredged and the displaced earth was used to fill in the creek bed. At the same time the problem of filling the creek was being solved, Dr. Anderson was having a hard time clearing titles to some of the land Flagler was trying to purchase in connection with the hotel. Flagler did not remain discouraged long, however, and sent the following message to his friend in St. Augustine, "It will be a disappointment, of course, if we have to stop operations, but you and I are too old and tough to be killed off by a thing of this sort [clearing the land titles].[20] The retired Standard Oil magnate was too well schooled in Rockefeller's principles to let one or two obstacles stand in his way. Had Flagler given in and stopped at this point, his Florida developments perhaps would never have become a reality. However, Flagler had great determination to accomplish what he set out to do. That vision and commitment were among the secrets of his success.

$\mathcal{F}$lagler and Anderson both hoped that the actual work on the foundation of the Ponce de Leon could take place in August or September. They wanted to have the building ready for use for the 1887 season, but there was much work to be accomplished before the realization of their dreams came true. One thing in which Flagler was intensely interested was the reaction of the officials of the city of St. Augustine to his plans. Making sure that everything was in readiness when the time came to build, Flagler instructed Anderson to see that the board of aldermen had no objection to his proposed program. Said Flagler,

> *We should be well advised on these points, for if I contract with the builders to do this work, and don't give them the ground at the time agreed upon, it may prove a very serious matter to me, as well as delay the completion of the hotel a year longer.*[21]

*A*nother question which entered Flagler's mind at this time concerned malaria. The disease was uncontrollable in certain places. Flagler feared that digging the foundation might create a malarial epidemic in St. Augustine. Anderson, however, being a physician, quieted his friend's fears by assuring him that if the lime were freely used by the workmen while digging, the possibility of spreading the disease would be minimized.

*L*ocally, much encouragement was given to Flagler's efforts. Most people wanted to cooperate. President Green of the Jacksonville, St. Augustine, and Halifax Railroad consented to extending his road farther into St. Augustine so that materials being hauled could be placed closer to the construction site. Permission was immediately granted by the city officials for the use of coquina rock from Anastasia Island, just across the Matanzas River from St. Augustine. However, that permission had to be approved by the United States government. Flagler was a personal friend of Secretary of State Whitney, who secured permission for him through the Treasury Department to use as much of the coquina as he needed.[22]

*W*hile Anderson and Flagler worked diligently on details pertaining to the building program, the architects, Thomas Hastings and John M. Carrère, worked on the blueprints. They remained at their office in New York all summer and consulted with Flagler almost daily.[23] The two young architects realized this was their opportunity to make a reputation for themselves. They knew Flagler had plenty of money; so they tried hard to reproduce, as far as possible, the atmosphere of old Spain—which was the builder's wish. As the architects finished the plans for each floor, a photograph was sent to Dr. Anderson. Flagler's letters to Anderson carried a note of eagerness as the blueprints neared completion. He was putting much of his time, money, and energy into the hotel. He hoped it would be the most beautiful hotel in the world. As he wanted its design to be a surprise, he requested that drawings of the building not be made public. He also wanted no indication of how much he was spending to be made known. He estimated that the work, if begun by September, 1885, would be finished by January 1, 1887. Because of the many particulars involved in the huge undertaking, the hotel was not completed on schedule and the construction completion was delayed for several months.

After learning that the work could not be finished on schedule, Flagler invited Dr. Anderson to visit him at his summer home at Mamaroneck for a two week vacation. The trip was made in August and the two men, who had already become friendly, enjoyed the many activities which Mamaroneck offered, including several ocean trips on Flagler's yacht, the *Columbia*. Their two weeks together gave them a better understanding of each other. It was an understanding and friendship which continued to grow as long as they lived.[24]

During Anderson's visit with Flagler they talked at great length about St. Augustine's future and what the resulting effects from a building program in that town would mean. After seeing all the splendor and wealth displayed at Satanstoe, Anderson was curious. He asked Flagler why he was interested in a musty old place like St. Augustine, when he had such beautiful surroundings at his New York home. Flagler's reply, in effect, was that his place at Mamaroneck was complete. It was finished. There was very little to be done to enhance its value. But St. Augustine offered all sorts of possibilities for development and he wanted to see what could be done with it.[25] It was Anderson's firm belief that his wealthy friend looked at the Ponce de Leon Hotel, his first undertaking in Florida, not wholly as a commercial enterprise. Anderson thought building the hotel was largely as a pleasure for Flagler, a plaything perhaps, or a means of satisfying his desire to see what he could create in the quaint old town. Flagler set out on his Florida enterprises without any idea of being able to obtain from them an income commensurate with his investment. The entire scheme seemed to be essentially a hobby. Sustaining his hobby, too, was another motive. Henry Flagler was a religious man imbued with a firm belief in a personal Deity. Dr. Anderson believed that Flagler felt obligated to use his wealth in such a manner as to create opportunities for others to help themselves. He believed Flagler regarded furnishing large numbers of persons with employment as the highest form of charity. This desire was, to a large extent, influential in shaping Flagler's efforts in Florida. Though Anderson was never officially connected with any of the Flagler enterprises, he was one of his most enthusiastic boosters.[26]

*F*ollowing the Mamaroneck visit, Anderson returned to St. Augustine in September to finish minor details before construction got under way. Flagler made a short visit to St. Augustine on October 22, but returned to New York on October 31.[27] The trip was merely to make routine inspection of what was going on and to finish arrangements for digging the foundation. The excavation began on the Ponce de Leon Hotel on the morning of December 1, 1885, with the majority of St. Augustine's 2,000 inhabitants on hand to see the initial stroke take place. Flagler arrived again on December 2 from New York and seemed satisfied with his project. He remained for nearly three weeks, going back to New York in time for the Christmas holidays.[28] All the information that had been kept secret concerning the hotel was now made public, and, as the great structure began to rise slowly from what had been wasted marsh lands, people throughout the East talked of the tremendous undertaking. Many people questioned Flagler's judgment in the matter, but he looked at the proposition from an entirely different angle. En route to Florida on one of his many trips in 1886 to see how the work was progressing, he was asked by a traveling companion why he was building a hotel in St. Augustine. Illustrating his answer with a story, Flagler replied,

> *There was once a good old church member who always lived a correct life until well advanced in years. One day when very old he went on a drunken spree. While in this state he met his good pastor, to whom, being soundly upbraided for his condition, he replied, 'I've been giving all my days to the Lord hitherto, and now I'm taking one for myself.' This is somewhat my case. For about 14 or 15 years, I have devoted my time exclusively to business, and now I am pleasing myself.*

*F*lagler's answer was typical of him and was, no doubt, one of his motives for beginning the development. The companion, however, answered jokingly, "You have been looking for a place in which to make a fool of yourself, and you've finally chosen St. Augustine as the place."[29]

This statement expressed the views of many of his close friends, but they knew that once Flagler had his mind set on something there was no way for anyone to change it.

*F*or a while it seemed to Flagler that the work was going terribly slowly, but it took time to get everything thoroughly organized. The building was one of the first large structures in the country to be made of poured concrete. St. Augustine offered no natural building stone other than the coquina, which in many instances was too soft. Ton upon ton of coquina gravel was brought over from Anastasia Island across the bay and was mixed with cement. Twelve hundred workers were engaged to tramp this mixture as it was poured into the forms. Hundreds of other laborers were employed to do the many other duties connected with construction. Slowly the four-foot-thick walls rose, cast in one solid piece. Certainly one of the biggest problems was transporting materials to the construction site. The short railroad from South Jacksonville to St. Augustine did a Herculean job. Some of the lumber was secured from the banks of the St. Johns River in the Palatka area, being brought to Tocoi by river barge and then to St. Augustine by rail. Coastal schooners were used in bringing heavy materials from Jacksonville via the Atlantic Ocean. A great portion of the magnificently carved and dressed oak finish for the interior of the building was prepared in New York and shipped to St. Augustine by boat.

*D*espite all the effort, Flagler soon realized that the gigantic task of completing the hotel would not be finished in time for the 1887 season. The architects had insisted from the beginning that it would be difficult to meet his proposed deadline. The contractors for the Ponce de Leon Hotel were James A. McGuire and Joseph E. McDonald. Both men were prominent New England contractors, each having come to Florida because of the rich field in construction they foresaw. McGuire had been brought down from Boston by Isaac Croof, a wealthy merchant, who proposed to build several hotels throughout the state. McGuire built for Croof the beautiful Magnolia Hotel at Magnolia Springs.[30] After this hotel was completed, McGuire was assigned to build the San Marco Hotel in St. Augustine. McDonald, who had just come to Florida, was also hired by Croof to work on the San Marco Hotel. The two men seemed suited to each other in their work and did a magnificent job in building the first modern hotel in St. Augustine. It was at the San Marco Hotel that

McGuire and McDonald first met Flagler. He admired their work from the beginning. After a short conference with the two men, they agreed to do the work on the Ponce de Leon. McGuire and McDonald became Flagler's official contractors, just as Hastings and Carrère were called upon to make the plans for Flagler's later building program in Florida.

*F*lagler carefully supervised the construction of the Ponce de Leon and spent much of his time between his office in New York and his first project in Florida. He received with enthusiasm news that the huge building would be ready for occupancy by January 1, 1888. Flagler was so anxious to see the hotel completed and furnished that this story, which bears the impress of truth, was told about him later:

> *The hotel's furniture was delayed several days. When the boats finally arrived at St. Augustine harbor, Flagler took off his coat and worked diligently to help transport the new furnishings to the newly constructed hotel. He liked to mix with the laborers; sometimes they were unaware of his presence. On this particular day, in conversation with a worker who thought Flagler was a day laborer, one employee said, "This Flagler is a pretty good fellow."*[31]

*I*t was worth the day's efforts for Flagler.

*A*nother story is told about Flagler's being refused entrance to the Ponce de Leon grounds while the structure was being built. He often walked around the unfinished building smoking a cigar. There were "No Smoking" signs placed here and there for the attention of the workers.

> *One day Flagler tried to enter, smoking his cigar, when he was stopped by a watchman. He quickly informed the watchman that he was Mr. Flagler, the owner of the hotel. The watchman replied, "I can't help that. There have been a good many Flaglers trying to get in here." He did not get in until one of the contractors, James McGuire, came by and rebuked the guard for not recognizing his boss. Flagler, however, complemented the young man on his efficiency.*[32]

*T*he Ponce de Leon Hotel was finished on May 30, 1887, and was formally opened on January 10, 1888, the beginning of the next season. The first dinner served in the $2,500,000 structure was given with an air

of celebration and gaiety.[33] Hundreds of visitors crowded the spacious rotundas, corridors, and tropical court. They viewed some of the most beautiful decorations ever introduced in a hotel anywhere in the world. A prominent band from New York was hired for the first season. Merry-makers celebrated the first of Henry Flagler's Florida developments.

Ponce de Leon Hotel, St. Augustine, 1889

$\mathcal{A}$s a visitor approached the hotel, the first impression was of size. The mammoth structure covered most of its five-acre lot. The Ponce de Leon, with its medieval towers, was situated not far from the center of quaint, old St. Augustine. It was fitting that the great structure should be named in honor of a discoverer whose romantic quest made his name symbolic of the adventurous spirit of his age. The architects had truly preserved the spirit of Old Spain. They had envisioned not merely a big hotel, but a pleasure palace. The building embodied characteristics of Spanish Renaissance architecture, with sunny courts and cool retreats. The fountains, towers, and decorations were all suggestive of the history of the city.[34] The Ponce de Leon was not a tall building in the modern sense of the word. It was only four stories high, but it was big and sprawling. The grounds were beautifully arranged with tropical gardens, overhanging palms, and appropriate shrubbery. Adjacent to the grounds were a large orange grove and a woodland section which served as a backdrop of dark green against the sandy tan color of the building.

$\mathcal{T}$he front entrance was arranged with verandas running along the street on each side of the main gate. On the grand arch were mermaids supporting the shields bearing the name of Ponce de Leon. There was a theme of the sea displayed at each entrance. At the East and West entrances there were fountains with water flowing from the mouths of dolphins. These were not only typical of the sea, but had local significance as well. The name of St. Augustine's River of Dolphins was bestowed by the Frenchman, Laudonnière, when he anchored in Florida in 1564. The dolphin and the shell designs were repeated again and again throughout the hotel. Even the door knobs were modeled after shells.[35]

*I*nside the front gate was an interior court, covering an area of 10,000 feet. It was surrounded by vine-clad verandas. In the center there was a multicolored fountain, around which were planted unusual evergreens. Directly across the court from the main entrance, the visitor entered the rotunda through the grand archway. The archway was 20 feet wide and above it there were a number of smaller arches supported by pillars of spiral shaped terra cotta.

*T*he spacious rotunda was the center of operations of the Ponce de Leon Hotel. It was inlaid with richly colored mosaics and its great dome was supported by pillars of massive oak. The figures and orna-ments, all of Spanish Renaissance design, emphasized eight subjects. Here were found allegorical representations of the elements: fire, water, air, and earth. The other four figures, typical of adventure, discovery, conquest, and civilization, were located on the pendentives of the ceiling of the second story. These figures were elaborate. Adventure wore a cuirass and on her helmet an eagle's crest. She held a drawn sword. Discovery was robed in drapery of the blue of the sea. In her right hand was half a globe; her other hand rested upon a tiller. Conquest, clad in martial red, with helmet and cuirass, firmly grasped an upright sword, significant of might and war-won supremacy. Civilization was clothed in white and wore a crown. In her lap was an open book, the symbol of knowledge. Her face had the repose of dignity and benevolence.[36]

*T*he offices and parlors were to the right of the rotunda and to the left was the grand parlor, decorated in keeping with the beauty of the hotel. Behind the dome of the rotunda was the grand dining hall. The stairs on the right and left walls leading to the dining room were of solid polished marble. The paintings represented the Landing of Columbus, the Conquest of Charlemagne, and the Introduction of Christianity.

*U*pon entering the large dining hall, visitors were impressed with its stained glass windows, magnificent columns of antique oak, and highly polished floors. The room was an oval, 70 by 150 feet in size, and had a seating capacity of 700 people. Two galleries were in front and one was in the rear overhanging the room.

*T*he ceilings in the dining room were handsomely decorated with designs of the 16th century. Dinner guests had only to look up to learn the tragic story of St. Augustine's first years. The paintings began with the persecutions of the French Hugenots, who sought refuge in the New World. The story continued by showing how Jean Ribault explored the coast of Florida in 1562, under a commission given by the admiral of France, in search of a location for a French colony. Ribault entered a river which he named the River of May, now known as the St. Johns, and erected a stone pillar there as a token of French possession. René de Laudonnière came with French colonists and they built a fort at the mouth of the river. However, by a more definite claim, Florida belonged to Spain. King Philip II did not want the French colonists there and sent his boldest adventurer, Pedro Menéndez de Avilés, to drive them out. Menéndez destroyed the French settlement and proceeded southward to the mouth of the River of Dolphins. It was there that he established a settlement for the Spanish. The paintings further told the story of a bloody massacre Menéndez performed shortly thereafter at an inlet south of St. Augustine. His men brutally killed a band of shipwrecked Frenchmen. The inlet became known as Matanzas (Spanish for "slaughter") Inlet. Later Dominique de Gourges got revenge for Menéndez's bloody acts, but by that time the Spanish were so well entrenched that it was impossible to uproot them.

*T*he history of St. Augustine could be seen and talked about while enjoying a marvelous meal. The ceiling art was done by one of the most prominent artists of the day, Virgilio Tojetti, and was one of the most unusual of its kind in America. The general scheme was an adaptation of the picture-writing of the American Indians.[37]

*W*ithin the hotel there were 450 sleeping apartments: some were suites of rooms, some single rooms, and some were bridal chambers with the most luxurious furniture. Electric lights, something of a novelty to most of the guests, were installed. Facilities for steam heat, seldom used in Florida, were also included in the building. There were numerous private parlors, reading rooms, game rooms, and refreshment rooms throughout the building. The furnishings in every room were beautiful. They included exquisite draperies; imported rosewood, walnut, and mahogany furniture; and Brussels carpets. Two miles of halls and corridors, serving as avenues, all led either directly or indirectly to the main rotunda.[38]

*W*hen Henry M. Flagler began construction of the Ponce de Leon Hotel, he did not know that it would lead to further development. He soon realized that the Ponce de Leon would need a companion hostelry catering to people who were not quite so wealthy. Accordingly, the Alcazar Hotel was built across the street. The Alcazar was started early in 1887 by McGuire and McDonald, the same contractors who were working on the Ponce de Leon. Its plans had been drawn by Carrère and Hastings, the Ponce de Leon's architects. For a time in late 1887, both hotels were being built by virtually the same workmen. Materials and furnishings came from common sources and many of the same ideas were used in both buildings. Both were in the Spanish Renaissance style, though the Alcazar had a distinctive Moorish stamp on it. It was opened with 75 furnished rooms late in 1888, but it was not fully completed until the next year, when its formal opening was held.[39]

*T*he Alcazar, an Arabic word meaning "royal castle," embraced some of the most beautiful architectural decorations from castles in Seville. The hotel rounded out perfectly the picturesque group of buildings on King Street—the Ponce de Leon, the Alcazar, and the Casa Monica, which was built by Franklin Smith. The Alcazar was somewhat smaller than the Ponce de Leon, its dimensions being 250 feet by 400 feet. The structure was four stories high and it was built around a court. Leading from the court were arcades. Stores, restaurants, shops, and salons opened onto the court. Above there were two floors of rooms supported by handsomely carved columns and symmetrical arches. The facade was a reproduction of the famous Alcazar in Seville, one of the royal palaces of the kings. In front of the building was a large tropical garden with flowers, trees, and fountains. In the rear of the hotel was a large casino. This part of the hotel was the "sporting section" and included indoor sulphur and salt water pools for bathing, indoor amusement courts, and game rooms. It was very popular and was often the scene of elaborate balls and parties. It was regularly used every season.[40]

*A*lthough the Alcazar did not accommodate as many guests as the Ponce de Leon, and had no rotunda or dining hall as famous as that which could be found across the street, many people, including Flagler, felt that it was just as beautiful. The cost of the Alcazar, including the casino, was only about half that of the larger hotel. European travelers in this country usually spoke of the Alcazar in terms more glowing than those used for the Ponce de Leon.[41] The difference was simply a matter of taste. As soon as the Ponce de Leon and Alcazar hotels were opened, they were filled with visitors from the North. Thousands of tourists poured into St. Augustine annually and the news of Flagler's work spread across the United States.

*F*lagler became increasingly pleased over the area's prospects. By 1888 there was no doubt in his mind about making additional investments in Florida. To add to his holdings he purchased the Casa Monica Hotel, located adjacent and to the right of the Alcazar. The hotel had been under construction from 1886 to 1888. When Flagler purchased it in 1889, he renamed it the Cordova. Until 1894 it was operated it as a separate hotel. A connection was then built between the Cordova and the Alcazar and it was operated in conjunction with the latter.[42]

*F*lagler's business interests in Florida were increasing rapidly. He and Ida Alice spent an increasing portion of their time in the state. There was always time for pleasure, even though he was busy. The warm climate made spending winters there quite pleasant. The Flaglers enjoyed St. Augustine and the gaiety which the old town offered. After the hotel opened, their suite at the Ponce de Leon was occupied each winter by family members and guests whom they brought from New York.

*T*he Flaglers' private railroad car, named the Alicia for Ida Alice, made traveling a pleasure. It was large and contained several bedrooms, a spacious sitting room, dining room, kitchen, and all the conveniences of homes of that day. In it, the Flaglers made many trips between New York and Florida. He often turned down opportunities to go to other places and resorts. Traveling was not a pastime with him, it was becoming a business. Besides a trip to Jamaica and a business visit to the Bahamas, he was never out of the country. He had no desire to go abroad or to visit distant places in the United States.

Since both of the Flaglers liked Florida so well, it was not long until they began planning to build their own home in St. Augustine. Named Kirkside, it was started in 1892, but they did not move in until March 1, 1893. Located only a few blocks from the Ponce de Leon Hotel, the newly-built Kirkside, was a beautiful structure. It was especially designed for winter living. It was spacious, roomy, and fitted for entertaining. Colonial architecture prevailed throughout the 15 room structure.

Kirkside. Henry and Ida Alice Flagler's St. Augustine Home (no longer standing)

The front elevation was two stories high. The roof was supported by Ionic pillars which were extremely rich and beautiful, corresponding with the cornices, brackets, and mouldings. The dwelling was white, with pale green blinds. Inside was exquisite furniture. A long hall ran through the house with brightly decorated rooms opening off each side. The salon, usually considered the loveliest room, was suggestive of Versailles in all of its splendor. Added features included bedrooms with connecting baths and dressing rooms. The specially designed chandeliers furnished electric light. The grounds of Kirkside were artistically laid out. Plants and palms grew around the concrete walks and drives. The entire lot was enclosed by a coquina wall four feet high.[43]

Life was good to the Flaglers throughout the 1880s and early 1890s. Because of his large holdings in the Standard Oil Company, the Flagler fortune increased by the millions. Ida Alice enjoyed being married to a man of great wealth. During their winters in St. Augustine she entertained lavishly at the Ponce de Leon Hotel and in their home. Although Henry cared little for social life, he usually tried to please her by participating in her entertainments. St. Augustine had come to be recognized as a vacation center for wealthy Easterners. Hundreds of them came each year to enjoy the climate and to take part in elaborate entertainments. Ida Alice tried diligently to lead the social life of the entire town, but had only moderate success.[44]

One of her most elaborate entertainments for the 1892 winter society season in St. Augustine was given on February 3rd at the Ponce de Leon Hotel. She called it the "Hermitage Ball." The festival was designed to commemorate Andrew Jackson and his contributions to the state of Florida. Nearly 1,000 persons attended the ball, including many dignitaries who were guests at the hotel. President and Mrs. Benjamin Harrison received special invitations but were unable to attend and ex-Governor Porter of Indiana, at that time United States minister to Italy, represented the President. Governor and Mrs. Francis P. Fleming of Florida were also there. Mrs. Flagler wore a beautiful gown of white tulle, *en traine*, the front bodice being embroidered in mother of pearl and gold and the skirt was bordered with pearl fringe half a yard deep. The bodice was decollaté, the neck being finished with white ostrich. Bows of broad white velvet caught up the short sleeves. Her necklace was many strands of pearls, and a spray of marguerites formed a fillet for the hair. As hostess, Ida Alice Flagler, in dress and manner, made herself the center of attention throughout the evening.[45]

On two other occasions during February the Flaglers hosted lavish social affairs, one of which was a colorful military ball on February 22nd. Over 700 expensively engraved invitations were mailed. Dinner was served to the guests. After the dinner brilliant fireworks were set off from the roof and grounds of the Ponce de Leon Hotel. Again Ida Alice Flagler's gown and her actions during the evening attracted attention from their guests. Though some of her guests did not approve of her conduct, she usually arranged to be the center of attention at her events.

The winter of 1893 saw even more entertainment by the Flaglers than the year before. *The Tatler*, a social sheet, or newspaper, in St. Augustine, listed five formal affairs given by the Flaglers between January and March. In addition, many of the small parties given at Kirkside were not listed. On March 23, 1893, Mrs. Flagler gave a dance at the Ponce de Leon which *The Tatler* called the "pearl dance" because of the unusual size and beauty of the pearls which she wore.[47] To Mrs. Flagler, St. Augustine was a playground. Her social interests were too fast paced for her husband and before long he began to withdraw from so much social activity.

*F*lagler's investments in Florida became so great that he invited his son to come to Florida to help him bear some of the responsibility.[48] Harry went reluctantly. It was Henry Flagler's plan for Harry to learn the hotel and the railroad business and gradually succeed him in the work. Flagler needed all the aid his 23 year old son could give him. For two years, Harry tried to make himself a business executive; but none of the work was pleasant to him. His father could not understand why Harry disliked the business world. However, Harry was determined to follow a career more suited to his tastes and in the end, he returned to New York where he became prominent in musical circles.[49] Flagler may have been overbearing in his dealings with his son. It was hard for him to realize that Harry was sincere in his distaste for the life that his father had chosen for him. Nevertheless, the misunderstanding caused a breach between the two which never fully healed.[50] The youth's alienation from his father was not easy for Henry Flagler to accept because Harry was his only living child.

*J*ennie Louise, Flagler's much loved daughter, had died on March 25, 1889. After her first husband, John Arthur Hinckley, died she had married Frederick Hart Benedict, a Wall Street broker on October 6, 1887. On February 9, 1889, she gave birth to a baby girl, but the child lived for only a few hours. Jennie's condition did not improve so her physician recommended that she go to Florida for rest and recuperation.[51] Her father-in-law, E. C. Benedict, well-known in yachting circles, offered his finest yacht, the *Oneida*, for the trip.

Jennie Louise Flagler Hinckley Benedict

*T*he doctors felt that the cruise down the coast would be less strenuous than a trip by rail. They also thought that the salt air might have certain healing qualities. Several days after the yacht put out to sea, Jennie Louise became much worse. Complications set in. Before the yacht could reach Charleston, the nearest port, she died. Her husband and her brother, Harry, were with her. Henry Flagler was in St. Augustine with Ida Alice. He went to Charleston and accompanied his daughter, her husband, and his son back to New York where Jennie was buried in Woodlawn Cemetery.

*J*ennie's passing was a source of great sorrow to Flagler. He determined to create a fitting memorial to her. The Memorial Presbyterian Church, formerly known as the First Presbyterian Church, was completed in 1890. The building was located at the rear of the Ponce de Leon Hotel. It was designed in the Venetian Renaissance style. It was one of the chief adornments of the city with a dome which contributed its dignity and grace to St. Augustine's picturesque skyline. Adjoining the church was a beautifully constructed mausoleum. Jennie's remains, along with those of her mother and her baby, were moved to the vault.[52] Space for Flagler's tomb was also provided for within the mausoleum.

*D*edicatory services were held in the new church building on March 16, 1890. The church, which contained 600 seats, was filled and overflowing for the occasion. Eight ministers were in charge of the services. A choir from New York provided the music. Among the many notables present were Mrs. Benjamin Harrison, wife of the President of the United States; the Vice-President of the United States, Levi

Memorial Presbyterian Church, St. Augustine

P. Morton, and his wife; the John Wannamakers; the Henry M. Flaglers; Harry Flagler; and Frederick Benedict, husband of the young woman in whose name the church was built.[53]

*F*lagler also befriended the Methodist and the Catholic congregations in St. Augustine. A disastrous fire almost destroyed the Catholic cathedral in the early 1890s, and his contribution assisted in large part in the rebuilding of the structure.[54] In the case of the Methodist Church, Flagler wanted the land on which the church stood. He offered the congregation a new building and parsonage about five blocks from the old church. Such an action was typical of Flagler.

*O*n many occasions Flagler provided important services to the town. He built a modern hospital and deeded it to the local board of trustees in 1889. The hospital was named Alicia for his wife[55] and Ida Alice was greatly interested in the undertaking. The hospital had a main building and two large pavilions. Flagler furnished it completely with beds, mattresses, and all the other necessities. In addition, he suggested the formation of an association of women to assist in maintaining it. The women's organization began in 1888, before the hospital was finished. By 1900 it had earned more than $30,000 by holding benefit balls, teas, sewing parties, and other functions. His gift of the hospital and the efforts of the women involved were particularly important since the hospital handled a great number of charity cases, for which the county paid only a small fee.

*A*mong other projects in St. Augustine to which Flagler contributed money and time were the building of City Hall and an African-America school. His funds were also used to pave streets, establish a water works, install electric lights, lay sewers, and construct a number of comfortable homes for his employees. Flagler also built his car shops there and, in this way, gave steady employment to hundreds of men.[56]

*B*y the early 1890s, it is fair to say that Henry Flagler was St. Augustine's greatest benefactor and perhaps its most prized resident. He had done more there in five years than most people had done in a lifetime. There was something about Florida and its untapped opportunities that Flagler could not shake off. There was a challenge ahead that he would not let go unheeded. At the age of 60, near Ponce de León's supposed fountain of youth, Flagler created a new career. He looked to the future with anticipation and enthusiasm.

Henry Morrison Flagler

9. Penetrating the Florida Frontier

During his first career with the Standard Oil Company, Flagler was never a railroad builder. In addition, there is little evidence that he was interested in hotels until he saw the need for better accommodations in St. Augustine. After retiring, his personal desire for a luxury hotel in the old city spurred him to action. Once the decision was made to build hotels, he naturally turned to transportation facilities. During his early visits, access to St. Augustine had been poor. Because of this fact, many eastern visitors to Florida traveled by train to Jacksonville and then by boat on the St. Johns River, patronizing hotels along its banks. St. Augustine, located some distance from the river, was not affected directly by increased or improving water transportation.

Flagler was well aware of Florida's poor railroads. However, the fact was brought to his attention distinctly when he began constructing the Ponce de Leon Hotel. The Jacksonville, St. Augustine and Halifax River Railroad ran from South Jacksonville to St. Augustine. It could have been in the position to serve St. Augustine effectively. However, it was a rickety, little, narrow–gauge railroad. It gave poor service and, consequently, was of little value to Flagler in meeting his construction needs. He tried without success to get the owner to improve the road. When that didn't work, he decided to try to buy the railroad and run schedules as he saw fit. Soon after the hotel's construction began, Flagler began negotiations to purchase the short road. His efforts were successful. The property became his on December 31, 1885; whereupon the road was immediately improved.[1] Flagler was now a Florida railway man.

The narrow–gauge tracks, consisting of 30 pound rails,[2] were torn up and replaced with 60 pound rails. New equipment was provided for the trains and, within a year, material for Flagler's building programs in St. Augustine was being shipped faster than ever before. Tourists also began to use the new route. Largely thanks to improved rail transportation, the Ponce de Leon Hotel was filled to overflowing almost immediately upon opening to the public.[3]

$\mathcal{D}$uring the next few years Flagler became increasingly interested in acquiring other railroad properties connecting St. Augustine. In 1888 he purchased two other short roads. The first was the St. Augustine and Palatka Railroad, which ran from St. Augustine to Palatka. He later acquired the St. Johns Railroad running from Tocoi on the river to St. Augustine. Both trains used the same tracks from St. Augustine to Tocoi Junction, a distance of about six miles. They then separated with one track going to Tocoi and the other to East Palatka. These purchases totaled more than 40 miles of railroad. They gave Flagler access to the St. Johns River at Tocoi and East Palatka, as well as a depot at South Jacksonville. As his St. Augustine building program continued, Flagler's fame spread.

$\mathcal{T}$he railroad purchases claimed considerable attention. From time to time, Flagler wondered if he should stop his investments in Florida. However, late in 1888, he acquired a logging road constructed by S. V. White. It traveled from East Palatka to Daytona via San Mateo and Ormond. This acquisition gave him a direct line from South Jacksonville to Daytona. At once, he began to remodel portions of the road. While railroad crews were busy along the route, no schedules were interrupted. Standard–gauge tracks were laid by 1889. With that job done, the entire railroad from South Jacksonville to Daytona was as modern as could be found anywhere in the South.[4] It was with this accomplishment that Henry Flagler seriously entered the field of railroads.

$\mathcal{T}$here were other developments Flagler foresaw in connection with his railroad. Since his tracks touched the banks of the St. Johns River at Jacksonville, Tocoi, and Palatka, he realized the need to build bridges at these points. Tocoi, however, was soon eliminated from his plans because of the nature of the river there and the work of bridging the St. Johns at Palatka was soon under way. It was completed in 1888.

$\mathcal{W}$ith the completion of the bridge, Flagler anticipated carrying his program of hotel development into Palatka.[5] He made several visits, but received little encouragement from the town's civic leaders. Their actions may have been prompted by their earlier failure to get him interested in purchasing town land in 1885. At any rate, Flagler was refused the right to purchase lots on the river front for a hotel. In addition, land farther from the river was so advanced in price that he became disgusted with his treatment and left.[6] At that time Palatka had two hotels, the larger one being the Putnam House, which was known for its splendor and beauty. It had served visitors to northeastern Florida for a number of years. Its popularity was due chiefly to its convenient location on the river. The Flagler touch on Palatka most certainly would have set off rapid growth in the little town. In fact, had Flagler's efforts been directed along the St. Johns River, we can only wonder when or if he would have proceeded down the East Coast.

*F*lagler did not permit his setback in Palatka to stop his efforts in that area. The bridge was laid with tracks and a depot was built in East Palatka. Rail cars shuttled back and forth across the river, serving both communities. He liked Putnam County and often visited East Palatka, San Mateo, and Hastings, purchasing a considerable amount of land in the latter two places.

*W*ith the Hastings land, Flagler established a model farm. His efforts helped give the town a name in the potato growing world. In San Mateo he used his land to build orange groves. Flagler was soon a friendly competitor to the other citrus growers in that section. Flagler, his railroad, and his groves were appreciated in San Mateo. On one occasion he favored all the residents of San Mateo, several hundred in number, with a free train trip to St. Augustine and dinner at the Alcazar.[7]

*S*oon after the East Palatka bridge was built, Flagler also made plans to bridge the St. Johns River at Jacksonville. Prior to building the bridge, passengers going by rail to St. Augustine and other points south had to be ferried across the river to South Jacksonville where they boarded their train. To eliminate this inconvenience, Flagler began construction of an all–steel bridge in 1889.

*W*hen the Jacksonville bridge was opened for traffic on January 20, 1890, it was one of the finest of its kind built in the South and it remained in use until 1925.[8] The completion of that bridge meant through trains could be operated between New York and St. Augustine, assuring the Ponce de Leon and Alcazar hotels of more guests during the winter season than ever before. All–Pullman vestibule trains had been operated between New York and Jacksonville for a year or so. At the end of each car there was a closed vestibule and one could go throughout the train without being exposed to the wind or weather. Perhaps the greatest wonder in connection with the all-Pullman train was that it was electrically lighted throughout. So widely heralded was this new route to Florida that Grover Cleveland, then President of the United States, yielded to an urge for fast travel. He made a visit to Jacksonville and St. Augustine in the winter of 1888, stopping at the newly–constructed Ponce de Leon Hotel.[9]

*I*n order to better to accommodate his passengers, Flagler built a modern railway depot in St. Augustine, not far from the Ponce de Leon Hotel. It was a two–story structure, 106 by 50 feet, and included all the conveniences the late 1880s could afford. It was built on a 30 acre lot which had been filled in because of its marshy nature.[10] Another expense Flagler undertook as a railroad promoter was the laying of a continuous wire fence on both sides of the tracks for almost the entire distance from Jacksonville to Daytona. Cattle claims had proved so numerous in the first years of rail transportation, that something had to be done to keep them off the tracks. Although an improvement, even the fence failed to clear the tracks completely of the roving cattle which seemed anxious to have the run of the woods as well as Flagler's trains.[11]

*D*uring the late 1880s, in a rivalry of civic pride, both St. Augustine and Jacksonville claimed Henry Flagler. Each place felt honored to have his presence or his money. Jacksonville became so interested in the attention he was giving Florida that the Board of Trade made an all–out effort to get him to sponsor a drive to bring tourists to their city. They appointed him to a local committee to plan and arrange a "Sub–Tropical Exposition." Its purpose was to attract people from all over the nation and to advertise Jacksonville as Florida's foremost city.[12] Flagler took only moderate interest in the movement and the scheme never developed as completely as the Board of Trade had hoped it would. In many respects Flagler was conservative in his spending. He did not open his wallet to everyone who called upon him.

*B*y 1889 Flagler had thoroughly embarked on his new career as a Florida builder and developer. His railroad, which served Florida as far south as Daytona, made connections with steamers on the Halifax River which penetrated farther into the rich citrus belt. His expenditures had run to a figure fully 10 times that originally contemplated. Money was being spent rapidly, sometimes almost without Flagler's realization. His vision was clear. One thing called for another. Each time he looked around, his energetic mind found new possibilities for development. Flagler's business interests continued to lead him southward in Florida. He headed into the heart of an undeveloped country. In this respect he was a frontiersman—a late 19th century pioneer.

*F*lagler's next move was to purchase an interest in a small hotel at Ormond, a town on the coast north of Daytona. It had been built by John Anderson, a native of Maine, and Joseph D. Price, from Kentucky. Money for its construction had been lent to the builders by the same S. V. White, long–famed Wall Street operator, who financed the construction of the railroad from East Palatka to Daytona. The venture did not prove profitable to Anderson and Price, and Flagler bought them out in 1890. The Flagler touch was what was needed. Flagler enlarged the building and beautified the grounds. The hotel was well located, between the Halifax River and the Atlantic Ocean, not far from either. One visitor declared that it was an extremely comfortable place and "more home like than any other Flagler Hotel, and the grounds have a more exotic look than those hotels in St. Augustine."[13] Among the many features at the Ormond Beach Hotel were the golfing facilities. A new 18 hole course was constructed. Although Flagler cared nothing for golf himself, he foresaw what an attraction a good course would be. Automobile racing fans also crowded the Ormond Beach Hotel to enjoy the sport which soon made the Ormond and Daytona beaches famous. Much enthusiasm was also shown for bicycling with special equipment furnished guests engaging in this and water activities.[14]

*D*own the coast was Daytona, another prospect for the Flagler touch. However, Daytona's business leaders, like those in Palatka, were not particularly cordial. Consequently Flagler moved on, although Daytona remained the terminal point for Flagler's railroad for a number of years. South of Daytona the East Coast of Florida was not inviting. Travelers rarely ventured into the region and only a few hearty settlers inhabited the banks of the Indian River. In those days, the Indian River, Lake Worth, Biscayne Bay, and other waterways provided the main thoroughfares of travel. Sail boats and other small craft, which were subject to the uncertainties of wind and weather, were the primary means of transportation.

*T*he area did show promise as an agricultural region. Oranges and pineapples were being shipped by boat from the Indian River region.[15] It is doubtful if Flagler intended to extend his railroad south of Daytona in 1890. His interest, as it had been since 1885, was primarily in the construction of hotels. He talked considerably about further hotel construction and a rumor circulated that he was thinking of building a big hotel in every Florida city. Enthusiastically, the *Weekly Floridian* insisted from the capital city of Tallahassee,

> *Come right along, Mr. Flagler: Tallahassee is the very place to locate one of them [hotels].*[16]

But Flagler was not interested in building hotels in places except where there could be possible resort centers.

*I*t is not known when Flagler decided to push his railroad into Florida's frontier. Prior to 1890, he hadn't built a mile of railroad. Instead he had bought up old railroad properties, improved them, built bridges, and increased their equipment. From 1890 to 1892 his road did a good business in connection with the Indian River steamer traffic. In addition, he bought a few small boats for the purpose of running regular schedules up and down the Indian River. These boats made connections with the Jacksonville, St. Augustine, and Halifax River Railroad at Daytona. The road, a consolidation of all the rail properties Flagler had bought to this time, was doing good business. Flagler was the president of the company, and Charles C. Deeming was its secretary and treasurer. The business owned 11 locomotive engines; plus 17 passenger cars; five baggage, mail, and express cars; and 90 freight cars—a total of 112 cars.

*M*any people soon urged Flagler to push his road southward into the Indian River section. They emphasized that a direct railroad line down the Atlantic Coast would be a better proposition to control and develop traffic than the existing route along the Indian River by steamer and from there by rail. Landowners offered some inducement. Some promised a right of way for a Flagler railroad extension. Flagler carefully studied the matter for two years. By the end of that period, he was thoroughly convinced that he would keep building the railroad—he had gone too far with his Florida developments to stop. In 1892 he obtained a charter from the state of Florida authorizing him to build a railroad along the Indian River as far south as Miami.[17] It is rather certain, however, that Flagler had no ambition at that time to take the railroad that far south. His immediate plans called for the road to go to Rockledge. Then, if things worked out right, he might build on down the coast to Lake Worth which was one of the most desirable areas on the East Coast.

*A*fter so much spent in consideration of the extended railroad, preliminary plans were hurriedly made and Flagler hastened to New York to make the necessary financial arrangements. Land was purchased, equipment gathered, and labor crews assembled for the great task. On June 17, 1892, Flagler telegraphed his superintendent to begin the construction of the railroad from Daytona to Rockledge.[18]

*W*orking under favorable conditions, the railroad was completed to New Smyrna by November 2, 1892. On that day, the first train puffed into the little village which had been founded by Andrew Turnbull in 1707, but had almost dwindled from the map.[19] It was a significant day in the history of the East Coast because it stamped Flagler as a builder and developer of railroads as well as hotels.

*A*bout the same time a more appropriate name was given the railroad. It was now called the Jacksonville, St. Augustine and Indian River Railway. The pace of construction was pushed with even greater rapidity into the heart of Florida's undeveloped East Coast. On February 6, 1893, Flagler's train rolled into Titusville. On February 27, 1893, the little towns of Cocoa and Rockledge were gaily decorated to greet the iron horse. Few people had ever dreamed of seeing a railroad running south of Daytona. Children clung to their mothers' skirts and grown–ups stared in amazement as they watched the little engine move slowly toward a makeshift depot .

*F*lagler's name had become a byword for progress. He could not stop now. Over 80 miles of new railroad had been constructed and put into operation in less than a year. He enjoyed seeing the two ribbons of steel roll southward. Flagler had employed more than 1,500 men to complete the task. But, once completed, Flagler knew that his task was only half finished. He would not stop until a thorough job was done. He realized that more pineapples and oranges could be marketed along the southern banks of the Indian River. What was needed was better and faster railroad freight service. Fruit cultivation was expanding rapidly, spreading farther south along the coast.[20]

*F*lagler could not resist the urge for further action. He gave orders to continue with construction of the railroad toward Palm Beach. He saw hidden possibilities in this seemingly empty land. Because Flagler wanted the road to follow the coast as closely as possible, there was considerable work to be done in laying the rails. Marshy places had to be filled in and built up. At other places track was laid on graded sandy soil. The rails weighed 60 pounds to the yard and were later replaced with 90 pound steel tracks.[21]

*T*he track was finished to Eau Gallie on June 26, 1893. By January 29, 1894, trains were operating to Fort Pierce. The residents of the little settlement at Palm Beach waited for the coming of Flagler's train. But much planning and building were necessary before that section could be operational. Finally, on March 22, 1894, workmen completed construction of the tracks to a point across Lake Worth from Palm Beach, which was to be the terminus of the Flagler railroad.

II

*I*n 1894, Palm Beach was only a small community. Its settlers had inhabited the narrow strip of land just off the Florida coast for many years. The area was separated from the mainland by an arm of the ocean, which was called Lake Worth. It was named for General William J. Worth by United States soldiers who had been sent there before the Civil War to settle Indian troubles.

*I*n October, 1867, George W. Sears cruised southward along Florida's East Coast. He was traveling from the Indian River to Miami and noticed what looked like an inlet to the ocean. Upon exploring the inlet, he found that it led inside a shallow pass into a beautiful tropical lake. The lake's shores were lined with overhanging trees, jungle vines, and foliage. Sears was astonished at what he saw. He considered the area a virtually untouched paradise. The only living beings in the Lake Worth area at that time were a few deserters from the Confederate Army who did not know the war had been over for two years.[22] Sears enthusiastically told the story of his discovery of Lake Worth to his friends. Soon others came to visit the place. It was not long before a small community had grown up on the island. Some drifted there because land was cheap, others because the winters were balmy, and still others because the neighbors were scarce. By 1878, there was not much promise that the settlement would ever develop into a thriving town.

*A*mong the early settlers who came during the late 1870s was Robert R. McCormick, a Chicagoan of harvester fame. He bought several large tracts of land and built a winter home on Lake Worth and was considered Palm Beach's first developer. The tropical gardens surrounding his home contained almost every tree, shrub, and flower that could thrive in the soil and climate.

*A*nother early resident of Palm Beach was Captain O. S. Porter, who saw the advantages of the tropical lake area. As years passed other people learned of the beauty of Lake Worth and winter homes increased there. All of the homes were built on the east side of the lake. The first post office was established in 1878 and the name of "Lake Worth" was given to the community. The first postmaster was V. O. Spencer. He had used a row boat to visit settlers around the lake in quest of signatures for the petition to the Post Office Department.[23]

*T*he name of "Lake Worth" was not permanent. Within a few years, E. M. Brelsford led a petition to rename the settlement "Palm City." The Post Office Department in Washington refused to accept that name and there was much protest made because the name had been rejected. A compromise was soon effected. Gus Ganford, a visitor from Philadelphia, was prospecting in the wild jungle country of South Florida. He heard about the rejection of the name and suggested that, instead, the community should submit the name of "Palm Beach." His reasoning was that there was no other city in the United States with that name. A petition was soon dispatched to Washington requesting the change. Three weeks later, in March, 1886, the name of Palm Beach, Florida, was confirmed by the Post Office Department.[24]

*W*ithin a few years more people learned about Palm Beach, situated between the lake and the ocean. The fertile soil and near–perfect climate made possible many kinds of tropical plants including the coconut palm and the royal poinciana. The area could make an ideal resort, but it needed the touch of someone who had the vision to see its possibilities. It needed a person with the will and the resources to change the vision to reality.

$\mathcal{F}$lagler visited Palm Beach on one of his trips to St. Augustine in the early 1890s. There were not more than a dozen or so houses in Palm Beach at the time. Palm Beach was about three days travel from Jacksonville. Unless one desired frontier conditions, one would not choose its surroundings. Even after seeing all this, Flagler was charmed with South Florida. The Palm Beach section was much to his liking and he decided to make further investigations.

In April, 1893, he made another trip to Palm Beach. After consultation with some of his lieutenants, he decided to buy some of the McCormick property for $75,000. He had decided to build another Flagler hotel.[25] The Palm Beach community was electrified when it heard that he intended to extend his railroad as far south as Palm Beach. They were stunned when he announced that work on the hotel would begin immediately and that the railroad would be extended as soon as possible. Flagler's purchase of land in Palm Beach was publicized far and wide. Prices of real estate increased to incredible figures. Land that had been virtually worthless was immediately priced from $150 to $1,000 an acre. The boom was on. Homesteaders, who had come to Palm Beach several years earlier, suddenly found themselves newly rich.[26]

$\mathcal{F}$lagler and his lieutenants moved swiftly to locate hundreds of workmen to come to Palm Beach. There were no housing facilities so the workmen were put into a makeshift community of tents and shanties. It was given the name of the "Styx." On May 1, 1893, work started on a new hotel, already named the Royal Poinciana. Here again, as in the case of the Ponce de Leon Hotel, transporting materials to the scene of construction was the biggest problem. Work on the railroad progressed simultaneously with that on the hotel. Therefore, Flagler had to provide other means for shipping materials to Palm Beach. Most of it was brought by railroad to Eau Gallie and from there to Jupiter it was sent by boat. From Jupiter to Juno, a distance of about eight or 10 miles, materials were shipped by way of a little railroad called the "Celestial Line." From there to Palm Beach water transportation was used. Some of the lumber for the Royal Poinciana Hotel was shipped by river steamers down the coast of Florida to Palm Beach and several Mississippi steamers were purchased by Flagler for this purpose.[27]

*A*s late as the spring of 1893, there were virtually no settlers on the west side of the lake in the area which is now West Palm Beach. Flagler saw the possibilities of establishing a commercial town there. His idea was to leave the east side, Palm Beach, for winter visitors. In April, 1893, he purchased several hundred acres of land, largely from Captain O. S. Porter, and laid out the town site for West Palm Beach. He planned to terminate the oncoming railroad in that place.[28]

*T*he Styx was moved across the lake and his workmen were housed in the newly–created town which grew rapidly. It soon became a thriving town. For a time, tents and shacks continued to spring up as more and more workmen poured into the area. West Palm Beach resembled a mining camp similar to those found on the frontiers of the far West, suffering some of the rough elements that pervaded those towns. Each work day, men rowed across Lake Worth in the morning to their jobs at the Royal Poinciana and then rowed back across the lake in the afternoon.[29]

*T*he town of West Palm Beach, as it was laid out in August, 1893, extended from the waters of Lake Worth some distance westward to Clear Lake. J. E. Ingraham, one of Flagler's most able assistants, was placed in charge of construction of the new town. Streets were given the names of trees, fruits, and flowers common to the area.

*O*ne of the first services in West Palm Beach was a fire department. Ingraham thought such an organization was especially needed since many of the shacks and huts were highly flammable. The fire fighters were called the "Flagler Alerts." A bell atop a building used as the city hall summoned the fire fighters to duty. When the bell was sounded, the "Alerts" jumped on bicycles, rushed to the city hall, donned helmets and coats, and then sped away to the flaming structure with a cart–like hose–reel and hand engine, sometimes hoping the fire had not burned out before they arrived. The day of the horse drawn fire engine was yet to come to West Palm Beach. [30]

𝒯he new city of West Palm Beach grew much faster than Palm Beach. Wooden stores were erected. One of the first merchants was George S. Maltby, a furniture dealer and undertaker who came from McPherson, Kansas. Another newcomer was E. M. Hyer from Orlando. He operated a small store. Captain E. M. Dimick opened the first drugstore.

𝒮everal of her first citizens worked diligently to ensure that West Palm Beach became an incorporated town. After a number of mass meetings, the town was incorporated on November 10, 1894. John S. Earman was elected mayor by its 78 voting citizens. George W. Potter, E. H. Dimick, J. M. Garland, J. F. Lamond, George Zapf, H. T. Grant, and H. J. Burkhardt were elected aldermen. For their city clerk the citizens selected Eli Sims and W. L. Torbett was made city marshal. West Palm Beach came into existence with comparative ease and a population of about 1,000 people. The laws of Florida provided that when two–thirds of the voters within a certain area decided to become incorporated, they could file a request with the clerk of the circuit court for immediate action. This was done without sanction from the state legislature. West Palm Beach was situated in Dade County at the time of its incorporation. In those days, the county seat of Dade County was located at Juno.[31]

ℋenry Flagler had been a major benefactor of St. Augustine. That was to happen again in the early growth of West Palm Beach. He helped in many of the civic projects as well as financing his own large private developments. Houses were built for his employees and the flimsy temporary dwellings were slowly torn down. Flagler contributed to public funds and helped in the construction of several of West Palm Beach's prominent buildings. He gave a plot of land for a municipal cemetery. In fact, at one time, he expressed a desire to be buried in West Palm Beach, but later changed his mind. Flagler also built the Catholic Church in the city because a large number of his employees, including Joseph McDonald, were Catholics.[32]

ℒargely as the result of Flagler's efforts, Palm Beach County was created out of Dade County in 1909 and West Palm Beach became the county seat. The newly–created county seat had a population of 1,700 people. West Palm Beach had outgrown Palm Beach in size and commercial importance. However, Palm Beach continued to cater to resort activities. It did not become a separate municipality until 1911 and this act marked the passing of the Flagler era in both of the Palm Beaches.

III

*F*lagler's greatest contributions to the Lake Worth region were the extension of his railroad down the East Coast and the construction of the Royal Poinciana and Breakers hotels. The railroad was completed to West Palm Beach on April 2, 1894. The Royal Poinciana was finished in record time and opened on February 11, 1894. This is particularly impressive since it had only been started on May 1, 1893.[33] The Royal Poinciana was located on the eastern shore of Lake Worth and was set on about 100 acres of beautiful land. The grounds were covered with one of the greatest varieties of tropical growth found in Florida.[34] Though the hotel's frontage was on the lake, the ocean was only several hundred yards to the rear.

*W*hen built, the Royal Poinciana was one of the largest wooden buildings in the world used exclusively for hotel purposes. It required 1,400 kegs of nails, 5,000,000 feet of lumber, 360,000 shingles, 4,000 barrels of lime, 500,000 bricks, 240,000 gallons of paint, and more than $1,000,000 to build. The hotel had 1,200 windows and 1,300 doors. One of Flagler's heaviest expenses was transportation, since his own road had not been completed.

Guests in front of the Royal Poinciana Hotel, Palm Beach, March 14, 1896. The hotel is no longer standing.

The lumber cost from $13.50 to $16.00 per thousand feet, shingles from about $2 to $3 per thousand, bricks about $12 per thousand, and lime about $1.35 per barrel. The wages for carpenters and other laborers ran from $1.50 to $2.25 a day.[35]

*I*t was necessary to build up part of the land on which the Royal Poinciana was constructed. By now, filling in swamps and hammocks was not unusual for Henry Flagler. His engineers dumped thousands of carloads of earth on marshy lands which later became a magnificent golf course adjacent to the hotel. Avenues of Australian pines were planted to enhance the dignity of the building and tropical shrubs and trees lent grace and beauty to the surroundings. The hotel was named for the royal poinciana tree, a native of Madagascar, which was common to the tropics. The royal poinciana is a beautiful umbrella–shaped tree which produces a scarlet and orange flower. It is extremely delicate, and stands very little cold weather.

*T*he building was a huge, sprawling structure with 540 bedrooms. It accommodated 800 guests when it was opened in 1894. The building was enlarged from time to time. The hotel's final capacity was around 1,200 guests and the dining room had a seating capacity for 1,600 people. At the time it was built, the Royal Poinciana was considered the largest resort hotel in the world. Although it was only six stories high, the structure covered several acres of ground. In the center of the building was a large rotunda from which ran several miles of hallways. There were spacious drawing rooms, lounges, parlors, and a casino. A large veranda ran across the front of the building.[36] The furniture was chosen with utmost care and taste, attracting the most fastidious travelers. The color scheme on the inside was green and white. Chairs were upholstered in green velvet and there was light green carpeting on the floor. The walls and ceilings in the more prominent rooms were painted light green with trimmings of white. The outside of the hotel was painted yellow with white trimmings.[37] The building was enlarged in 1899 and again in 1901.[38]

*T*he Royal Poinciana was the gathering place for persons of wealth, fashion, and society. The hotel was known throughout the United States for its service and its food. Wealthy patrons were charged high rates for their lodgings which included meals. However, the hotel was designed to also accommodate less affluent guests. Some less expensive rooms were available and their prices differed from season to season. As in the other Flagler hotels, there were a great variety of accommodations, depending entirely upon one's desires and one's ability to pay. Approximately 1,400 employees were kept busy during the months when the hotel was open, usually from December to April. A waiter was employed to serve every four diners. There was a chamber maid for every few rooms. A bell man was on call in every hall. Highlighting the social season each year was the Washington Birthday Ball, held on February 22. This event was always the most brilliant and the most anticipated of the year. Thousands of dollars were spent preparing for the affair each year. Among other social activities available for the guests each season were cake walks, teas, balls, and dinners. The term the Gay '90s was certainly appropriate at the Royal Poinciana.

Outdoor activities were probably even more popular at the Royal Poinciana than the social affairs inside the hotel. Each evening found people on the lawn, in the gardens, or strolling informally along the lake front. The ladies wore dark skirts and white blouses with leg–of–mutton sleeves. The men were dressed in light trousers or tight–fitting knickers, dark coats, stiff collars, and caps. Golf was the popular sport among the visitors. Two 18 hole courses were available for the guests' use. There were also numerous tennis courts, motor boats, wicker wheel chairs, bicycles, and more. Courteous, well–trained attendants were provided by the hotel to help the guests enjoy the recreational activities available. In addition, a trolley car to transport guests to and from the beach was drawn along a track by a mule. The trolley was always a special treat for the children.

A variety of cultural and religious activities were also provided for the guests. Perhaps the most stressed was religious worship. Guests frequently heard talks given by the Reverend E. B. Webb. The Reverend Webb came to Palm Beach in 1895. Flagler engaged him to lecture weekly and built an annex to the Royal Poinciana where people might assemble to listen to his sermons. Guests at the Royal Poinciana and the newly completed Breakers Hotel, regardless of their religious affiliations, visited the chapel regularly. After Reverend Webb's death in 1900, Flagler remodeled the small chapel. He asked George M. Ward, who at that time was the president of Rollins College in Winter Park, Florida, to become the minister. Reverend Ward, who became one of Henry Flagler's best friends, served in this capacity for 31 years.[39]

*T*he second of Flagler's hotels in Palm Beach was the Breakers, although it was not always known by this name. For a few years it was called the Palm Beach Inn. The hotel building was started during the summer of 1895. Located one–quarter of a mile east of the Royal Poinciana, on the ocean shore, it opened in January, 1896. The Inn was not pretentious. After the first few seasons the building was enlarged and

beautified. At that point, its name was changed to the Breakers and a more modern structure was completed in 1900. It was ruined by a fire in 1903 and replaced in 1906. When the new Breakers opened, it was as luxurious and popular as any Flagler hotel.[40]

Guests enjoy fishing from the pier in front of the Breakers Hotel, Palm Beach, ca. 1907

*F*lagler also built a number of cottages along the ocean in Palm Beach, as well as his own home which was situated on Lake Worth. In 1896, he built a railroad and footbridge across Lake Worth thereby connecting the two Palm Beaches. This made it possible for visitors to come to West Palm Beach on his railroad and have easy access to either of his hotels in Palm Beach. The tracks across the lake reached the Palm Beach side at a point just south of the Royal Poinciana. From there, guests could continue on to the Breakers. For several years trains deposited passengers at the south doors of both hotels. The railroad across the lake later became an automobile bridge and Flagler's railroad terminated in West Palm Beach.

*T*here was much speculation. Would Flagler go farther south with his developments? Those who knew him best contended that Flagler would never be satisfied until he had reached the southernmost tip of Florida. He did not give any indication of what he proposed to do, but Flagler was a man of action. It would not be long before he made known his next development plans.

10. The City That Flagler Built

*B*efore Henry Flagler arrived there was a little settlement. It was located where the Miami River empties into Biscayne Bay. The area gave little promise of growth, despite its beautiful location. For many years the spot had attracted only a few frontiersmen. As early as February 27, 1808, the Spanish government, which then dominated in Florida, granted 100 acres of land to John Egan. The land granted was on the Miami River, the name Miami was an Indian word meaning "Sweet Water." Egan, a hardy pioneer, persuaded a few other settlers to join him. They made their homes on the banks of the beautiful river, in view of the bay. This was the beginning of Miami.

*A*fter Florida was transferred to the United States in 1821, James Egan, a son of John Egan, laid claim to a large portion of the land in the Biscayne Bay area. He made that claim because of the grant his father had been given by the Spanish government in 1808. John Egan presented his petition to the United States Commissioners at St. Augustine and they deemed his claim valid. The federal government gave John deeds to 640 acres of choice land along the shores of Biscayne Bay.

*W*hen young John Egan traveled to his land, he found only a few settlers in the vicinity. The population grew soon after the outbreak of the Seminole Indian Wars in 1836 when other settlers arrived. The federal government established Fort Dallas at the mouth of the Miami River. Governmental activities radiated from that point. Settlers came to Fort Dallas seeking protection and hundreds of troops were sent to the area. The soldiers became familiar with early Miami. Many of them liked the area and decided to make it their home after the fighting stopped. The war itself helped to open up other portions of the Miami River to settlers.[1]

*B*efore the Civil War, no efforts were made to advertise Fort Dallas, as the settlement was called, or to publicize south Florida to the outside world. After the Civil War, the Biscayne Bay Company and several other land companies bought up tremendous tracts of land, including the Egan grant. Their purpose was to develop the region.

One syndicate was formed to raise bananas along the Miami River. It hoped to make millions from banana sales. At the time, Cuban bananas were selling for $1.00 a bunch plus transportation. The owners of the syndicate believed they could raise bananas as well, and less expensively, than the Cuban growers. What they didn't know was that Florida bananas would not grow to the size of Cuban bananas. The plan was soon abandoned. Developers then decided that the future of Fort Dallas lay in her possibilities as a commercial and resort center, rather than as a banana plantation.[2] In the meantime, the Biscayne Bay Company continued to sell land around the mouth of the river. At the same time, a few other settlements were growing up in the area. At Coconut Grove, six miles south of the Miami River, a lighthouse keeper and several families had located and a few fishermen lived along the bay.

One of the first settlers to buy land from the Biscayne Bay Company was William Brickell. He moved to Fort Dallas in 1871 and located south of the river. Brickell was a hearty adventurer who depended at first on fishing and salvaging for his livelihood. Later he established a trading post at the mouth of the river very near old Fort Dallas, which had virtually become abandoned by this time. Brickell traded mostly with Indians and fishermen. He lived the life of a typical pioneer in a section whose possibilities had not yet been opened up to development.[3]

The next pioneer to settle at Fort Dallas was Mrs. Julia D. Tuttle. About the same time that Brickell came to the area, she arrived with her husband and her father, Ephraim T. Sturtevant. Julia was fascinated with everything about south Florida. She especially liked the Miami River and beautiful Biscayne Bay. When her father and husband made plans to return home to Cleveland, Ohio, Julia Tuttle decided to remain in Florida for a time. She purchased 640 acres of land from the Biscayne Bay Company on the north bank of the Miami River and built a small cabin. She enjoyed the backwoods life of the wilderness region. She returned to Cleveland when her husband died, but only stayed there for a short while. Julia Tuttle returned to Fort Dallas on November 13, 1891, and remained there until her death on September 14, 1898.[4]

Mrs. Tuttle bought and remodeled the old fort. She made a comfortable home out of it. She liked Fort Dallas and tried to attract other settlers to the area, particularly those settlers who would purchase part of her property. For several years she was unsuccessful. Taxes began to amount to large sums; so both Julia Tuttle and Charles Brickell began to redouble their efforts to sell portions of their properties which were located on opposite sides of the river. The Tuttle property was on the north side of the river and the Brickell property was on the south side.

Julia Tuttle

*J*ulia Tuttle was a clever woman who possessed many good business qualifications. She had heard of Henry Flagler since most of Florida was experiencing, either directly or indirectly, some benefit from his developments down the East Coast. There is also some possibility that Mrs. Tuttle had known Flagler before he left Cleveland. At any rate, she certainly knew of his reputation in connection with the Standard Oil Company. Julia Tuttle had land and saw her opportunity. She decided to contact Flagler about Fort Dallas. She hoped that he would be interested in extending his railroad south. At this time the road was not quite completed to West Palm Beach. If Flagler should begin to buy land in Fort Dallas, reasoned Mrs. Tuttle, his purchases would set off a land boom.

*H*er first move was to visit Flagler in St. Augustine. She did this in 1893, but the trip was in vain. Flagler considered her just another salesperson of land. At the time, he did not entertain the idea of building his railroad farther south than West Palm Beach. Mrs. Tuttle went back to south Florida. Although she was discouraged, she did not let Flagler's refusal get the better of her. She wrote him letters offering to divide her large property holdings north of the river with him. Her persistent pleas fell on deaf ears. With the receipt of each letter, Flagler's opinion of Mrs. Tuttle lessened. In the end, however, her efforts brought much success to both Flagler and herself. Providence and her own persistence favored her.[5]

*F*lorida experienced her coldest weather in over 100 years during the winter of 1894-1895. The first freeze occurred on December 24, 1894. On the night of December 28, 1894, the temperature fell to 19° in central Florida. The cold spell lasted for several days. Then, on February 6, 1895, another hard freeze hit the state.[7] Farmers were hardly over the first spell when the second crept down from the North Pole. These hard freezes ruined the citrus crop and killed vegetables and coconut palms as far south as Palm Beach. Property was damaged to the extent of millions of dollars. Hundreds of people were left without income since their crops had been ruined. Many persons who had come to Florida to raise fruit packed what they could carry of their earthly possessions and began the trek North. They left their houses to the bats, the owls, or perhaps the tramps.[8]

*W*hat the people of North and Central Florida lost most in the freeze was their confidence in the state. They lost their confidence in its potential to become a great citrus-producing section. Mrs. Tuttle, taking advantage of the freeze, reminded Flagler of the fact that the Miami River region had been untouched by the cold weather. She emphasized that the settlement at the mouth of the river was in a tropical region. She pointed out that it could easily become the center of a great citrus belt if Flagler would only lend a hand.

*A*t last, Henry Flagler began to think back over Julia Tuttle's propositions. He was in St. Augustine at the time and instructed J. E. Ingraham, who was in Palm Beach, to make a trip to Biscayne Bay and investigate conditions there. Ingraham immediately visited Mrs. Tuttle. He was surprised and delighted to find that the freezing weather had not reached that far south. Flowers were in full bloom. Not a single orange tree had been killed. He, like Julia Tuttle, concluded that the climate was ideal for raising citrus fruit and reported his findings to Flagler. Soon after, Henry Flagler decided that it was at least worth a trip there himself. He left St. Augustine in the company of some of his lieutenants, including Joseph R. Parrott, McDonald, and McGuire. In West Palm Beach they were joined by Ingraham. The entire group was headed for Biscayne Bay to see persistent Julia Tuttle.

*F*lagler had been in the Miami River area only once before. As he had remembered, the 66 miles between Palm Beach and the Miami

River was practically an unbroken wilderness. Mail was delivered to Fort Dallas once a week and was carried by a barefoot mailman who walked the entire distance between Palm Beach and Fort Dallas. Flagler and his party traveled from Palm Beach to Ft. Lauderdale by launch. From there on they rode in a cart drawn by a mule. When they arrived at Fort Dallas they knew that much better transportation south of West Palm Beach would be necessary before any development could be seriously considered. But, at that time, Flagler did not feel he was the one to provide the means.

*U*pon arriving at Fort Dallas the party was entertained by Mrs. Tuttle. Flagler was soon convinced that the region had limitless possibilities. He conferred briefly with his associates. Before he went to bed the first night, he made up his mind to extend his railroad from West Palm Beach to the Miami River.

*M*rs. Tuttle was most persuasive about the area's potential. She backed up her talk by offering Flagler 100 acres of her land for a railroad terminal, railroad yards, and the hotel site. She kept for herself 13 acres north of the Miami River, which today is the heart of the city of Miami. Another 527 acre lot was laid out in alternate strips, half of which she gave to Flagler and half of which she kept for herself. In return for these considerations, Flagler promised, on June 12, 1895, to extend his railroad to Biscayne Bay. He agreed to build a terminal station, lay out streets in the proposed town, and build a municipal water works.[9] Flagler also acquired other large holdings of land throughout the area. Mrs. Tuttle had finally succeeded in getting him interested in her section of Florida. All he had needed was a little time and a hard freeze.

*T*he freeze of 1894-1895 caused other events to happen in Florida. Flagler was sympathetic with the people up and down the East Coast who had lost their livelihood. He gave thousands of dollars to individuals to help them replace what they had lost. Through these benevolent deeds he restored peoples' confidence in the state. When money agencies, banks, and corporations realized that Flagler had faith in Florida, they, too, returned needed capital into the state.

*T*here was one incident which involved a Captain Sharpe who had a large orange grove on the Indian River. Sharpe wrote Flagler a letter telling him that his crop was ruined and requesting aid. Flagler had J. E. Ingraham visit Captain Sharpe and his wife at their home. Ingraham found the Sharpes to be worthy and deserving. Arrangements were made to rehabilitate the grove. Sharpe was given money. Flagler was to be repaid when the grove was productive again. The money was furnished without question. Captain Sharpe, however, insisted that Flagler take a mortgage on the property. Finally, Flagler accepted the mortgage. Later, when the grove was again bearing fruit, Sharpe invited Flagler to stop and see the oranges. Flagler accepted and his special train was brought to a stop on the grove siding. The two men rode among the trees in the Captain's old buggy which was drawn by a mule. The Sharpes entertained Flagler royally. Sharpe never paid the mortgage off because Flagler would not let him. The two men became fast friends. As long as Sharpe lived he sent fruit from the grove to the Flaglers during each winter wherever they were.[10]

II

*W*hen Flagler contracted with Julia Tuttle to extend the railroad to the Miami River he realized that the undertaking was a big one. Mrs. Tuttle had insisted that he complete his new hotel within 18 months and Flagler had agreed to that requirement. Biscayne Bay was a long way from the more populous sections of Florida from which he had to draw most of his labor. He had one of his assistants insert advertisements in papers throughout the state proclaiming that laborers of all kinds could find employment in Miami, as the community was called by this time. An army of workers descended on the little settlement, but could not find adequate living facilities. William Brickell, who had the only place of business in Miami, sold out his stock completely. He had to close his doors until new supplies could be shipped. Flagler began hasty preparations to bring more supplies and material to Miami. He was eager to get started because he had promised Mrs. Tuttle that he would try to complete the road to Miami by February 1, 1896, and also to have the hotel ready for the winter season.[11]

*F*lagler began surveys for the extension south of West Palm Beach in June, 1895. It took several weeks to complete the preliminary arrangements, but full-scale construction was soon underway. Several steamers which had been running on the Indian River were transferred to the inland waters between West Palm Beach and Miami, giving service to the various railroad camps that were under construction between the two places. Portions of the inland waterway in south Florida were dredged. This was necessary so that larger steamers could make their way up and down the coast carrying materials and supplies to the construction sites. The laying of track south of West Palm Beach began in September, 1895. The distance of nearly 70 miles was covered in record time.

*A*s the rails were laid southward through the undeveloped stretch of country, several small towns were laid out. Workmen needed places to live and Flagler aided them in establishing places where they might bring their families while they were employed on the railroad construction. The first town to be developed was Delray; then Deerfield, Fort Lauderdale, and Dania were established. Fort Lauderdale was the first of the towns to grow to any considerable size. It was located on both sides of the New River and offered good farm land. In 1897 Flagler built a railroad station there. It soon became the most prominent town on the road between West Palm Beach and Miami.[12]

*D*espite the level land over which the road was built, there was a considerable amount of grading which had to take place. Flagler contracted for this grading job in units and it was one of the most expensive undertakings relative to the building of the railroad. But the expense did not seem to bother him. His stock in the Standard Oil Company was becoming increasingly more valuable as the years went by and Flagler's fortune was steadily becoming larger.[14]

*O*n April 15, 1896, the railroad was completed to Miami. As a result, more people poured into the little town daily. At last the Flagler railroad was anchored securely in south Florida. While Miami, on one end of the line, was just awakening, Jacksonville on the other end of the line, 366 miles to the North, was already enjoying the benefits of the railroad.

*T*he year 1896 was a prosperous one for Jacksonville. The city set aside seven days in the spring as "Gala Week" to celebrate growth and progress. The occasion almost reached the proportions of a New Orleans

Mardi Gras. The New York Giants held spring practice in the "Gateway City" to Florida. Jacksonvillians were singing a brand-new song, "Take Me Out to the Ball Game." Huge crowds marvelled when George N. Adams set a world's bicycling record at Panama Park. Sports were becoming prominent everywhere.

*I*n the meantime, on September 7, 1895, the name of the railroad was changed again. Instead of being known as the Jacksonville, St. Augustine and Indian River Railroad, the new name became the Florida East Coast Railway. This change was necessitated by the accumulation of property which Flagler had bought and the continued developments which he contemplated. The new name of the road was appropriate. It was suggestive of the territory which it served. The charter was granted on September 13, 1895, and was signed by Henry L. Mitchell, Governor of Florida.[14] Although trains were operated from New York to Miami, the Florida East Coast Railway was a Florida institution and it escaped Interstate Commerce Commission regulations. This was especially beneficial to Flagler as he was able to charge a higher freight rate than most of the other roads could demand. Then, too, whenever the line crossed a bridge, he charged an extra freight rate. Such business methods earned for Flagler many a critic among his shippers. In the long run he made little money out of the Florida East Coast Railway.[15]

*D*uring the first few years of the Florida East Coast Railway, Flagler spent much more in operating his trains than he made. Engines burned wood instead of coal and within one year his trains consumed 15,305 cords of fuel, or an average of 56 miles per cord. The wood, which was chiefly fat pine, was cut and stacked at various places along the road. At these intervals the train had to stop and get a new supply of wood. Flagler would not contract with a single lumberman for fuel, but bought from various ones all along the route. The engineer, after receiving his supply of wood left a "wood ticket" with the lumberman. From time to time these tickets were presented to the railroad for payment. By 1900, the fat pine along the road was getting scarce. It had to be brought long distances to the railroad and the wood burners were changed to coal burners.[16]

*T*he coming of the railroad to Miami was the biggest single event in the city's history. After the railroad, the territory around Miami began to unfold rapidly. A region which had been a veritable wilderness began to show signs of life and a new city began to appear. Mrs. Tuttle and William Brickell did not have to wait long to see their economic dreams come true. Among

Getting ready to roll. An early train to Miami, ca. 1897

the early arrivals in Miami was Joseph A. McDonald, who came there on February 15, 1896. His job was to superintend all of Flagler's construction in the town. John B. Reilly came soon after as bookkeeper and cashier to McDonald and John Sewell soon arrived from Kissimmee as foreman of the Flagler interests. Sewell said later that he found Miami all woods. He believed that Mrs. Tuttle had done some developing but not much. She had started building a sort of hotel, but it was more like a barn where men slept.[17] Sewell spent his first night in Miami on a floating houseboat on the Miami River, but soon moved to Mrs. Tuttle's rooming house where he found the living conditions crude and uncomfortable.

*O*ther settlers who came to Miami in 1896 were G. E. Sewell, brother of John, who opened a clothing store and Frank Budge, who operated a hardware store. J. E. Lummas opened a general store; Isadore Cohen, a clothing store; John W. Watson, a hardware store; E. L. Brady, a grocery store; L. C. Oliver, a lumber yard; Salem Graham, a hotel; and William Burdine, a general store.[18] Flagler encouraged all these early inhabitants and gave them what aid he could in making a success from their respective businesses. He also encouraged different people over the state to go to Miami by giving one free round trip ride on his railroad to any purchaser of land in the area.[19]

*M*iami was incorporated on July 28, 1896, with 502 voters. This action took place about four months after the arrival of the first Florida East Coast train. The name Miami was appropriate and pretty. It had been in use for some time, although not officially. At the time, there was growing sentiment to call the town Flagler, but he expressed a desire that the old Indian word be retained. Flagler did not want the publicity which might result from having a town named for him. So Miami remained Miami, but the new town showed little resemblance to the old community. John B. Reilly was chosen the first mayor on a compromise ticket. The town's two most prominent citizens at the time were J. A. McDonald and John Sewell. McDonald, Fred S. Morse, Daniel Cosgrove, and Walter S. Graham were elected councilmen. Jack Graham became the first city clerk.[20]

*P*erhaps the first new building erected in Miami after the railroad was extended was a home and office building for J. A. McDonald, Flagler's assistant. McDonald originally came to Florida as early as 1881 and was associated with James A. McGuire. For years, both contractors worked almost exclusively for Flagler. However, after McDonald came to Miami he liked the area so well that he refused to leave. McDonald became one of Miami's most loyal citizens and went into the lumber, ice, and transfer business. He built the Biscayne Bay Hotel in Miami, one of the city's first rooming houses.[21]

*A*fter Flagler paved a few of Miami's existing streets and laid out some new ones, his first big undertaking was the construction of a luxury hotel comparable to the Royal Poinciana and the Ponce de Leon. In his agreement with Mrs. Tuttle, a hotel had been one of the things he had promised to do. Mrs. Tuttle had reasoned that an adequate hotel in Miami would be a drawing card for wealthy people who might come there and purchase land. They decided to call the new hotel the Royal Palm because of the large quantity of those trees found around Biscayne Bay. Work started on the new hotel two months before the railroad reached Miami. J. A. McDonald supervised the beginning of the work on February 15, 1896, but after a few days McDonald became ill and was unable to go on with his assignment. Flagler then sent John Sewell to Miami. He took charge of the construction until McDonald recovered.

*J*ohn Sewell remained in charge of construction for some time. His brother, George, also came to the area to work on the Royal Palm Hotel and later opened a business of his own.[22] As in the case of his earlier developments, Flagler did not allow any phase of the construction to lag. He chose men to do the work in whom he had the fullest confidence. One of the employees of the Royal Palm Hotel was J. J. Brinkerhoff, whom Flagler had known since his days in Cleveland. Flagler had been responsible for Brinkerhoff's investing in the Standard Oil Company. They had been good friends since that time. J. F. Lewis was placed in charge of the plumbing. Dan Cosgrove supervised the steam and gas fittings. A. T. Best was the head electrician, Robert H. Horter the head painter, and E. W. Talmadge was in charge of the brickmasons.[23]

$\mathcal{T}$he Royal Palm had the most nearly ideal location of all the seven Flagler hotels. Its grounds covered 15 acres of beautiful land where the Miami River emptied into Biscayne Bay. The new hotel opened on January 16, 1897, but it was not in its completed state. Henry W. Merrill, the

The Royal Palm Hotel, Miami

manager, continued to work with busy painters and plasterers for several months thereafter. The opening of the hotel was a significant date in Miami's history. It was positive proof of Flagler's faith in the future growth of the little town and was an occasion equally as great as the day the railroad to Miami was completed. People were present in large numbers to see the first guests register.[24]

$\mathcal{T}$he new hotel was 680 feet long and 267 feet wide.[25] It was five stories high. A large court was formed by wings running from the main building. From its verandas and from the upper floors, one could see a vast expanse of bay, ocean, keys, pine woodland, and marshy Everglades. Royal palms grew in profusion about the building, forming attractive walks and roads leading to the bay and river.

$\mathcal{T}$he Royal Palm Hotel was only a small portion of Flagler's Miami developments. The prevailing Flagler characteristic, that of seeing a project finished in record time, was evident in all of his Miami undertakings. It had taken Flagler some time to decide to invest in Miami, but once he got started there was a strong urge to continue until he had built a thriving city on Biscayne Bay. Once again, Flagler was a real benefactor of the new town. He did much more than build a railroad and a hotel. He paved the streets and made sidewalks. He saw the need for an electric light plant and built it. At that time, electricity was a novelty to many of the residents. Its use was indicative of Flagler's advanced ideas and the scope of his vision for the town of Miami. He also began a system of sewage and waterworks of which few towns of Miami's size could boast.[26] With the start Flagler gave her, Miami grew rapidly.

*I*n addition to building the physical infrastructure of the community, Flagler soon saw the need for public schools and churches. He worked to establish them and donated the land on which the first public school was built. In addition, he contributed most of the funds for the school's construction.[27] A short time later he was instrumental in the building of four churches, one each for the Baptist, Methodist, Episcopal, and Catholic congregations. He gave the land on which all of these churches were built and contributed heavily to their support. His interest in the Episcopal Church was aroused through the efforts of Mrs. Tuttle, who was a member of that church. Joseph A. McDonald solicited his interest for the Catholic Church, John Sewell for the Baptist Church, and E. V. Blackman for the Methodist Church.[28]

*T*he church to which Flagler was most helpful was his own, the Presbyterian Church. It was organized in Miami on April 1, 1896. Initially, there were only four members and a Presbyterian missionary, the Reverend Henry Keigwin. The Reverend Keigwin had been sent to south Florida to minister to the frontiersmen. At first the tiny Presbyterian Church organization grew slowly, but in 1897 Flagler began to contribute heavily to its support. Services were held in a shack with a tent-like top, but Flagler soon built a handsome church building which he deeded to the congregation. Until his death in 1913 he donated generously to the First Presbyterian Church in Miami.[29]

*F*lagler gave several lots to the city of Miami. They were for municipal buildings in the center of the community. He also donated the land for the city market.[30] On March 20, 1896, as a result of his encouragement, a weekly newspaper was begun. He gave it a name, the *Miami Metropolis*. That paper later became the *Miami Daily News*.[31]

*H*e soon became interested in constructing houses for his workmen. On one occasion when he was visiting Miami while the Royal Palm Hotel was being built, he expressed surprise to find that so few workers had built permanent homes there. John D. Reilly explained that most of the people employed were men who had lost heavily in the freeze.

Flagler realized at once that it took all that these men could earn to supply themselves and their families with the basic necessities of life. He hastily made an investigation to see where comfortable homes might be built. The bay front location was not chosen because he believed wealthy people would buy lots and later erect homes there. Finally, he decided on reserving two streets, 13th and 14th, where he constructed dozens of modest, comfortable homes for his employees.[32]

*A*s Miami grew, it rapidly became a commercial center and served as an outlet to many of the islands nearby. Flagler kept boats running to Key West and Nassau. When he started his developments in Miami, the channel in Biscayne Bay was not safe for vessels which drew more than six feet of water. Flagler came forward. He put dredges to work cutting a channel down the bay to Cape Florida. With a wider and deeper channel, ships were able to come into the mouth of the Miami River. In 1898 it was found that the entrance to the Miami River was impracticable for ocean going steamers; so Flagler decided to move the docks up the bay from the river. A new channel was dug to a point near Sixth Street where he built a large dock and wharves. For many years Flagler kept the channel dredged; however, later when the city took over the port, it also built municipal docks.[33]

*M*iami rapidly became the biggest town in south Florida. As this change occurred, there was increasing demand made for the county seat of Dade County to be moved there. Juno, a little town at the North end of Lake Worth, had been the county seat. Not only was Juno small, but it was at the extreme northern tip of what was then Dade County which extended south all the way to the tip of Florida. After Flagler's railroad opened up most of the East Coast, the voters in Miami outnumbered the voters in Juno. In 1899 the county seat was moved to Miami. Soon thereafter Palm Beach County was carved from the northern portion of old Dade County.[34]

*A*nother disastrous freeze on February 7, 1897 quickened Miami's growth. It was the second of the great Florida freezes. Vegetables which were nearly ready for shipment from central and northern Florida were killed. Again, as in 1894-1895, Miami was spared from the cold weather. News that Miami was totally frostproof traveled quickly and more settlers moved to south Florida. Flagler, as before, came to the aid of the stricken farmers. He issued free seed packets to those who had been hurt by the cold. Fertilizer and crate materials were hauled free of charge on his railroad. J. E. Ingraham was sent to the area hardest hit by the front and was instructed to use $200,000 as necessary to help the people.

*M*iami's growth was arrested for a time starting in the summer of 1899 when a yellow fever epidemic broke out. The epidemic started as a result of ticks which had been brought in by a cattle boat from Cuba. The fever became more and more severe and 14 of the 263 people who had been stricken died. Miami was quarantined from October, 1899, to January 15, 1990. While the quarantine was on, Miami experienced some extremely hard times. Virtually every activity in the city stopped.

*F*lagler felt he had to do something. He poured money into Miami by giving work to hundreds of people who had been made idle by the quarantine restrictions. It was at this time that he financed the construction of new streets, sidewalks, and various other municipal improvements. He kept many people from going hungry and saw that all payroll funds were supplied. During the quarantine, anything that John B. Reilly or John Sewell wanted done for the city Flagler ordered carried through. Although the epidemic was deplored at the time, in the long run it resulted in many new developments for the rapidly growing Miami.[35]

*B*y 1902 Miami claimed a population of over 5,000 and construction was still going forward. By the time Flagler died in 1913 the little community into which he injected life in 1896 had a population of 10,875 and ranked fifth in size in Florida.[36] It had three banks, two elementary schools, one high school, six churches, and nine hotels. The city that Flagler built was not only a prominent commercial center but was also a rapidly developing resort community. From December, 1909, to May, 1910, more than 125,000 guests registered at Miami hotels. Julia Tuttle and Flagler had foreseen the future and Miami was still to see her period of greatest growth.

11. *Turbulent Years*

*D*uring the years of Miami's infancy, Flagler was having serious domestic troubles which took much of his time and attention. His family had always been a great source of pleasure for him, but the death of his first wife left him sad and lonely. For a number of years after Mary's death he tried to forget the past. He then centered his affections on his second wife, Ida Alice. She accompanied him on most of his business trips to Miami, Palm Beach, and New York. Ida Alice liked yachting, boating, and entertaining. Flagler tried to provide her with everything that might make her happy. At one time they owned two yachts, the sloop *Eclipse* and the schooner *Columbia.*[1] In addition Flagler belonged to two or three yacht clubs so that Ida Alice might enjoy their privileges.

*T*he *Alicia* was perhaps the finest yacht the Flaglers owned. It had been designed by Harlen and Hollingsworth, prominent New York builders.[2] The *Alicia* was a beautiful craft and was very fast. Its length was 160 feet, yet it was easy to handle. Although seen often in Florida waters, the *Alicia* was used more during the summer when the Flaglers were at their Mamaroneck home. They often used it to visit friends in New London, Connecticut, a fashionable summer resort.[3]

*I*t seemed that Ida Alice was happiest when she was busy doing something. She was nervously inclined and had an abundance of energy. The first time Flagler questioned his wife's conduct was on one occasion when she entertained a group of ladies with a yachting party off the coast of New England. On this cruise a storm arose. Ida Alice refused to allow the boat to be put into port.

*F*lagler worried about her behavior and her judgment. Several days later he expressed to a friend his fear for Ida Alice's safety and his concern over her peculiar action.[4] The next few years passed during which time she apparently lived a normal life. Only occasionally was her conduct a little out of the ordinary and that seemed to occur when she was in the company of a large group of people. Although Flagler was often puzzled at her ways, he said little to anyone about it.

*M*rs. Flagler's mental condition first attracted serious concern from her husband in 1894. He still hoped it would not call for widespread notice. Her talk aroused the suspicion of Dr. George G. Shelton, a prominent New York physician and personal friend of the family. At an appointed time Shelton made a personal call on the Flaglers at their Mamaroneck home. There were other guests in the home at the time, but the presence of her physician friend inspired her to confide in him about more "secrets." Stating that she had something important to tell him, she invited Dr. Shelton to go with her to a secluded corner of the porch. They walked down the long piazza of the home and she began telling him about a prominent New York court case at that time being tried.[5] She spoke with so much freedom that the doctor got up from his seat and looked to see if anyone could be listening, fearing the servants would not understand why she should talk so openly and freely to him.

*D*r. Shelton was embarrassed and tried to change the conversation; but Ida Alice did not observe the caution. In fact, she increased her vehement talk. She referred to a well-known New York woman as the illegitimate daughter of a prominent nobleman of Europe, whose name at the time was before the public. Shelton was amazed at her statements.

*E*xcusing herself a minute, Mrs. Flagler hurriedly went to her room and came back with three little pebbles. She asked him if he could not see "certain marks" in the pebbles. When he answered in the negative, she became infuriated. Finally she jerked the stones out of his hands and exclaimed, "Of course you cannot see them; there are only three people in the world who can, and only members of a secret society possess them and the power to interpret them; they are talismans; they are very, very old." Then picking the first one up in her two fingers she continued, "This one has cured many forms of paralysis, and this one," pointing to the second stone, "will produce pregnancy in a barren woman if she carries it with her for a month." The fact that she was childless had no doubt affected her mind. Dr. Shelton realized this because he had been the one to tell her several months before that she would never be able to have children. He finally excused himself, thinking that his departure might snap her out of her nonsense; but before he left, she insisted that he take two of the stones and put them in his pocket for safekeeping. This he did. "The other one," she said gleefully, "I am going to send to the Czar of Russia."[6]

*D*r. Shelton went back to his office in New York a stunned man. Henry Flagler was his personal friend, but should he tell him what he knew of his wife's mental state? He called Flagler in to receive the grim news, but the latter was not surprised. He had suspected long before that his wife's mental disorder was growing steadily worse. They talked freely about her condition. The fact that Flagler knew now what he had for some months suspected about his wife's health opened the way for further action.

*F*lagler brought Ida Alice from Mamaroneck to their Fifth Avenue home. He felt that she could get better attention from Dr. Shelton there. Ida Alice was encouraged to call the doctor when she felt ill; so she became nothing less than a nuisance to Shelton. Often she called to report a "slight headache;" but if he diverted her attention toward a new hat or some social matter, she would show no evidence of pain. He repeated such an experiment many times with the same results, spending a great deal of his time in the Flagler's Fifth Avenue home. Flagler seemed to be more contented when Dr. Shelton was around.

*M*rs. Flagler began to have delusions, one of which was in regard to her wealth. One day she gave her manicurist a check for $1,000. The manicurist was alarmed and reported the incident to Dr. Shelton. Shelton remonstrated with Ida Alice, but to no avail. She referred to the sum as a mere pittance of her vast wealth. Her thoughts ran to infidelity. Besides her husband, she accused many prominent New York people of all forms of immorality and crime. Scandal and gossip seemed to fill her mind. Her delusions increased and one never knew when another was coming on. She carried on conversations with imaginary people. She laughed and joked with relatives who were nowhere near.[7]

*D*uring the first week in October, 1895, Mrs. Flagler began to speak of her great love for the Czar of Russia. She explained that she had been informed by her Ouija board that the Czar was madly in love with her. Ida Alice divulged the information that she intended to marry the Czar immediately upon Flagler's death. She did not say when she expected her husband to die, but Dr. Shelton became fearful of Flagler's safety and took every precaution to prevent a tragedy. One day soon thereafter she visited one of New York's large jewelry stores and purchased a $2,000 cat's-eye diamond ring, which she sent to the Czar. The ring was intercepted by telegram and never reached its destination. Mrs. Flagler's mental illness became more critical every day.[8]

*H*enry Flagler grew increasingly miserable as his wife's condition worsened. He did not seem to fear for his safety, but her illness was difficult for him to accept. At times his grief was hard to bear. There can be no doubt about his deep concern over her. He left nothing undone that would insure her comfort.[9] On October 24, 1895, Dr. Shelton, acting on Flagler's wishes, called in for consultation Dr. Allan Starr and Dr. Frederick Peterson, specialists in the field of mental disorders. On that day, Mrs. Flagler became violent. After a tantrum she locked herself in her room and barricaded the door. Dr. Peterson, who, in addition to his private practice, was president of the Lunacy Commission of New York State, tried to force his way into the room. Ida Alice would not admit anyone except her maid. Peterson began a patient vigil in an adjoining room.

*S*oon Mrs. Flagler sent her maid out of the room to call a detective. The maid related the story to Peterson. He directed her to go back into Ida Alice's room and report that a detective would be there shortly. In 15 or 20 minutes Peterson went in. The maid told Mrs. Flagler that he was a detective from the central office. With that the patient began to tell her own story. She said the house was full of Russian spies; that she was engaged to be married to the Czar of Russia; and that she constantly had communications with him through the Ouija board which she had on the table. She manifested certain delusions of persecution, one of which was her belief of an attempt on the part of her family to poison her and made homicidal threats during the course of the conversation.

*A*fter the examination, Dr. Peterson told Mrs. Flagler that he would go get several more detectives to help clear the house of spies. He said that when he returned he would rap three times on the door and that would be a sign for her to open it. She consented to do that. Dr. Peterson retired to the living room where he consulted with Dr. Starr. The papers for her committal to Choate's Sanitarium in Pleasantville, New York had already been drawn up by Dr. Shelton. The three physicians pronounced the case as delusionary insanity and recommended that she be sent to Choate's private asylum immediately.[10]

$\mathcal{D}$r. Peterson went back to Ida Alice's room and gave the three raps on the door as promised. The door was opened. With one male attendant and one female attendant, Mrs. Flagler was taken by force down the stairs and put in a waiting carriage at the door. She was carried to the station and transferred to a special railroad car which sped her to Pleasantville, New York.[11] After Ida Alice's departure, Flagler was urged by Dr. Shelton to go to Florida and remain there for the winter. Shelton felt that Dr. Anderson in St. Augustine could do much to mend his spirits. Said Dr. Shelton to Dr. Anderson in a letter written the day after Mrs. Flagler was committed to the Pleasantville asylum,

> *Mr. Flagler proposes to start for Florida next week. I have advised very strongly that he do that because he is almost prostrated with grief and anxiety. I have seen him in deep trouble, but never has anything taken such a hold upon him as this. I hope you will keep him in the South until the edge of his grief wears off . . . . I believe you can cheer him more than anyone.[12]*

$\mathcal{F}$lagler took Shelton's advice and went to St. Augustine, but he was restless and dissatisfied. He tried to forget his troubles by prolonged work. He went to Palm Beach and Miami. He tried working hard and he tried complete relaxation. When he was in New York, he yearned for Florida. When he was in Florida, he wanted to go north. It was a long, dreary winter. Flagler kept in touch with Dr. Shelton. At Flagler's request the doctor made two trips to Pleasantville to see Ida Alice. At first she seemed to get no better. She continued to manifest delusions of grandeur and to speak of her love for the Czar of Russia. She despised seeing Shelton and threatened him for putting her in what she styled "that hole." Realizing that his visits did nothing but aggravate her condition, he discontinued his trips to the asylum.[13]

$\mathcal{I}$n the spring of 1896, Flagler returned to New York. He talked personally with the doctors about his wife's mental disorder. Dr. Starr made an examination in May and found her much better than he expected. Ida Alice talked freely with him about her delusions. In only one instance did she revert to the abnormal state, and that was the incident about the ring for the Czar. She talked to Starr freely about that. She thought her husband was still in Florida; however, he had been in New York for several weeks. She told Dr. Starr to tell Flagler that she still loved him and that she was now clothed in her right mind. Dr. Starr reported to Flagler that it might be possible to bring her home within a short time, but warned against overoptimism. He explained that Ida Alice could have a relapse in two to six months and made no prediction beyond that. Flagler was happy to know that his wife was better, but disappointed because he was given no assurances that she would be permanently well. In a letter to Dr. Anderson, he said, "I shall try to keep up courage and make the best fight in her behalf that is possible."[14]

*F*lagler planned to open their Mamaroneck home in time for Mrs. Flagler's arrival. He hoped that would be before June 5, their wedding anniversary. Arrangements were made to bring from the institution one of her attendants as a companion. Only a few visitors were allowed inside the gates at Satanstoe. Flagler hoped to continue Mrs. Flagler's rest cure there and planned to stay with her as much as possible himself. Dr. Starr warned against giving her the opportunity of meeting men acquaintances. She was to be given full liberty of action, to ride or go on the yacht, but her husband was always to be with her.[15]

*O*n May 29, Flagler talked with Dr. Choate in New York about Ida Alice. The owner of the asylum did not share Dr. Starr's fears concerning a relapse. At that point, definite arrangements were made for Ida Alice to rejoin him on June 5. Said Dr. Choate, "I regard Mrs. Flagler as entirely cured."[16] Henry and Ida Alice were happily reunited on June 5, 1896, in White Plains, New York. Dr. Choate accompanied her to this point, where she was met by her husband. The meeting was natural and without restraint. There was much to talk about, since their separation had been of nearly eight months' duration. Flagler was not able to detect the slightest flaw in her mental action. He discussed freely with her every phase of her former delusions and declared that he now believed in miracles because he thought her to be her normal self again. Joyfully he reported to Dr. Anderson several days after they reached Mamaroneck, "I am surprised and need not say delighted at the outcome—it seems too good to be true."[17]

*T*he next few weeks were joyous ones. It was the first time Flagler had been happy since the preceding October when his wife was sent to Pleasantville for treatment. There were many amusements and diversions at Mamaroneck. Flagler had a number of fine trotting horses, which he purchased for the use of the family and their guests. He built a quarter-mile track and it attracted much attention in the community.[18] Time was spent in a new pleasure which had become popular in many parts of the country—bicycle riding. Mr. and Mrs. Flagler hired a tutor to instruct them in the art of mounting and dismounting. They rode seven to 10 miles each day.[19]

*F*lagler liked to read and was enjoying *Ham and Dixie* which Dr. Anderson sent him from St. Augustine. While he read, Ida Alice did handwork. She busied herself with an afghan she was making for the latest arrival at the Andersons' home, Baby Clarissa. She kept an album in which she had the pictures of many babies. Clarissa's picture was at the very front of her collection. "It seems an irony of fate," wrote Flagler to Dr. Anderson, "that Alice, who is so fond of babies, can't have one of her own."[20] This fact constantly preyed upon her mind. She often spoke of her husband's vast wealth which he would leave to so few of his own.

*T*hroughout the month of June, Ida Alice's mental state was normal. Her happiness at Mamaroneck seemed complete. She asked her husband to sell their city home in order that they might divide their time between Mamaroneck and St. Augustine. Flagler thought it a wise course to pursue, since the memories of the Fifth Avenue home were none too pleasant. The house, however, was not sold immediately. Flagler spent one or two days each week at his office in the city, but was away from Ida Alice as little as possible.[21]

*M*ost of the time the Flaglers were alone. None of their relatives were invited to Satanstoe, except for the Eugene M. Ashleys of Lockport, New York. Mrs. Ashley before her marriage was Eliza Adriance, a second cousin of Flagler on his mother's side. Of all his cousins Eliza Ashley was his favorite and she was especially fond of him.[22] Her husband, Eugene was a prominent lawyer. He and Flagler had much in common. The Ashleys arrived at Satanstoe on July 1 for an indefinite stay. It was Flagler's hope that they would help divert Alice's attention to things which tended not to disturb her. They understood the case and their presence was a great satisfaction to everyone concerned.[23]

*S*oon after the Ashleys arrived, Mrs. Flagler began to show signs of a relapse. She begged for a Ouija board. She tried to bribe the servants to find one for her. Otherwise she seemed perfectly well, but Flagler knew that he could expect the worst. It was the Ouija board that had thrown her off balance the preceding year. After a week of apprehension, Eliza Ashley and the nurse began to notice Mrs. Flagler's odd actions. Mrs. Ashley confided to Flagler that his wife was as full of delusions as she had been before she entered the institution at Pleasantville. Once again Ida Alice expressed her great love for the Czar of Russia. She also carried on in the same manner about her husband's lack of fidelity and her loss of respect for him. Alhough she talked in derogatory terms about him to Mrs. Ashley, she was very attentive and affectionate to him when they were alone. When not in her husband's presence, she talked glibly and nonsensically. Flagler tried to act normal around her, but his spirits began to ebb. In a letter to his friend, Dr. Anderson,[24] upon whom he leaned heavily for comfort and advice, Flagler said, "It almost breaks my heart to write this sad news. Please do not mention it to anyone.... Mr. MacGonigle [Presbyterian minister in St. Augustine] writes me occasionally expressing his joy over my happiness. You may tell him about Alice's relapse, for I don't believe I can bear to receive any more congratulations, but don't say anything to others yet."[25]

*D*r. Choate had died only a short time after Ida Alice returned from Pleasantville to Mamaroneck. Doctors Starr and Shelton were both vacationing in Europe, but Dr. Peterson was available and was consulted immediately. He warned Flagler of impending danger because he knew of the homicidal threats Mrs. Flagler had made the year before. When Flagler told him how critically his wife watched every move he made when he was near her, the doctor advised that he occupy another room at night. Flagler, however, did not think it wise to make any change. He thought it might excite her suspicions. In view of this fact, he decided to go on as usual, "depending," as he said, "upon God's mercy to keep me from harm." In his regular letter to Dr. Anderson, he continued, "I cannot tell you how this destruction of my hopes affects me."[26]

*T*hrough July and August, 1896, Ida Alice's condition changed very little. At times she grew worse and her delusions became more pronounced, but after a day or two they would cease. Flagler was hopeful one day, but was filled with despair the next. He dreaded the thought of having to send Ida Alice to an institution as he had done before. In August Flagler consulted Dr. Seldon H. Talcott, superintendent of the asylum at Middleton, New York. On August 24, Talcott examined Mrs. Flagler and gave her husband encouragement. The doctor's words merely raised false hopes. Mrs. Flagler became worse. In the absence of other available doctors at that time, Flagler consulted Dr. Carlos F. MacDonald in an effort to find someone who might help her. Dr. MacDonald was the new owner of the sanitarium at Pleasantville, once run by the late Dr. Choate. He had met Mrs. Flagler when she was confined there in October, 1895. After a thorough examination he told Flagler that he doubted she had been cured the first time. He reminded Flagler that his wife was going through a trying time of life. His advice was to give her time; a year or two might tell whether she was to be permanently well or insane. He laid quite as much stress as Dr. Peterson had done on the fact that she might commit homicide. Flagler contended that it would be impossible for him to occupy a separate bedroom without exciting a suspicion in the direction he wanted to avoid. To the casual observer Mrs. Flagler manifested no delusions. To her husband she was the embodiment of affection and tenderness. The watching and waiting on the outcome was nerve-wracking. The Ashleys were a great help. As best they could, they tried to keep Flagler's mind on anything other than his troubles.[27]

*F*riends advised Flagler to send his wife back to the asylum, but he had made up his mind to do this only as a last resort. He assured Dr. Anderson, "I shall not let her leave home until it becomes absolutely necessary."[28] Dr. Talcott called occasionally and always left a ray of hope. After Dr. MacDonald's visits, however, there was little but gloom. It was decided that the family should not go back to the city, or to St. Augustine, as was the custom in September, but that they should remain at Mamaroneck to await the outcome of Mrs. Flagler's illness.

*O*n October 10, Ida Alice obtained a Ouija board from a neighbor's wife. She secluded herself in her room with it. Within 10 minutes her mental equilibrium was completely destroyed. She played with the board constantly. Flagler's first impulse was to take the board away from her by force, but Eliza Ashley warned against this for fear that Ida Alice might hurt her husband. He consulted Dr. Shelton, who was back from Europe, as well as Doctors Starr and Peterson. It was decided to confine her at the Satanstoe home. Four nurses, one male and three female, were secured and sent to Mamaroneck to be on constant guard. The exclusive services of an experienced physician, Dr. Roland du Jardins, of New York, were secured. Du Jardins, with his wife, went to live at the Flagler home. The doctor was to have charge of the patient and the nurses and Mrs. du Jardins was to supervise the servants and the house.

$\mathcal{F}$lagler then left Mamaroneck and moved to the Manhattan Hotel in New York. "Mr. Flagler looked very bad," his secretary told Dr. Anderson. "The strain upon him was great indeed. However, now that the shock has come, he looks more composed. The feeling that he can now sleep without any apprehension must afford his mind some relief. It is indeed a sad case."[29] Soon after he became settled at his hotel in New York, Flagler wrote to Dr. Anderson, "The year last past has taught me the truth of your remark, that, 'Living one's misfortunes down is a terribly slow and painful process.' I am learning this lesson by a slow and painful experience and I often feel that I should break down if it were not for the messages of love and comfort you so generously send me. I receive similar ones from others but none touch my heart as yours do."[30] Dr. Anderson, in replying, tried to reason with Flagler and insisted that he must quit worrying and become resigned to Ida Alice's illness. To which Flagler responded, "I know that all you say is true, that having done everything for my poor wife that human skill can devise, my duty to myself and the enterprises upon which the welfare of so many depends, is to accept the situation and make the best of it—this I shall try to do. I realize that I am morbid, for sometimes I forget my sorrow for the moment and afterwards reproach myself that I could do so."[31]

$\mathcal{T}$he winter at Mamaroneck was a long one. Flagler went to Florida in November but was back in New York before the first of the year. He paid frequent visits to his summer home, but at no time was he allowed to see his wife. The doctors felt that it would not be for the good of either of them, since he was the object of most of her homicidal threats. The Ashleys remained with Flagler much of the time. The reports from Dr. du Jardins were anything but encouraging. Mrs. Flagler was in a violent state part of the time. It was necessary to take away from her such articles as knives and forks. At one time she assaulted Dr. du Jardins with a pair of scissors she had hidden on her person. She bruised the doctor about the face and badly lacerated one of his hands before he could withdraw from the room.[32] She seemed to be a hopeless case. The crisis had passed and she was left insane.

On March 20, 1897, Doctors Shelton and Peterson went to Mamaroneck to examine Mrs. Flagler for commitment to the asylum again. She recognized them as the persons who had carried her to Pleasantville in October, 1895; so she was extremely difficult to handle.[33] Preparations were made to take her to the sanitarium of Dr. MacDonald, successor to Dr. Choate, at Pleasantville. She was committed there for the second time on March 23, 1897.[34] Upon entering the sanitarium, Mrs. Flagler insisted that her name was Princess Ida Alice von Schotten Tech and that she bore the evidences of her royal heritage. Concerning her husband, she said she had been married to Henry Flagler, but he was now dead and she proposed to marry the Czar of Russia at an early date. Her delusions of persecution continued. She insisted that Dr. Shelton had tried several times to poison her. She also had the idea that many of her friends had turned enemy to her and were trying to take all of her money. Throughout 1897 her mental aberrations became more pronounced. She would sit at a window in an attitude of attention and smile and gesticulate in a way indicative of hearing voices. She painted her cheeks with red coloring matter extracted from woolen yarn. She blackened her eyebrows with burnt cork and rubbed the cream served with her coffee into her hair for a tonic.[35]

At times Mrs. Flagler was quiet and composed and for weeks at a time the attendants had no trouble with her. Occasionally her brother, Charles F. Shourds, visited her. During these visits she revealed to him a variety of delusions as to her age, her personality, her relations with the Czar of Russia, and as to her having been drugged and surgically operated on.

There was no change in Ida Alice's condition during 1898. She filled numerous blank books with what she called poetry, and improvised music and lyrics, which were largely incoherent scribblings. She collected thousands of pebbles, which she called minerals, and on which she recognized faces and other mysterious characters. These pebbles she preserved with great care in a bag which she had made of bits of silk. She ate and slept well, and, physically, kept well and healthy. Her husband was asked never to visit her; however, he had flowers sent to her twice each week. She spoke one day of her husband's being dead; the next, of his being alive. Visits made to her by Drs. Shelton and Talcott, at Flagler's requests, were never satisfactory. She disliked Shelton especially and often refused to speak with him. Occasionally she upbraided him for unheard-of-things.[36]

*A*dvised by the physicians that Ida Alice would never again be normal, Flagler decided to have the courts make an official declaration in order that a legal guardian could be appointed. He filed a petition with the New York Supreme Court on June 28, 1899, asking that Ida Alice Flagler be declared insane and incompetent. A commission composed of W. J. A. McKim, Allan Finch, and James Meng was appointed to hear the witnesses. Doctors Shelton, Talcott, and MacDonald, together with William H. Beardsley, appeared before the commission and swore that Mrs. Flagler was suffering from paranoia, a mental disease from which she would never recover. On August 4, 1899, the court ruled her insane. The court appointed Eugene M. Ashley committee of her property and Dr. MacDonald committee of her person. Flagler arranged for her to be provided for through channels set up by these two friends.[37]

*B*y 1901, Mrs. Flagler's mental disease had progressed so far that it had reached what Dr. MacDonald termed the "third state." She was beginning to show enfeeblement of her mental faculties as shown by the impairment of memory, the loss of the power of attention, and the general lessening of her will power, affections, and emotions. Flagler had watched her slowly reach that point and with all of his might he made himself accept her illness. No one could doubt his love for Mrs. Flagler; but after she lost her mental equilibrium, there was no basis for companionship. Their separation was final on March 23, 1897, when they carried Ida Alice to Pleasantville. He never saw her again and his mind gradually focused on other things. At times he even showed signs of happiness, although he was lonely at heart. His developments in Florida helped to absorb his attention and to make life a little more pleasant.

*F*or some time, Flagler had been pondering the matter of a divorce from his insane wife. He knew the storm of criticism it would bring when once announced publicly. Many of his friends could see his side of the issue, but many advised against divorce. As time went on, he became more determined. It was impossible to secure a divorce in New York or Florida, using insanity as the basis for the procedure. He had accomplished things virtually impossible before and he did not mean to fail in this attempt. Florida was the easier of the two states in which to petition for a divorce. With this in mind, he moved his citizenship from New York to Palm Beach. His intentions were announced in the *Florida Times-Union* on April 23, 1899. Its editor commented favorably on "Florida's new citizen." The reason given for his change of residence was that his business interests in Florida could better be served. It was also stated that he wished to escape the excessive inheritance tax imposed by the state of New York. Business purposes were sound reasons for changing one's residence.[38] They were entirely legitimate; so far, the public suspected nothing.

*I*n March, 1901, Flagler visited Dr. Anderson in St. Augustine. During this trip, he saw only a few of his intimate friends. Apparently a decision of importance was made in consultation with the doctor.

*O*n April 9, 1901, a bill was introduced into the Florida State Senate "to be entitled an act making incurable insanity a ground for divorce for husband and wife, and regulating proceedings in such cases." On April 17th, the bill passed the Senate with little opposition. Meeting a little opposition in the House, it passed this body by a vote of 42 to 19 on April 19th. The way had been well cleared for its passage in both houses. Governor W. S. Jennings signed the bill on April 25, 1901. The law declared that insanity in either husband or wife had to exist for four years prior to the filing of a bill of divorce. It also provided that the person accused must be judged insane by a competent court, that a committee or guardian must be appointed for the insane person, and that in case of a wife she was to be well provided for by her husband.[39] All of these provisions Flagler could meet.

*I*t was apparent by this time that Flagler was the instigator of the law. He was accused of buying off the legislature and many of his friends throughout the state were singled out for criticism.[40] Newspapers opened a double-barreled attack on him and on the legislature. They dubbed the law the "Flagler Divorce Law." Few newspapers took Flagler's side in the controversy. However, the *Ocala Banner*, edited by Frank Harris, upheld him and the new law. Harris argued, editorially, that all states should pass sensible divorce laws. He continued, "Man and woman were made one and the two together were given dominion over the whole earth, but neither was given dominion over the other."[41] The *Palmetto News* accused Harris of getting some of the $20,000 which it was believed Flagler spent in getting the law passed and said that "Harris needs the prayers of the brethren of the press."[42] The *Bronson Times-Democrat* and the *Citrus County Chronicle* denounced the Ocala paper for its stand, as did the *Pensacola Journal*. The latter paper accused Harris of "selling out" to Flagler, as well as the members of the legislature.[43]

*T*he *Pensacola Journal* brought to light more evidence of what it called "Flagler's influence in state affairs." Soon after the law was passed, Flagler made a gift of $10,000 to the Florida Agricultural College at Lake City for a gymnasium, provided the State would appropriate $2,500 for equipment. In 1903, when the institution was renamed the University of Florida, he gave another $10,000.[44] Frank Harris was one of the trustees of that institution and may have been responsible for Flagler's liberal gift. At any rate, coming at the time it did, the gift took the form of a thanks offering to the state for what it had done for him.[45]

*T*he public was aroused over the divorce law. Few people thought Flagler would start divorce proceedings in the immediate future. He, however, tossed more timber on the fire on June 3, 1901, when he filed a bill of divorce against his wife with Judge Minor S. Jones in the Circuit Court, Seventh Judicial Circuit of Florida.[46] Flagler was a citizen of Florida and incurable insanity was a ground for divorce. His wife had been declared incurably insane. The way was clear for the final act.

*N*o man could have made himself better known to the people of a state than Flagler had to the people of Florida. During the summer of 1901 his name was a household word. There were many critics; but, on the other hand, many stood by him. It was Flagler's nature to get what he wanted. He had been schooled in that philosophy. The case went through without any delay or hindrance.

*F*lagler had left no stone unturned. Every angle of the case had been well prepared and carefully reviewed. The law firm of Nicoll, Anable, and Lindsay of New York represented him and Delancey Nicoll personally attended the trial. Nicoll and George P. Raney acted as counsel for the complainant. Also in attendance were Francis P. Fleming, guardian *ad litem* for the defendant; Eugene M. Ashley, committee of the property of the defendant; Carlos F. MacDonald, committee of the person of the defendant; and H. H. Buckman, solicitor for said committees.[47] The hearings took only one day, August 12, 1901. Those testifying on behalf of the complaintant were Doctors Carlos F. MacDonald, George G. Shelton, Seldon H. Talcott, and Frederick Peterson—all of whom were familiar with the case. Each testified in positive terms that Mrs. Flagler was suffering from paranoia, otherwise known as chronic delusional insanity, and that there was no possible chance of her ever being normal again. Declared Dr. MacDonald, "It invariably occurs in persons having what is known as a nervous or insane temperament, whether through heredity or inherited predisposition or whether acquired in early life. Such cases do not recover." He explained that this insane tendency lay dormant in Mrs. Flagler until she married. After that time she tried to live a life equal to the standing Flagler had given her, but failed in the attempt and the tendency became active.[48] Eugene M. Ashley, J. R. Parrott, and George Wilson also testified in Flagler's interest.

*F*lagler's own testimony was interesting but pathetic. He reviewed the entire case. He stated that in the last four years, he had not seen his wife and that since he would not be permitted to see her again, it would be better for them both if they were entirely free. He reminded the court that during the last few years he had given her over $2,000,000 worth of property and securities.[49] Eugene M. Ashley, who had charge of her property, reported to the court exactly what Mrs. Flagler had in the way of stocks, bonds, and money. She owned 2,420 shares, worth $795 each, in the Standard Oil Company and 153 shares of Natural Gas Trust certificates, worth $200 each. She also possessed Natural Gas Trust bonds, worth $15,300; cash amounting to about $570,000; and small securities amounting to $68,322.03. In addition, she had considerable property in St. Augustine which did not contribute to her support. Ashley said the total in his hands was $2,373,137.42. All of the securities were in the state of New York and were annually accounted for by him to the Supreme Court of New York. Mrs. Flagler's annual income was about $120,000. Her expenses at the sanitarium amounted to $15,600 per year. Additional comforts were about $5,000. The remainder of the income went into the principal.[50]

*T*here was no question about the adequacy of the income which Flagler provided for her. The financial statement, which was published in all the Florida newspapers, allayed the fears and suspicions of some;

still others could see nothing good or pleasant coming out of the divorce case. There was no effort on the part of Mrs. Flagler's family or friends to interfere with the procedure. There were no testimonies in her behalf. The divorce was officially granted in Miami on August 13, 1901.[51] A long and turbulent chapter in Flagler's life had come to an end.

*T*he divorced Mrs. Flagler never realized what action the court had taken. She continued to live in her world of delusions and hallucinations. She gave no thought to her enormous income, her family, her friends, or her ex-husband. Many years later she was moved by Eugene Ashley to a private sanitarium at Central Valley, New York. There she was given a special cottage on the grounds of the institution and was provided with an attendant and with all the comforts she could enjoy. Physically, she continued to live in good health until July 10, 1930, when she died of a cerebral hemorrhage, at the age of 82. She was buried in New York.[52]

II

*O*n August 21, 1901, seven days after Flagler's divorce was granted, newspapers throughout the South and East carried an announcement of his engagement to Mary Lily Kenan. The news was received with mingled feelings. People who knew them both were expecting it, but yet were amazed when the information was actually released. Commented the *Atlanta Journal*, "The announcement caused no surprise, because the affair has been talked about and gossiped over for the past two years, although rumors concerning the engagement could never be confirmed."[53] Public opinion crystallized rapidly and was anything but favorable to the match between the twice-married 71 year old Flagler and the 34 year old North Carolina belle.

*M*ary Lily Kenan was a pleasing young woman who was born of an old North Carolina family on June 14, 1867. Wilmington was her home, but she had spent much time in other places in the state. She studied music at Peace Institute in Raleigh and had become an accomplished pianist and vocalist.[54] There were three other children in her family, Jessie, Sarah, and William R. Kenan, Jr.[55]

*F*lagler was first introduced to Miss Kenan in 1891 when she was visiting the Pembroke Jones family in St. Augustine. Pembroke Jones was also a North Carolinian. After making a fortune operating rice mills, Jones retired and spent the winters in Florida and the summers in Newport, Rhode Island. Mrs. Jones and Miss Kenan were close friends and spent much of their time together.[56] Flagler was impressed with Mary Lily from the start. At that time, Ida Alice Flagler also admired her for her pleasing personality and her elegant manners. The first winter she was in St. Augustine Ida Alice Flagler entertained for her and the two became friendly.[57]

*T*he Flaglers saw Miss Kenan occasionally during the next few years in St. Augustine as well as in Newport. They were pleasant meetings for them all. Then came Ida Alice's mental breakdown. During this time, Mary Lily became close friends with Eliza Ashley, Flagler's relative, who spent much time in Florida at his invitation. Because of Eliza, Flagler was often thrown in company with the two young women. They traveled to Palm Beach and Miami with him on business trips and as Flagler was trying to make the best of his wife's insane condition, he escorted the young ladies to places of interest. He enjoyed showing them a good time because it was the best way he had found to forget his troubles.

*I*n 1897 Eliza Ashley and her husband were invited to spend the winter at Palm Beach as Flagler's guests. They occupied a beach cottage. For a large part of the winter, Flagler was also there. The Ashleys invited Mary Lily to spend most of the winter in Palm Beach as their guest. Mary Lily had a charming personality. Her musical talent was greatly admired by Flagler and he often requested that she sing his favorite songs. The friendship between them became warmer and more intimate. Flagler and Miss Kenan were thrown together more each winter season. Palm Beach society began to gossip. The news spread to Miami, then to St. Augustine, and finally to many of the fashionable places in the country.

*I*t was not long before the public knew what Flagler planned to do. In 1899, when he first tried to get a divorce from Ida Alice in New York, the laws of that state would not permit it.[58] Florida did grant the divorce after his residence was established there. The couple lost little time after Flagler was divorced. Their wedding on August 24, 1901, was

Mary Lily Kenan Flagler at Satanstoe

elaborate, but done in the presence of only a few friends and relatives. They were married at Liberty Hall, in Kenanville, North Carolina. It was a typical antebellum home where dozens of Kenans had been born and reared. Liberty Hall was situated on the brow of a long rolling hill in the midst of a magnificent grove of oaks, sycamores, and elms. For this special event, it had been thoroughly renovated and repainted during the early summer. Peyton H. Hoge, of Louisville, Kentucky, read the wedding vows in the spacious hallway which connected all of the rooms downstairs.[59] The bride's wedding gown was of white chiffon over white satin, trimmed with point appliqué with a veil of the same material, adorned with orange blossoms. She wore no ornaments. Her only attendant was a niece, Louise Clisby Wise. Flagler looked dignified in a Prince Albert coat with light trousers.

*S*oon after the wedding, the couple boarded Flagler's private train car at Magnolia, North Carolina, the nearest railroad point, and sped away to New York. The honeymoon was spent at Satanstoe, Mamaroneck, their summer home.[60] There were many messages of congratulations which greeted the Flaglers on their arrival at Mamaroneck. These gladdened the aging man's heart. Naturally he was interested in what his friends thought about his marriage. Perhaps some of the communications were not sent in any degree of sincerity. At any rate, Flagler was thankful for the friends who genuinely rejoiced with him in his good fortune.[61] Not all of his own family accepted graciously the new member of the Flagler clan, but that was to be expected.[62] The general public had little mercy for either of them and contended that his fortune had entered strongly into the match. Less critical persons accepted the marriage. There was much to say in Mary Lily's behalf. She was Flagler's equal socially and intellectually. She was a good wife to him. She was socially inclined and loved excitement and a good time. Such was afforded her whenever she desired it.[63]

*I*f lavished wealth was what she craved, Mary Lily Flagler had reason to be happy. Flagler spared no expense to give her anything that money could buy. She had always wanted a marble palace, so Flagler built her a mansion in Palm Beach which she called Whitehall.[64] It was begun several months after they were married and was finished in a record time of eight months. The home was planned by the same architects and built by the same contractors Flagler employed on the Ponce de Leon Hotel. All of the interior work and furnishings were executed from designs of the Pottier and Stymus Company, under the personal supervision of William P. Stymus, Jr. Flagler had first thought of reproducing a typical Cuban house. He had seen the home of Dominquez Cerro, one of the most imposing structures in Havana, and hoped to reproduce it. However, it soon became apparent that the conditions Flagler had established as to size, height, and arrangement would interfere with his original scheme. Beyond the general plan of an interior patio or court, there was not much left of the original idea in Whitehall. The Spanish court, typical of Cuban homes, contained rare varieties of palms and shrubs of all kinds. In the center were built a fountain and pool.[65]

*F*rom the outside, Whitehall was typical of great wealth and beauty. It sat amidst grounds of flowers, shrubs, palms, and graceful Australian pines. Broad marble steps led to the colonnade which extended across the front of the building.[66] Great bronze grille doors led into the

*Whitehall, Palm Beach.
Now the Flagler Museum*

Marble Hall, Whitehall, Palm Beach

Marble Hall. Occupying the center front of the house, it was designed with a superb double staircase of white marble. The white marble hall, 110 feet long and 40 feet wide, was relieved by lines of black marble which formed panels. There were also heavily inwrought capitals that surmounted the columns separating the two flights of steps in the center of the hall and upholding the ceiling at either end of the passage.[67] The chairs and important pieces of heavier furniture in the hall were richly carved in Louis XIV design and were covered with tapestries and silk velvets. The clock, made by Francois Linke, was nine feet high. It was made of rich bronze and represented "time" riding the world in a cloud. Across the room from the clock was an Italian Renaissance-style chest. Its decorative panel represented the marriage of the Adimari family.

*W*indows in the Marble Hall were draped in Spanish tapestry of green. Four slender pyramid trees, 10 feet high, were placed near the windows to complete the color scheme. The interior of the house presented an atmosphere of the Old World. Agents searched France and Italy for superb furnishings and rare works of art. Rugs that usually required years to create were woven in months. Furniture was made in record time to fulfill the great builder's desires.

*S*haring the first floor with the Marble Hall were the salon, ballroom, library, music room, breakfast room, and grand dining room. Of these, the dining room was perhaps the most elaborately decorated.

The room, 44 by 23 feet, was treated in François I design and finished in satinwood. The ceiling was divided into panels and ornamented with molded plaster in tones of green coloring, relieved by gold. The walls were hung in two shades of green tapestry. The windows were draped with plain green silk velours. Chairs in this room were covered with Aubusson tapestry, which was made especially for each. Window curtains were of rich Colbert lace; and the rug of Savonnerie, the center being plain green, with a rich border representing fruit and game. Four bronze and crystal chandeliers lighted the room.[68]

*T*he library occupied the southeast corner of the house with full views of Lake Worth from the broad arched windows. The spirit of the Italian Renaissance period prevailed in this room. The walls were hung in rich Spanish tapestry and over the windows were Arabian laces. A large oil painting of Flagler was over the mantel. Aubusson tapestry covered furniture, carved walnut chairs, richly carved tables, and a Savonnerie rug in rich tones of red completed the furnishings of the library which also housed many rare and valuable paintings—as well as books. One of its pieces was a magnificent painting by Thomas Moran representing the landing of Ponce de León in Florida.

*T*he music room also served as an art gallery because many fine paintings were displayed there. It was 64 by 24 feet in size and was designed after the Louis XIV period. Its domed ceiling, treated with a decorative canvas panel of the aurora, was lighted by recessed electric bulbs. The pipe organ which graced one end of the room was reputed to be, at the time, the largest ever placed in a private home in the United States.

*F*or grandeur the ballroom had few equals. It was characteristic of the type found in the time of Louis XV. Its dimensions were 91 by 37 feet. Its color scheme was white and gold, the whole effect being soft in tone. A mezzanine for the orchestra was erected at one end of the room. Handsome mirrors, richly ornamented and divided into panels, were placed between the long windows. Introduced above the doors and windows were alternating Watteau-style pastoral scenes and Boucher-style scenes with cupids. The window draperies were in two shades of rose de Berry silk damask. The jeweled chandeliers and brackets were the same as those used in grand salons in the 15th century.

Flagler had a private suite of rooms overlooking Lake Worth, at the southwest corner of the house, which he used as offices for himself and his secretaries. The furnishings here were of mahogany, the walls and ceilings being treated to match, with floors of oak.[69]

On the second floor were 16 guest chambers, nearly all of which had a different style and design. Each represented an epoch in world history. Italy, France, Spain, England, the Orient, and American Colonial mansions were studied in order to carry out this distinctive plan. From each of these 16 rooms, there was a private hallway leading to the main hall. The average size of the guest chambers was 24 by 18 feet. The beauty of the walls especially impressed the guests. The walls of one room had cream moiré panels; a second was in shades of cream and white stripes; another represented a green lattice on which pink roses appeared to be growing; while another was covered with gold silk damask. The furniture in all the rooms varied, having been brought from France, Spain, and other European countries. Only one bedroom was in modern American style. The floor coverings in the bedrooms ranged from small scatter rugs to large gold-colored Angora carpets. The window draperies, for the most part, were of silk tapestry. In passing from one room to another one was impressed with the perfect harmony in the color schemes. The fireplaces, andirons, locks, and fixtures for lighting were skillfully designed to be in keeping with the rooms for which they were selected.

The Master Suite was the most beautiful of all the bedrooms. The walls were done in silk damask. The window draperies were of the same material and the curtains were of silk lace. The furniture, in two tones of pearl gray, represented the period of Louis XV. The bed was draped with a gold damask canopy. Each corner of the bed was ornamented with a woman's head and shoulders in bronze. The maple floor was covered with an Axminster rug. The bath, which opened from the Master Suite, was 17 by 11 feet, and contained a sunken tub. The floor was laid with marble tile. From this room opened a clothes closet fitted with armoires having glass doors to show the gowns. There were also compartments for jewelry, laces, and lingerie. In this suite there was also a dressing-room for Flagler.[70]

Mrs. Flagler enjoyed entertaining. Her husband entered as gracefully as he could into the pastime, although he was getting old and wished many times to be away from crowds and excitement. A certain amount of entertaining had to be done, however, in keeping with their standing in the community. Their common pleasure was music and each winter some prominent organist was employed to give regular weekly programs at their home. The musician who filled most of the engagements was Russell Joy, who had been organist for a while at Memorial Presbyterian Church in St. Augustine. He not only presided at the console at Whitehall but also played at the Royal Poinciana Chapel. Organ music was a feature of all the social functions given by the Flaglers regardless of the formality.

*P*erhaps the most brilliant social season for the Flaglers was the winter of 1901-1902. They had been married only a few months when they arrived in Palm Beach. It did not take Mrs. Flagler long to create a place in the social register for herself. All the affairs given by her were in keeping with the vast wealth of her husband. She entertained at elaborate bridge parties, teas, and banquets throughout January, February, and March at the Royal Poinciana Hotel, since Whitehall was not completed. At one of the bridge parties she gave as prizes a cut glass scent bottle set with an amethyst stone in a gold top, a gold buckle set with pearls, and a bouquet of lilies of the valley in which was hidden a hat pin set with pearls and turquoise.[71]

*W*hitehall was completed before the 1902-1903 season and became a mecca for socially prominent visitors. Flagler gave several stag dinners and Mary Lily entertained at several elaborate affairs. Her guests always represented the wealth and fashion of the nation. Among the notables who were entertained by the Flaglers at Whitehall were Sir Gilbert Carter, Governor of the Bahama Islands;[72] Admiral George Dewey, hero of Manila Bay;[73] Elihu Root, cabinet member of Theodore Roosevelt;[74] John Astor; Henry T. Sloane; Lyman J. Gage; and P. C. Knox. Their friends were many and their interests always varied.

*O*ne of the most welcomed winter visitors at Whitehall was the famous English actor, Joseph Jefferson. He was a lovable character who was always witty, funny, and sensible. Flagler liked his companionship and grew to rely heavily upon him for entertainment. Others who frequented the Flagler mansion from time to time were Eliza and Eugene Ashley, of New York; Jessie Wise, of Georgia, sister of Mrs. Flagler;

Senator Camden of West Virginia; William R. Kenan, Jr., of North Carolina, brother of Mrs. Flagler; and the Andrew Andersons of St. Augustine. Whitehall was seldom without visitors.

*M*ary Lily Flagler was a charming hostess. The art of entertaining became second nature with her. Her parties were well planned and always enjoyed by those attending. She was especially fond of Christmas Eve and New Year's Eve parties because of the gaiety engendered by the holiday season. She served expensive wines of which she was especially fond. However, her husband never touched strong drink and was always much opposed to it.[75] She was a graceful dancer, too, but in this form of entertainment her aging husband usually defaulted in favor of some younger partner. Her clothes were beautiful, without exception, especially her party frocks. Most people liked her tastes in other matters as well as clothes. She was respected by her contemporaries in Palm Beach, and though there were a few critics among her so-called friends, she mixed freely with the best of society in Palm Beach and also at their summer home, Satanstoe, in Mamaroneck.[76]

*A*fter several years very little entertaining was done at Whitehall. Flagler's age kept him from entering actively into any social life while Mary Lily found social attractions elsewhere. House guests were not as frequent as they had been, and the mammoth marble structure seemed more like a tomb than a home.[77] Flagler deserved a place for rest and relaxation during his latter years, for his domestic life had long been anything but settled.

Henry Flagler, 1909

158

12. Flagler's Folly

*T*he last phase of Henry Flagler's railroad construction in Florida, the overseas railroad extension from Miami to Key West, was his most expensive and his most daring undertaking. It was in operation for 20–odd years, but it was never a paying proposition. Flagler's friends advised him against building the overseas extension. His critics rebuked him for sinking so much money along the Florida Keys. However, his intense desire to build something great and magnificent got the better of him. At the age of 75, Flagler had seen many of his great dreams for Florida's East Coast become reality. However, he had one more dream. He had one more idea about how to link the entire East Coast of Florida. The overseas extension would be one of the engineering marvels of its day. As the railroad neared completion, Flagler became more and more eager to realize the completion of his last Florida construction project.

A railroad connecting Key West with the mainland of Florida had been talked about for a long time. Years before Flagler's era, some people had urged and others had prophesied the building of an overseas extension to Key West. From a commercial and a military standpoint it was practicable. As early as 1831, in a report to the upper House of Congress, a Key West newspaper had advocated building a railroad to the island town. The editor had explained the great advantage the nation would derive from such a railroad. He argued that Key West was a strategic location and was in a position to serve as a great naval base. Nothing was done for a long period of time. In 1883, General John B. Gordon, of Georgia, secured a franchise to build a railroad to Key West. Gordon built 50 or 60 miles of railroad on the Florida mainland, but the work was abandoned before the Florida coast was ever reached.[1]

*D*uring the 1890s there was much speculation as to the possibilities of such a railroad being built. Early in that decade the Trustees of the Internal Improvement Fund in Florida engaged an engineer, H. S. Duval, to inspect the railroad south of Daytona and to make recommendations as to the advisability of building further railroads in South Florida, and if so, how far south. Duval made the following report::

It does not appear where the final terminus of this road [Flagler's Road] is to be, but no doubt when the great capitalist [Flagler] learns that the Florida Keys are islands enclosed in a harbor made by natural submerged breakwater called the Florida reefs and are therefore not really exposed to the violence of the outer sea, and may be connected with ordinary creosoted trestle work as now existing across Escambia Bay, he may rise in a culminating spirit of enterprise and moor Key West to the mainland.[2]

*T*his was the first time that anyone had even mildly predicted that Flagler would extend his road to Key West. However, the report began to center public attention on him. From then on, there was a feeling among those who knew Flagler best that someday, if he lived long enough, he would undertake the tremendous task.

*A*fter the Florida East Coast Railroad was completed to Miami, speculation increased over Flagler's next move. The *Bartow Courier–Informant* on April 3, 1895, predicted that a railroad would be built at an early day from some point, "on the lower East coast of Florida across the many keys which skirt the mainland, to the city of Key West." The paper made known the fact that competent engineers had announced the project a practicable one and that Flagler had agents working out details for the building of the road. The *Courier–Informant* also revealed that he had purchased about one–half of Key Largo, which was the first important island off the mainland at the southern end of Biscayne Bay. In the county clerk's office at Key West deeds had been filed for small tracts of lands on 63 different keys. All the deeds were in the name of one purchaser, whom the Bartow paper believed to be an agent of Flaglers. It was also reported that Flagler would build an immense hotel on Key Largo at once.[3] Most of the information divulged at this time came from Flagler's associates. It was unofficial and somewhat premature, but it was made in the light of how Flagler had accepted other great challenges in the field of development.

*P*eople in Key West were more anxious for the extension than anyone else. In 1894, Jefferson Browne wrote:

The hopes of the people of Key West are centered in Henry M. Flagler, whose financial genius and public spirit have opened up 300 miles of the beautiful east coast of the state. The building of a railroad to Key West would be a fitting consummation of Mr. Flagler's remarkable career.

There were between 15,000 and 20,000 people living in Key West by 1895. Most of them hoped that their town would be connected to the mainland by railroad. In September, 1895, two of Key West's leading citizens, George L. Babcock and George Lowe, were sent to St. Augustine and Jacksonville to solicit interest for the project. Citizens of both cities talked encouragingly to the Key West delegates.[4]

As was his style, Flagler did not hurry in making his final decision to build the extension. He wanted to know more about the possibilities and the practicability of building such a road. For several years his agents made surveys, produced figures, and estimated costs. He gave himself plenty of time to appraise these reports. There were several reasons for Flagler's final decision to proceed with the overseas extension. First, he had a flair for doing great things and the Key West extension would be a grand climax to all his other Florida developments. He realized that such an undertaking would cost a tremendous amount of money. He knew that it would take many years for the extension to pay for itself. But, as in the case of his other developments, he felt sure that it would be a good investment. He also believed that an overseas extension would be the means of linking Florida and the United States with Central and South America. He felt that Key West would become a sort of "American Gibraltar."

The Spanish–American War, in 1898, had virtually placed Cuba in the United States' hands and Key West could easily serve as an outlet to the former Spanish island. Flagler believed that as the years went by the American government would be compelled to maintain closer relations with Cuba.[5] In addition, he was particularly interested in Cuban trade. He had made a number of visits to the island and had expressed a desire to invest in cultivation of Cuban oranges. He had also bought shares in several Cuban railroads. All this made him vitally interested in the economic future of the island.

The decision by the federal government to build a canal across the Isthmus of Panama also helped to influence Flagler. For a number of years, America had anticipated the building of the canal across some narrow portion of Central America. When the way was finally made clear for the construction of the Panama Canal, Flagler began to think seriously in terms of connecting Key West with the mainland. During this time, he was in touch with Elihu Root, Secretary of War and a friend for many years. They communicated concerning the proposed extension. It was Root's feeling that United States interest in the Caribbean would be strengthened considerably with the building of the canal.[6] Flagler may have been influenced by Root's predictions as to our future in that section of the world.

*F*lagler and his agents began to study the preliminary surveys and engineers' reports in a new light. The assurance that the Panama Canal would be built made the Florida Keys, and Key West in particular, a most promising area. Key West was almost 300 miles nearer the point where the eastern terminus of the canal was to be located than any of the other Gulf of Mexico ports. It was a natural base for guarding and protecting the canal on the East.

*B*y fall, 1904, it was certain that Flagler would build the extension to Key West, but no official announcement had been made to that effect. Railroad, business, and news people hounded Flagler to see what he was going to do. Newspapers prematurely announced the decision. During this time, surveyors and engineers were still working to provide Flagler with data and information.[7] On January 30, 1905, Flagler and a group of his associates left Miami by steamer for a tour of the proposed route of a Florida East Coast Railway extension. They went to Key West where Flagler spent several hours in conference with the leading citizens of the town. He promised these people that the construction would begin within a short time. Key West buzzed with excitement over Flagler's proposed program, which meant so much to the tiny water–bound city.[8]

*O*n July 31, 1905, the *Miami Metropolis*, official mouthpiece for Flagler and his associates, published a special Key West edition. In it, the newspaper announced the plans and unfolded the entire scheme. The *Metropolis* told, for the first time, all about the unique and daring overseas extension. Flagler's plans included not only the extension, but he also hoped to construct in Key West twelve piers each 800 feet long and 200 feet wide. These piers were to be covered by sheds with basins

200 feet in width, each basin affording berths for four large ships. The paper also announced that Flagler expected the road to be in operation by January 1, 1908.[9] The program was actually not completed until about four years after that date.

*S*everal years before Flagler's decision to build the overseas extension, he had started extending his railroad south of Miami on the mainland. In 1903, he had tapped the vast unsettled lowlands with a 12 mile extension. This short line was known as the Cutler Extension. It was used primarily for shipping fruits and vegetables out of the region. In 1904, the line was extended into what was known as the homestead country, 28 miles south of Miami. A small community grew up where the road ended. It was known as Homestead. As in the case of many of the other small towns which Flagler built, it derived its existence primarily from the railroad. The road went no farther until Flagler made up his mind to span the keys. Construction was idle and the terminus of the road remained unchanged until the final jump was made to Key West.[10]

*F*or a time, Flagler was undecided as to what route he should take to Key West. One possibility was to extend his road only a few miles south to the eastern tip of Florida, taking off from the mainland at Jewfish and from there across the keys to Key West. The other was to construct an extension from Homestead to Cape Sable at the Southwestern tip of Florida and from there take off over open seas to Key West. Cape Sable was closer to Key West than Jewfish, but if he chose the latter route he would not have the advantage of all the keys. Engineers advised strongly against this route. Flagler soon abandoned any idea of extending his road across the swamps and jungle through the Everglades to Cape Sable.[11]

*P*reliminary surveys, mappings of channels and water courses, observations of winds and storms, and the charting of the route over the keys from Jewfish were completed early in 1905. Construction began in the summer on an undertaking which many financiers had termed as "unthinkable" and which scores of engineers thought "impossible." Flagler announced to his friend, George M. Ward, that he had decided definitely to build a railroad over the keys to Key West. His friend, by then an elderly churchman, felt the need to respond. Thinking of what a preposterous idea it was, he emphatically remarked, "Flagler, you need a guardian."[12]

The Florida Keys over which Flagler built his railroad were small patches of land which were completely surrounded by water. They numbered in the hundreds. The keys extended like a long finger, pointing about 128 miles from the mainland to Key West. They were composed of coral and lime rock formations and were part of an extensive reef. Many of them were in lonely places. Some were uninhabited and unexplored. For a long time, the intricate network of channels among these keys had formed an ideal retreat for pirates who had preyed upon the rich commerce of the Spanish Main. It was also along this route that Florida wreckers hid like vultures to pounce on stricken ships that were grounded by storms and winds. Smugglers and renegade sailors also used the keys as havens of refuge.[13]

Native vegetation on the keys was distinctly subtropical in character. It was of much interest to naturalists. Most of the trees were stunted in growth and included a variety of mahogany, dogwood, wild rubber, and bay. The chief commercial products were limes, fish, and sponges. The shoals, channels, and Gulf Stream, whose course lay only a short distance from these islands, abounded in all sorts of marine life. Between 500 and 1,000 varieties of fish were found there, some of which rivaled the rainbow in coloring and resembled the ever–changing water. Big game fishermen looked upon the keys as one of the most productive spots on the Florida coast. The difficulties which confronted Flagler and his associates when they began the extension were many and complex. One of the first things they did was to advertise for bids on the construction in the leading newspapers in the United States. After giving ample time for those who desired to have the job to send in their bids, Flagler was astonished to find that only one contractor was willing to talk about the task and he wanted a cost–plus contract to do the job. Flagler refused to sign such a contract. He decided to have his own lieutenants, headed by Joseph R. Parrott, undertake the task.[14] No other person would have worked more diligently and more faithfully. No one except one of Flagler's faithful, longtime associates would have undertaken the job.

Labor was a problem throughout the seven years of construction. It was hard to get men to work under the existing conditions. Yet, at one time, the work force reached a maximum of 4,000 men. An average of nearly 3,000 men were working all the time. The intense heat and vicious mosquitoes were two of the biggest hindrances. Since workmen were not to drink at the camps, the only places they could get liquor were Miami and Key West or from a "booze boat," as they were called, which would occasionally travel around the keys leaving intoxicants with the workers in the water–bound camps. Operators of these boats ran the risk of being caught and were handled with as little ceremony as pirates.[15]

$\mathcal{R}$ecruiting labor was done wherever it could be found. A few Spaniards from Cuba were hired, as were a few blacks from the Cayman Islands. Now and then a Norwegian was employed. The bulk of the workmen were secured through agencies in New York and Philadelphia. Many of the workers were derelicts and hoboes looking for adventure. Some of them skipped camp as soon as they were paid and went to Miami to drink up their earnings. About 80% of the work crews came from cities in the North. One of Flagler's associates commented, "One of our most trying problems has been to take a big body of low–grade [low-skilled] men, take care of them, and build them into a capacity for performing high–class work."[16] Among the highly skilled workers was a group of Greek divers who worked faithfully throughout the project. There was some loss of life among the workmen, but very little in comparison with the size of the undertaking. There were no epidemics and no prevailing sicknesses among the laborers.

$\mathcal{T}$he camps where the men lived were located at various places along the keys, depending upon the location of the work at any given time. Each camp was under the supervision of the engineer in charge and regular discipline was maintained. Each worker received board and lodging in addition to a salary. Flagler's officials maintained close supervision over these camps and saw to it that no lowering of fixed standards took place. The diet was substantial, wholesome, and bountiful. The occasional visitor found it decidedly appetizing. The steward in charge of the dining rooms ordered all of his supplies from the chief steward at Marathon where the road's depot was located. Supply boats were dispatched three times each week from that place.[17]

$\mathcal{F}$lagler provided his men with proper hospitalization for all emergencies. In each camp there was a first–aid station, staffed by two trained persons. It was at these stations that people were taken for emergencies and ordinary illnesses. In case the patient needed more specialized treatment, the workman was sent immediately to the company's hospitals at Key West or Miami where he received service free of charge. The Miami hospital was especially well equipped to care for sicknesses and injured patients. Flagler realized this would be an attraction in trying to secure workmen. Dr. J. M. Jackson, Jr., was selected as the chief physician in charge of the extension work and Dr. J. A. Heitlinger, of Bellevue Hospital, assisted him.

The matter of drinking water was of importance. A satisfactory solution had to be found since freshwater wells could not be dug on the keys. Several diggings were made as deep as 2,000 feet without any success. Two special trains of flatcars carrying large tanks of water operated daily from the little station of Everglades, not far from Homestead, to the various camps down the keys. The water in most instances was transported over 100 miles. At one time experts thought they could cut down on this distance by hauling it from Manatee Creek, only about 50 miles from the main camp. A water station was located there, but before it was put into operation along came a northwest wind and blew all the water out of the bay. When that happened, it was impossible for boats to get within two miles of the water station. The station was abandoned until the water regained its natural level. Three weeks later, the wind came from the opposite direction and piled the water up in the bay in such quantities as to drive them out again.[19] That was the end of that attempt.

Among the interesting features connected with the construction of the overseas extension was the equipment which was used. Some of it was lost in storms, some sank at times for lack of repairs since most of the machinery had to be put on floating units. Before he began work Flagler purchased the following equipment: 27 launches, ranging from five to 50 horsepower each; eight stern–wheel Mississippi River steamers; three tugs; 12 dredges; eight concrete mixers for work over water, two concrete mixers for work on land; nine pile drivers for water work; two track pile drivers; one skid pile driver; 10 power excavators; one catamaran for handling coffer dams; eight derrick barges; 150 lighters; two steel barges; six locomotive cranes; and two seagoing steamers. All of the floating equipment was fitted with dynamos for generating electric light because a great deal of the concrete work could not be interrupted by the coming of night. Part of the crew worked almost regularly at night.[20] All of the equipment was expensive and at the end of the eight–year period had been put to such heavy use that it was of little value to any other engineer.

*F*lagler thought he had made all the necessary preparations before the work started, but as construction progressed many problems arose which had to be worked out. For one thing, nature's resistance had to be reckoned with, the known factors of her force computed, and the unknown factors provided against. Another riddle was the growth of the average wave over miles of sea. This had to be measured, and the wind force had to be taken into consideration. New methods of construction had to be devised to meet the needs in various places and special materials, answering special purposes, were brought from long distances.[21] Permission had to be obtained from the federal government to build certain draws and also to close the spaces between the different keys. With the help of his faithful associates, Flagler was able to meet all of the requirements necessary for the completion of the work.[22]

*F*lagler and Parrott chose Joseph C. Meredith as the constructing engineer on the project. His selection proved to be an excellent one. Meredith was from Kansas City and had attracted considerable attention for his work at various places over the country. Just prior to accepting the job with Flagler, Meredith had been employed by the Mexican government to build a pier at Tampico.

*W*hen Meredith was offered the job with Flagler, he accepted immediately. He stated that he liked to undertake daring tasks which other engineers tended to shun. Meredith took over and worked for several years with skill and determination, facing every danger and meeting every difficulty without hesitation. He was always on the job, flitting in and out of the various construction camps in a launch, giving orders here and there. He was usually standing, with binoculars to his eyes, like a military leader observing the movement of his troops. The exhaustive pace at which he worked brought him to an early death on April 20, 1909, several years before the great task had been completed.[23] There was no associate of Flagler's who worked harder on his assigned task than Meredith. His great desire was to see the extension completed before Flagler's death; but the engineer himself did not live to see the job finished.

$\mathcal{W}$illiam J. Krome, a young, muscular giant, was assigned to finish the task which Meredith had started. Krome had attended the University of Illinois, but left to study engineering at Cornell University where he made an outstanding record. He went to Florida in 1902 and worked for several years helping make the preliminary surveys in preparation for the construction of the overseas extension. For two years, he had been one of the engineers who toiled and sweated through the jungles and swamps of the Everglades to Cape Sable and had been chiefly responsible for the Cape Sable plan's being abandoned. When Meredith died, Krome, who was already serving as first assistant, was made engineer–in–chief. He grasped the meaning of the great undertaking before him and set about to finish Meredith's work. Possibly even more responsibility rested on Krome's shoulders than on Meredith's because the latter phases of the work were so difficult. It was the happiest moment of his life, Krome declared, when Flagler's special train reached Key West on its first run.[24]

$\mathcal{E}$ngineer Krome was backed by capable assistants whose loyalty was equaled only by their ability to meet constantly recurring emergencies. The work evoked so much interest among them that each man gave the project his unqualified effort and support. These able assistants included P. L. Wilson, C. S. Coe, R. G. Smiley, and Ernest Cotton, division engineers; R. W. Carter, bridge engineer; E. H. Sheeran, general foremen; and B. A. Deal, auditor of construction. Work on the extension lasted seven years and nine months. Most of the assistants remained on the project throughout the time.[25]

$\mathcal{C}$onstruction over the first 28 miles south of Miami to Homestead was comparatively easy. The next 20 miles to Jewfish Creek, the jumping–off place, was through the marshy Everglades and heavy mangrove swamps. There was insufficient water to float dredges. There was not enough solid ground for wheelbarrow work. It was necessary for the engineers to make channels to accommodate dredges so that a roadbed could be built up. Two excavations were made wide enough to contain dredges with a depth of 2.5 feet of water. Two machines then made their way down the sides of an embankment, digging their own channels, using the material excavated for rearing the embankment. The work was hampered and delayed at many points by rocks and solid formations which came so near the surface that it was necessary to float the dredges over them. Six dredges were used in this particular phase of the construction. Some worked northward and others southward, meeting at a midway point between Jewfish Creek and Homestead.[26]

Miami to Homestead	28.00	miles
Homestead to Jewfish Creek	21.39	miles
Jewfish Creek	.02	miles
Key Largo	16.64	miles
Tavernier Creek	.06	miles
Long Island	4.88	miles
Windley's Island Creek	2.01	miles
Matecumbe Key	14.05	miles
Long Key	4.05	miles
Long Key Viaduct	2.68	miles
Grassy Key	15.57	miles
Knights Key to Little Duck Viaduct	8.95	miles
Bahia Honda Key	2.22	miles
Bahia Honda Viaduct	1.04	miles
Big Pine Key	28.41	miles
Boca Chica Viaduct to	1.68	miles
Key West	4.19	miles
Total	155.84	miles

The Route of the Overland Extension between Miami and Key West

𝓕rom this point on, the work became even more difficult. It was at Homestead that the railroad left the mainland and began hopping islands. More than 30 islands were used for stretches of construction, some as long as 15 or 20 miles, some less than a mile in length. The first concrete bridge off the mainland crossed Cards Sound at the south end of Biscayne Bay to Key Largo, the first key touched by the seagoing railroad. Key Largo, the largest of all the keys, was 27 miles at its longest point, but construction there was not so difficult as in many other places. However, in Key Largo, as on all the keys, the work was a web–footed proposition. The engineers expected marshy swampy earth on each key by which the railroad crossed.[27]

Workmen building the railroad

ℬelow Key Largo there was Tavernier Creek, less than a mile in width, before another low key was reached. Across the low keys the roadbed was built of natural coral reef. Where the reef was exposed to the destruction of the winds and sea water during storms, a heavy application of marine marl formed. This marl, which is of a calcareous nature and soft in consistency, flows out, forming a smooth leathery slope that hardens soon after exposure to the air and is able to withstand the heaviest seas. Matecumbe Key was the next formation of earth of much size, being 14 miles in length; however, six of those miles were creeks and swamps. It was eight miles south of Key Largo, and adjacent to Long Key on the South.[28]

𝒮outhwest of Long Key the first of the three great viaducts on the extension began. It was called Long Key viaduct and was 2.68 miles long. The viaduct was built of concrete in water from 10 to 30 feet deep. In most places it was exposed to the full gales of the Atlantic Ocean. At times the concrete had to be mixed on barges and placed in position by powerful boom derricks. At other places molds were formed by driving piling which held watertight framework in place. This bridge, which was one of the most expensive, had a series of 180 arches, 80 feet long, built of reinforced concrete. The spans, which gave the appearance of a Roman aqueduct, rested on piers set into solid rock. From the water to the crown of the arch was a distance of about 25 feet. The distance was usually determined by the depth of the water. The engineers had to determine the size of the waves in rough weather, so as to build the viaduct out of reach of the watery spray.[29]

ℱrom the Long Key viaduct the railroad ran to Grassy Key, a strip of land about 15 miles long, and from there to Knights Key, less than a mile long. It took four years to finish the road to this point. On January 22, 1908, the first train on this lap of the overseas extension arrived at Knights Key, a distance of 83 miles south of Homestead, 112 miles south of Miami, and 477 miles south of Jacksonville. When the railroad was opened to Knights Key, steamships from Havana and Key West transferred passengers and freight there, saving 112 miles of water route north to Miami.[30]

The work was halted for only a short time at Knights Key while more materials and supplies were gathered and more men were recruited. Some of the hardest and most tedious work on the extension was yet to be done. Between Knights Key and Bahia Honda Key, the next strip of land of any size, there were seven miles of almost unbroken open water. The viaduct over these seven miles was the second of the great bridges built on the extension.

Roughly speaking, the viaduct was one long bridge, 35,815 feet in length. However, it was divided into four sections—the original Knights Key bridge; Pigeon Key bridge; Moser Channel bridge, or Little Duck viaduct; and Pacet Channel viaduct. The first three short bridges actually constituted one long bridge made of concrete piers with steel girder spans laid on top to carry the track. The Moser Channel section was the longest portion of the bridge, being 13,947 feet or well over two miles in length.[31] The last section, the Pacet Channel viaduct, which was two miles long, was constructed on steel arches. The rails were laid 29 feet above the mean low tide.

There were ten other gaps of ocean, some large and some small, after the railroad passed the Pacet Channel viaduct. The greatest problem of construction presented itself when the Bahia Honda bridge, which connected Bahia Honda Key and Big Pine Key, a distance of about a mile, was built. This bridge, constructed in the deepest water the engineers encountered on the entire project, was 5,056 feet in length. The engineers not only had to support the concrete piers on solid rock, but they were determined to anchor each one there immovably. As in the case of the other bridges, the location of the pier was first determined, after which a coffer dam was floated into place on a catamaran. After the coffer dam was made to rest on the bottom, the soft mud was pumped

Knights Key Bridge

A Train Travels over the Viaduct

out. Then a steel punch was driven into the rock to make places for the wooden piles which followed. These piles which were driven into the rock as far as they could be forced were used as anchors for each pier. Twenty–four piles were driven for each pier. The next step was to sink a large quantity of cement through specially prepared pipes to the rock bed. The cement was imported from Germany because it had a special quality for hardening under water. It formed a solid union with the underlying rock and made the coffer dam virtually watertight. This was then pumped dry, and the piling, which was already encased in the cement foundation, was sawed off below the ordinary low tide level. Then the form or mold for the pier base was put into place and was filled with the same specially treated cement. It took seven days to dry completely. The coffer dam was then removed and it was upon this foundation that the pier was built. Alternate arches were constructed and allowed to harden for four weeks. The missing arches were then filled in and joined to those already in place by an interlocking device which held each firmly in position and closely bound to its neighbor. Since each alternate arch was a separate piece of concrete and was constructed at different times, its shrinkage and wear could not affect that of any other. In this bridge there were 13 spans, each one 128 feet long; 13 other spans, each 186 feet long; and nine arches of concrete, each 80 feet long.[32]

*T*he Bahia Honda bridge connected Big Pine Key, another larger body of land. This key was connected to Key West by the Boca Chica viaduct, the last bridge of any length before the terminus was reached. The total distance from Miami to the Key West station was 155.84 miles; from Homestead it was 127.84 miles. Of this distance, 75 miles of the overseas extension was built over water or extremely marshy land. Across some of the keys the ocean was far enough away so that construction closely resembled that of ordinary road building. Occasionally, there were dense jungles to be penetrated, but such terrain did not present the problems equivalent to those of the open sea.

*F*lagler built the overseas extension with the full encouragement of the federal government. The government made one request and that was the construction of a draw in the Knights Key bridge in order to create a direct passage connecting the Atlantic Ocean with the Gulf of Mexico. The draw had been originally planned for the Bahia Honda bridge, but Flagler was glad to comply with that request. In addition, three other draws were built between Homestead and Key West: one was at Jewfish Creek, one at Indian Key, and one at Key West.[33]

*D*uring the construction of the overseas railroad, there were several hurricanes which hampered the work considerably. One came in 1904 during the surveys, two in 1906, one in 1909, and one in 1910. The October storm of 1906 was by far the most destructive. The facilities were far too inadequate to resist such a strong blow and at that particular time there were more men working on the extension than perhaps at any other time. Most of the floating camps broke loose from their anchors. In one case more than 70 men were blown out to sea and never heard of again. The Italian steamer *Jenny* and the British steamer *Alten* picked up many other workmen. For days and even weeks after the storm, news of other rescued workers kept coming from distant ports such as London and Buenos Aires.

*T*he October, 1906, hurricane winds reached a velocity of 125 miles per hour, yet the concrete trestles that were being pushed out in the sea from coral island to coral island stood. Even with the tragic loss of life, Flagler became more convinced than ever of the ultimate success of his theretofore untried railroad.[34] As soon as the sea was calm again, engineers began to hurry the completion of the extension with more determination than ever before. The hurricane of 1909 was even more severe than the previous storm. However, it was not as destructive as the one in October, 1906, because more care was taken to guard the lives of the men and secure safety for the company's property. By this time most of the workmen were living in large stormproof dormitories, which were an improvement over the floating camps. The storm of 1909 taught Flagler's engineers a valuable lesson. They had calculated on the allowance that had to be made only for the ebb and flow of the ocean tides, and had not taken into consideration the great amount of water that would pass under the open arches and piers of the bridges in times of great winds. Most of the winds from these Caribbean hurricanes forced the ocean water through the Gulf of Florida. The Gulf of Florida stretches out a hundred miles wide between Cape Sable and Key West, but farther northward, along the Southeastern coast of the mainland, it narrows gradually until the keys meet the southern tip of the state. This great force of water had to be reckoned with, and the engineers solved the problem by building stronger bridges where the force of the water was greatest.

*B*efore the work was finished the engineers believed they had mastered the threat of the storms. They kept in close touch with the Weather Bureau at Washington and watched their barometers more frequently than they did their watches. During the months of August, September, and October, when the tropical hurricanes were most likely to occur, the inquiry most often passing over the telephone wires connecting their various offices and stations was, "How does your barometer read?" During the "hurricane seasons" no women were allowed to remain in the camps. Even engineers who frequently had their wives and daughters in their quarters were cautioned against letting them stay after the first day of August each year.[35]

*F*lagler encouraged families of the workmen to visit the scene of construction at certain safe times throughout the year. He provided them with comfortable places to stay and realized that in many cases his employees would be much happier with their loved ones near. Fishing camps with good accommodations were built at logical points along the extension, attracting many sportsmen as well as sightseers and relatives of the workmen.[36] Flagler acquired the new Russell House in Key West, which for a number of years had been a third–rate hotel, and renamed it the Key West Hotel. It was practically rebuilt and entirely refurnished and was used by many persons from the mainland, many of whom were indirectly connected with the construction.

*A*s the work on the extension neared its end, Flagler was noticeably becoming more and more inactive, but his interest was as keen as ever. In February, 1911, the question of finishing the road for traffic in the shortest possible time came up. Engineer Krome was asked by J. R. Parrott if he could complete the work so that Flagler could ride into Key West in his private car over his own rails on his next birthday, January 2, 1912. Flagler would be 82 on that day, and he was most anxious to see the extension completed by that time. Krome promised to do the job if no great storm or other unforeseen delay should overtake him. He kept his promise with 24 hours to spare. However, the first train did not arrive in Key West for several weeks. Flagler's construction job across the keys was finished.

On the afternoon of January 21, 1912, the bridge foreman closed the crossover span at Knights Key trestle. It was the last link in the line of rails connecting the overseas road with the main line of the Florida East Coast Railway. Soon thereafter, the pilot train from Knights Key

Henry Flagler at Knight's Key Dock, 1908

left for Key West. It gave the road a thorough testing and found it in prime condition for the opening. Engineers J. F. Norton and Ed Goehring, Pilot William Nichols, and Fireman Jack Basskopp had the distinction of having carried the first train into the island city.[37]

There was one specific regulation which these first trainmen, and all others who piloted trains over the extension, understood and that was concerning the cancellation of schedules in times of high wind. No train was allowed to travel over the road during times of high wind because such pressure might sweep a moving train from the tracks, though the road itself was built to stand extremely strong wind. The viaducts were fitted with wind gauges which measured the velocity of the wind on every part of the great stretch of masonry and steel, and by electricity registered it at each end. This register was attached to a block system which automatically set the switch against the approaching train when the recorded wind velocity reached 50 miles per hour on any section of the bridge. There were many other safety precautions, one of which was the speed limit. No train was permitted to run over the bridges of the extension faster than 15 miles per hour. Engineers said the strength of the greatest viaducts would warrant speeds of 70 miles per hour, but the possibility of an accident from a broken rail or imperfect car equipment demanded extraordinary precautions for safety of life and property. Normal train speed was resumed after the viaducts were passed. With the prescribed limit of speed, half an hour was required to cross the Knights Key bridge and almost 15 minutes to traverse the length of the Long Key viaduct and its approaches.

*T*he first official train to cross the overseas extension arrived at Key West on January 22, 1912, at 10:43 A.M. Ten thousand people were present to see the first section of a number of specials arrive. Many of the residents saw a passenger train for the first time, as they had been born either in Key West or the Bahamas. The waiting crowds yelled and cheered themselves hoarse. Added to the noise were the sounds of people speaking many languages, including Spanish and French. On the first official train with Henry M. Flagler were several of his close associates and many dignitaries. The most notable personage was Robert Shaw Oliver, Assistant Secretary of War, representing President William Howard Taft. In the throngs that cheered the arrival of the two sections of the train were also representatives of numerous foreign embassies and legations, including Italy, Mexico, Portugal, Costa Rica, Ecuador, Guatemala, San Salvador, and Uruguay. General Jose Marti, representative of President Gomez, of Cuba, accompanied by a Cuban band, arrived at Key West on board a Cuban gunboat and was followed soon thereafter by a delegation of residents of Havana and other Cuban cities.[38]

*A*s soon as Flagler's train arrived, Mayor J. N. Fogarty went aboard with the celebration committee. Brief ceremonies were held on the observation platform of the rear car. Flagler made his way to the edge of the platform and briefly surveyed the throng of people. He was rapidly becoming a feeble old man. His once keen eyes were weak and blurry. The years had mellowed him and there was a kind smile on his face. His shoulders were slightly stooped and he wore his ever–present gray cap. The mayor welcomed him to the island city in a fitting speech. Then George W. Allen presented the railroad builder with a tablet of silver and gold, containing a likeness of himself, as a gift from the residents of the city. Another tablet was presented to him, which was also of gold, on behalf of the men who did the actual work of constructing the railroad over the sea. Flagler replied to each with a brief speech. One of the other features of the welcome to Flagler was a children's chorus, composed of 1,000 school children, who sang patriotic songs. After the

Florida visionary left the platform he was escorted to the front of the children's bandstand where he greeted each boy and girl. The aging man was overcome with emotion by the demonstration given him.

*S*everal other sections of the "first train" arrived in Key West at various intervals all during the day. On one, a solid Pullman train, came a congressional delegation, foreign diplomats, high army officers, and other distinguished guests. Another section of the train bore officials from various cities in the South, particularly Florida. One of the sections was a through train from "New York to Havana"

*Welcoming ceremonies for Henry Flagler,
January 22, 1912, Key West*

and had been advertised as such. The passengers were carried close to the dock in the train and there they transferred to the American steamer, the *Governor Cobb*, which sailed about four o'clock in the afternoon.

*M*any Floridians made the trip. The Miami and Jacksonville specials were the last trains to arrive in Key West. Thousands of people remained at the station to welcome the throngs of visitors who came for the celebration.[39] Governor Gilchrist of Florida arrived on the last train.

The celebration lasted for several days. It included balls, receptions, and other social events. Perhaps the most brilliant affair was the military ball which was given in honor of Flagler on the evening of the first day. Governor Gilchrist spoke and a message was read from President Taft. When Flagler was introduced he was given a thunderous ovation.[40] One of the receptions given in honor of Flagler was preceded by a political rally, the affair being well planned and arranged. At the time, Florida was experiencing a hotly contested race for the governorship. The two leading candidates, Park Trammell and J. W. Watson, were on hand to take part in the rally. Each, in his turn, tore into his opponent with the vigor of a frontier preacher admonishing the devil.

Key West and her 20,000 inhabitants had never experienced such a celebration. The streets were gaily dressed with American flags and buntings. Homes were arranged with evergreens, palms, and coconuts. Tropical foliage was hanging around the verandas. In the show windows there were miniature trains going over the viaducts and bridges, all of which received much favorable comment from the visitors. A circus from Cuba performed stunts equal to those of the great Ringling Bros. & Barnum and Bailey shows. There was a Spanish opera and moving pictures. A carnival set up on the terminal grounds in sight of the tracks where the trains were stopped performed to capacity crowds. In the harbor were seven warships, including the fifth division of the North Atlantic squadron, commanded by Rear Admiral Bradden A. Fiske.[41]

The *Miami Herald* enthusiastically called Flagler's overseas extension the "Eighth Wonder of the World"[42] and spoke in glowing terms about what it would mean for Key West. Said the *Florida Times–Union*, "Today marks the dawn of a new era. The Old Key West—one of the most unique of the world's historic little cities—is shaking off its lethargy and from today the spirit of progress and development will be greater than ever."[43] Other newspapers throughout the nation were also enthusiastic in their predictions for the future of Key West.

Key West had come a long way since its charter of incorporation was issued on January 8, 1828. Its history had shown a slow but steady growth. It was built on a coral island standing boldly between the Atlantic Ocean and the Gulf of Mexico. About seven miles long and one mile in breadth, Key West was possessed originally by the Spanish; however, it was transferred to the United States when Florida was purchased from Spain in 1821. In its early days Key West was merely a fishing and wrecking hamlet, but the establishment of several large cigar factories changed it completely. Key West slowly developed into a city of some importance. But Key West did not grow into the great metropolis most people expected. It did not become the "American Gibraltar" as had been predicted. The overseas extension never enjoyed the volume of business for which Flagler had hoped. This was because very little freight came out of Cuba and the South American countries.

*F*lagler did not live to realize the folly of his great undertaking; he died believing his road would be the making of Key West. Key West's population remained in the 20,000 population range for some time. In 1945 it had less than 15,000 population, a population far beneath the dreams of those who lived during the Flagler era.

*T*he overseas extension was not destined to last forever. It served Key West and Florida for 22 years. On Labor Day, 1935, an unusually strong hurricane lashed the Florida Keys. Miles of embankment were washed away. The track over part of the route was left a torn and twisted wreckage. In some places the track was washed a great distance from the roadbed. The large bridges, however, survived the storm with only minor damages. The efforts of many years had been laid waste in the short period of a few hours. The Florida East Coast Railway had not survived the depression too well and the expense of repairing the damages to the extension after the storm was one the company could not undertake.

*W*as the overseas extension worth another try? The state of Florida thought so. The State Road Department acquired the partially wrecked extension and built a modern highway where once the railroad had been. The overseas highway was completed in 1938. Much of the road was constructed on the sturdy viaducts and bridges which were built by Flagler and his associates so many years earlier.[44] Key West was once again connected to the mainland.

Florida East Coast Railway

— Jacksonville to Key West
— Numerous inland extensions

Florida East Coast Hotel Company

— Ponce de Leon Hotel, St. Augustine
— Alcazar Hotel, St. Augustine
— Ormond Beach Hotel, Ormond Beach
— Royal Poinciana Hotel, Palm Beach
— Breakers Hotels (old and new), Palm Beach
— Royal Palm Hotel, Miami
— Continental Hotel, Atlantic Beach
— Colonial Hotel, Nassau, Bahamas

Model Land Company and its subsidiaries including

— Chuluota Land Company
— Fort Dallas Land Company
— Perrine Grant Land Company
— Okeechobee Land Company

Newspapers

— *Florida Times-Union*, Jacksonville
— *Miami Metropolis, Miami Herald*
— *St. Augustine Record*

Utilities

— Miami Electric Light Company
— West Palm Beach Water Company

Highlights of the Flagler System

13. The Flagler System

*T*he combination of all of Flagler's enterprises in Florida was known as the Flagler System. Each enterprise was incorporated and functioned as a separate unit even though they were all administered by the same group of officers. Flagler remained actively in charge of all his various incorporated units until April 9, 1909. At that time the presidency was given to James R. Parrott, the most prominent man in the organization besides Flagler himself. He was a vital part of the Flagler System.

*P*arrott had been born in Oxford, Maine and spent his early years in the East. He graduated from Yale University with an A.B. degree and also a law degree. "Polly" Parrott, as he was affectionately known by his classmates, was an all-round good fellow. He was a member of his college varsity crew team and won considerable recognition as an athlete. While at Yale, Parrott was thrown in with several young men from the South, one of them being S. Price Gilbert, of Columbus, Georgia. From Gilbert's accounts of his native state, Parrott became interested in moving to Georgia. He liked Atlanta especially and wanted to open a law office. However, the necessary arrangements could not be made.

*P*arrott's second choice for his law office was Jacksonville, although he had never been there. Gilbert assured him that it offered many opportunities for a young lawyer and wrote on his behalf to a friend of long standing. That friend, Duncan U. Fletcher, had just begun to practice law there. Fletcher spoke encouragingly about Jacksonville and the legal profession in that city. On the day after he graduated from Yale Law School in 1885, Parrott set out on the long journey to Florida. Quite by coincidence Henry M. Flagler had just begun his program of development in Florida.[1]

*D*uncan U. Fletcher gave the young lawyer a warm reception to Jacksonville. Parrott got off to a good start and with Fletcher's aid was soon doing fairly well in his profession. Parrott became acquainted with the more influential citizens of the town and it was due to these connections that he was made attorney for the small Jacksonville, Tampa and Key West Railroad. The railroad had undertaken a tremendous program of expansion, but found it impossible to carry through. Consequently the line fell into the hands of the receivers. Parrott was appointed by the court as a receiver less than five years after he arrived in Jacksonville. He did a good job and made the road do more than pay expenses.

*A*bout 1890 Flagler heard of Parrott and decided he was just the man for his organization. The great building program was well under way, but he needed brilliant young men with a passion for work and advancement. Parrott was hired as a legal advisor to the Flagler enterprises. Thus began a long and valuable period of service as Parrott made good in every respect. He launched out in the work and was inspired by the optimism which characterized the spirit of the undertaking. He gathered about him a corps of competent workers and entered into every enterprise with zeal and enthusiasm, as did Flagler. Neither man recognized the word failure. They made a fine team.[2]

*I*n 1892 Parrott was made vice-president of Flagler's short line. After a period of growth, in 1899, he was made vice-president and general manager of the Florida East Coast Railway as well as president of the Florida East Coast Hotel Company. Three years before Flagler's death, he accepted the presidency of all the corporations.[3] Through all of his service to Flagler, he never gave up his duties as head of the legal department. The fact that Flagler virtually turned over all his enterprises to Parrott is proof of his confidence in him. When Flagler died in May, 1913, he directed in his will the continuance of Parrott as president of the Florida East Coast Railway. Parrott was also made one of the three trustees to carry out Flagler's plans as stated in the will.[4] However, he lived only five months after Flagler's death in 1913.

*A*nother valuable young man connected with the Flagler enterprises was William R. Kenan, Jr., who later served as president of the Flagler System. His dealings with Flagler were somewhat more intimate than those of Parrott. His sister, Mary Lily Kenan, became Flagler's third wife in 1901. Kenan, who was a North Carolinian by birth, was the youngest of the Flagler lieutenants, but that was no handicap. He graduated from the University of North Carolina in 1893, after making an impressive record. Although little of his formal training was done in the engineering field, he had great skills in the field. One of his early jobs was with the Carbide Manufacturing Company at Niagara Falls, New York. While with this firm Kenan was sent to Australia for the business of constructing a carbide plant in one of the larger cities. On this trip he returned by way of Berlin, and although only 26, he remained there for several months as a consulting engineer to the German Acetylene Company. After returning to this country, he first located in Wisconsin and Michigan. On June 1, 1900, he became associated with the Traders Paper Company, Lockport, New York, as an assistant manager. While employed by this firm he made a number of trips to New York and on one of these trips he became acquainted with Henry Flagler.[5]

*F*lagler was impressed with the young engineer from the outset. He soon invited him to help with certain construction projects in connection with his Florida developments. Kenan's first assignment was to build the power plant at the Breakers Hotel in Palm Beach. After considerable study, Kenan made an estimate of the cost of the plant which was less expensive than the one Flagler had figured. He was pleased with Kenan's first assignment since it had saved more money than he expected. From this time on the elderly capitalist depended strongly on the opinion and judgment of his younger associate.

*K*enan had no official title in the Flagler System at first because he gave only part of his time to the organization. However, in 1904 he resigned his job with the paper concern in Lockport, New York, and became a full-time officer, serving directly under Flagler. In addition to building the power plant at the Breakers, he also installed the ice machinery and laundry. Kenan directed the work of the power plant at several other of the hotels and served as a consultant in connection with the vapor heating, electric lighting, water, and laundry plant at Whitehall. His official position was that of consulting engineer.

*I*n March, 1904, he was made a director of all the Flagler corporations and also a vice-president. He became influential in the Flagler enterprises. Kenan was given authority by Flagler to sign papers or checks at any time and to do anything which he thought was for the best interest of the Flagler developments. Kenan made important decisions for Flagler without needing to consult with his boss. This fact alone attested to the confidence which Flagler had in him.[6]

The two oldest corporations within the Flagler System, ones in which Flagler, Parrott, and Kenan were most closely concerned, were the Florida East Coast Hotel Company and the Florida East Coast Railway Company. These were the parent organizations, but as various schemes were undertaken other corporations were formed.

The Florida East Coast Hotel Company was the first of the corporations. The great chain of Flagler hotels that stretched along the East Coast of Florida created one of the most popular resort areas in the United States. It was evidently Flagler's purpose and ambition to make his hotels collectively and separately the finest in the world. He chose the most beautiful spots in Florida on which to construct the buildings and he summoned as his advisers some of the foremost landscape artists and architects of the time. Flagler urged them to employ their highest skill.

The Flagler hostelries offered wide variety and catered to various tastes. Some hotels were the winter gathering places of wealthy and fashionable people from the North. At the Ponce de Leon, the Royal Poinciana, and the Royal Palm visitors moved in exclusive circles. Some guests preferred sporting activities along with their social interests, so they chose the Ormond Beach Hotel, or the Breakers, or perhaps the Alcazar.

Flagler also built the Hotel Continental at Atlantic Beach, which was about 20 miles from Jacksonville. It was opened to the public in 1902 and its construction made the only digression in Flagler's hotel building, aside from one in the Bahamas. Instead of opening each year between the middle of December and January 10th, and closing between April 1st and 15th, the Continental opened late in March as the others were closing. It remained open through August, taking care of summer visitors who came to that vicinity. The reason for the summer opening of the Continental lay in the fact that Atlantic Beach got the full benefit of the breezes from the North and the cooling ocean currents.[7]

In 1898, Flagler left his pursuit of the Florida coast line and the sands of the beach long enough to jump nearly 200 miles over the ocean to Nassau in the Bahama Islands. It was there that he purchased the Royal Victoria Hotel and soon thereafter established a steamship line between Nassau and Miami. When Flagler first thought of the plan to buy the property at Nassau he made an offer to the British authorities to purchase the hotel building at their own price. The authorities wanted to know what Flagler would do with the hotel if it were sold to him. When he made it known that he would rebuild a larger hotel on the site, the plan was so startling to Sir William Haynes-Smith, the governor, that he refused to entertain the idea. However, after corresponding with his government in England, Sir William changed his mind. It was thought that Flagler had two motives in mind when he invaded the Bahamas: one, to prove to the American people that it was not necessary for them to go to Europe if they felt determined to get out of the United States for a vacation; and second, to establish a steamship line which made direct connections with his railroad running down the East Coast of Florida.[8]

*F*lagler paid $50,000 for the Royal Victoria Hotel and there resulted much rumor and speculation as to what he might do with the building. This move was not one that many people had anticipated. In fact, Flagler himself had thought very little of adding foreign property to his growing list of business interests which he was acquiring in Florida. He went to the Bahamas to expedite the flow of building material from the British Islands to the construction site in Florida. While there, he became interested in making the purchase. After gaining control of the hotel, Flagler spent an additional $50,000 rebuilding the structure. It was renamed the Colonial Hotel and opened for business in 1899, attracting vacationers from all over the world.[9]

*O*ver 1,000 workmen were sent to the Bahamas to hasten the completion of the newly named Colonial Hotel. The 500 room structure, built on a hillside, was made of stone quarried both in America and in the Bahamas. It was only two stories high, but was equipped with elevators and electric lights, luxuries known to few people in the islands at that time.[10] Although it was one of the last of the Flagler hotels, the Colonial brought as much satisfaction to its owner as any of the group of the Florida East Coast Hotel Company.

*J*ust prior to his purchase of the hotel in the Bahamas, Flagler inaugurated steamship service from Nassau, which was the central part of the British Islands, to Miami. The distance was 175 miles and the line gave excellent service after the Colonial Hotel was opened. Flagler extended his steamship service by opening a line from Miami to Havana, which was extended on to Savannah. Prior to this time, Henry B. Plant had also proved himself as a Florida developer.

*H*enry Plant came to Florida from the North soon after the Civil War. In 1877, he reorganized the Atlantic and Gulf Railroad of Georgia and renamed it the Savannah, Florida and Western Railroad. The line served northern Florida. The road was completely remade and new equipment and steel rails were installed. He next became interested in the St. Johns River and soon began operating steamers from Jacksonville to Sanford. From this his attention turned to railroad construction on the West Coast of Florida, resulting in the building of the Plant system of railroads.[11] In 1902, Flagler's East Coast Steamship Company consolidated with the Plant Steamship Company to form the Peninsula and Occidental Steamship Company in which Flagler and Plant held equal interests. The newly-organized company put on added schedules, and largely because of Flagler's efforts, expanded their services even more.[12]

*F*lagler's second corporation, the Florida East Coast Railway, included more than the main line which ran from Jacksonville to Key West, a distance of 522 miles. Several short branch lines were purchased and immediately rebuilt and more adequately equipped. Some of the branch lines reached inland and tapped rich agricultural lands or commercial points on the St. Johns River; however, none of them extended very far out of the East Florida area. Flagler had no desire to go west of the St. Johns River and Lake Okeechobee. The Plant System extended throughout west Florida and Flagler respected the monopoly of his fellow developer in that section of the state.

*I*n 1899, Flagler bought a small narrow-gauge railroad running from Jacksonville to Pablo Beach at the mouth of the St. Johns River. Several years later, he rebuilt the short line and renamed it the Jacksonville and Atlantic Railway and extended it to connect Jacksonville Beach, Atlantic Beach, and Mayport with the city of Jacksonville. At Mayport, he constructed large coal and lumber docks, hoping that his road would serve as a vital link between the beach town and Jacksonville.[13] Many of Flagler's friends thought he would build a large hotel at Pablo, but instead he built the Continental Hotel at Atlantic Beach. Another branch of the Florida East Coast Railway system was completed in March, 1893. In that year, Flagler acquired the Atlantic and Western Railway, extending from Blue Springs, a point on the upper St. Johns River, to connect the main line of his road at New Smyrna.[14] Six years later Flagler absorbed another short line, the Atlantic Coast, St. Johns and Indian River Railway, which ran 47 miles in length from Enterprise on the St. Johns to Titusville on the Indian River.[15] This was an important acquisition to his system of railroads. It brought to five the total number of points where Flagler's roads touched the St. Johns River: South Jacksonville, Tocoi, East Palatka, Blue Springs, and Enterprise. A traveler could easily reach the coast from the St. Johns at any of these places.

*P*erhaps the most important of all the beach lines of the Florida East Coast Railway was the extension from New Smyrna through Maytown southward into the interior of Florida. This was known as the Okeechobee division. It was begun in 1911, only two years before Flagler's death. The line reached the little town of Okeechobee, on the Nosohatchee River, two miles northeast of Lake Okeechobee, in 1915. It was thought best to put the terminus on the river, where shipping could be protected, rather than in the open waters of Lake Okeechobee. At the time of Flagler's death in 1913, the road had been built no farther than Kenansville, a small settlement which Flagler named in honor of his wife's family. The great builder would have been happy to have lived to see this division reach its destination, but death cut short his hopes.[16]

*S*everal years after the Okeechobee division was completed, the road was extended around the eastern shores of the lake as far south as Lake Harbor. That extension opened to rail one of the richest agricultural sections in the state. The region is known as the Florida Everglades. The soil is composed of a rich peat-muck and is almost solidly decomposed vegetation. Before the new extension was built, there was comparatively little farming done in the region because of inadequate transportation and drainage. The establishment of this line, combined with the extensive work done in drainage and flood control, made the Everglades area a tremendously productive region. The Florida East Coast Railway soon began to haul hundreds of cars of vegetables each year from that area. More than 50% of the produce carried were beans, the balance being made up of cabbage, peas, tomatoes, and miscellaneous produce. The Everglades also became an important sugar producing area, and many tons of sugar and molasses were shipped each year over the Florida East Coast Railway.[17]

$\mathcal{B}$esides vegetables, the railway handled a large volume of Florida's citrus freight. From the start, oranges were the biggest item of freight. However, in the 1890s, another money crop came into existence along the southern banks of the Indian River. Pineapples were being grown successfully. Producers were finding a ready market at profitable prices. The crop expanded satisfactorily and spread farther down the coast. For a number of years, pineapples proved so important as a source of freight that a picture of a pineapple was carried as a sort of trademark on the company's letterhead.

$\mathcal{S}$oon after the Spanish-American War, however, low wage competition and improved transportation from Cuba and Hawaii caused a serious setback in the production of Florida pineapples. In the area between Stuart and Delray 5,000 acres of rich pineapple land were soon almost untended. Many people accused Flagler of helping to kill pineapple production in Florida because they believed he was allowing Cuban pineapples to be shipped over his road at a cheaper rate than Florida pineapples. This was partially true. Large pineapple producers in Cuba were using Flagler's steamship line from Havana to Miami and from that point they shipped by the Florida East Coast Railway. Flagler catered to the Cuban producers because of the longer distances which they had to ship. Flagler never felt that Florida would excel in the production of pineapples when competing with Cuba and, furthermore, it was simply a business matter. His critics did not see it that way.[18]

$\mathcal{T}$he Florida East Coast Railway, when finally completed, consisted of 765 miles of track and represented a building project carried on by one individual. Flagler tied up a large portion of his fortune in the railroad, advancing the funds throughout the period of construction. The railroad was not bonded until the extension was built, and then only the railroad company was affected. These bonds were sold to brokers in the North and East as the builder needed the money. Because of the immense cost of building the Key West extension, the Florida East Coast Railway represented an extremely large outlay of capital, and though the road did a fair volume of business its earning power remained low throughout Flagler's lifetime.[19] All the other corporations remained free of any debt. Flagler set up the capital structure for his railroad in such a way that his investments were adequately safeguarded against loss which might result from any temporary setback. During Flagler's lifetime, however, the road was still in the stage of promotion, construction, and development. The total value of the properties rose, although the gross revenues rose slowly. Every indication points to the fact that Flagler received little compensation during his lifetime as a promoter of the railroad. His other Florida interests proved much more productive.

*O*ne of Flagler's most profitable pursuits was the acquisition and subsequent sale of large tracts of land throughout the East Coast area. The state of Florida, under an act passed by the legislature, gave railroad builders a certain number of acres of land for each mile of track laid. By May, 1889, the state had given, through the Trustees of the Internal Improvement Fund, between 8,000,000 and 10,000,000 acres to the various railroad companies.[20] Thousands of acres of land had been granted to the various small railroads between Jacksonville and Daytona which Flagler bought prior to 1890.[21] After Flagler began his railroad building in 1892, he claimed from the state, under a law passed in 1893, 8,000 acres per mile of railroad. His total claims amounted to 2,040,007 acres, this being in addition to the alternate sections of land previously granted by the state.[22] It was estimated that a grand total of between 1,500,000 and 2,000,000 acres of land were granted to the company while the road was under construction.[28]

*F*lagler established a special department of the Florida East Coast Railway Company to handle the sales and management of his land acquisitions. However, on February 6, 1898, this unit was incorporated as the Model Land Company, a separate organization. Other subsidiary land companies were the Fort Dallas Land Company, chartered on March 17, 1896; the Perrine Grant Land Company, chartered on May 6, 1899; and the Chuluota Land Company, chartered in 1912. The Model Land Company, and its associated organizations, controlled land from Jacksonville to Key West and contributed in large measure to the agricultural and industrial growth of Florida's East Coast. The company and its group of experts gave liberally of time, money, and experience in assisting the development of the soil areas. Expert agriculturalists, horticulturists, and stockmen were employed to give years of attention to the practical development of the East Coast country.[24]

*S*erving as president of the Model Land Company was James E. Ingraham, who had worked previously as the land commissioner of the railroad system. Ingraham was a Wisconsin native and had spent his early years there. For a short time he lived in St. Louis. In 1874, he moved to Florida and was employed by Henry S. Sanford. As a young engineer, his early work in Florida consisted of building the South Florida Railroad from a point near Sanford to Kissimmee. Ingraham became president of this road in 1879 and continued in that capacity until 1892. For a while he was associated with Henry B. Plant and helped to plan the construction of a road through the Florida Everglades. Ingraham was entrusted with the important job of making a survey through the Everglades from Fort Myers to Miami. As a result of the survey, he found that a railroad in that area was impracticable. The report, although not favorable to the building of a railroad, did point out the possibilities of a road on the East Coast.

*F*lagler heard of Ingraham's survey and conferred with him about it. As a result, Ingraham was offered a responsible position with the Flagler enterprises.[25] He undertook the pioneering work for the construction of the railroad and was responsible for the establishment of towns along the proposed route, as well as the accumulation of technical data. His greatest contribution to the Florida developments was in his position as land commissioner for the railroad.[26] Ingraham had complete charge of the Florida East Coast land department, and later the Model Land Company. More than anyone else, Ingraham was credited with advertising Flagler and his developments all over the nation. Ingraham published booklets, pamphlets, and a magazine called the *Homeseeker*, in which he told about the advantages of the East Coast and described the lands which were for sale at most of the points. These lands were sold at relatively low prices, ranging from $1.50 to $5.00 per acre. The terms were in three to four yearly payments at 8% interest. Special prices were given on large tracts of land, for land paid for in cash, or for groups of people colonizing.[27]

*I*ngraham made his headquarters in St. Augustine. He had a splendid corps of assistants working for him all along the East Coast. In some cases, railroad agents at various stations would serve as representatives for the Model Land Company. This was in addition to their other duties. Most of the agents were fairly well versed on soils, crops, and production. They usually gave out reliable information to persons in their vicinity. Flagler realized the importance of bringing people to the East Coast. The freight and passenger traffic which they produced would help his railroad. He once said that every new settler along his road was worth $300 to him since such an inhabitant had to bring in everything he used and had to send out everything he produced over the Flagler railroad.[28]

*M*any of the settlements along the Flagler railroad grew out of the efforts of small groups to create colonies at various points. In 1895, the settlements at Linton and Boynton were established by pioneers who purchased land from the railroad. Two years later, Boynton had 70 settlers and 13 of them had located there with their families. Over 100 acres of land were being cultivated. At Linton there were 177 settlers, only 40 of whom did not own land, and there were 130 acres planted in vegetables and 60 acres in fruit. Another small colony called Modelo was established in the same vicinity. It was a Danish colony and newcomers were mostly from Illinois, Michigan, Wisconsin, and Iowa. Holland was another colony in lower Florida. It was settled in 1897 and was composed mainly of Swedes. After the first few Swedes arrived, drainage ditches were put in, lands staked out, and sales begun. Other settlements were also under consideration. The following Florida towns grew up as a result of colonization: Delray, Deerfield, Fort Lauderdale, Dania, Ojus, Perrine, Homestead, Chuluota, Kenanville, and Okeechobee, in addition to the two principal towns of Miami and West Palm Beach.[29]

*F*lagler made many concessions to people who came to colonize. In order to encourage and stimulate the planting of lemon, grapefruit, and orange groves in Brevard and Dade counties, the railroad magnate made a temporary reduction of 50% in freight rates on nursery stock shipped over his lines to points south of Titusville. The Model Land Company frequently gave a variety of seeds to people in the area. At one time it was believed that tobacco could be raised with some ease in Florida. In 1895, Sims W. Rowley, of San Mateo, raised 2,800 pounds of leaf per acre with plants donated by Flagler and Ingraham. Rowley, who planted it between rows of young orange trees, argued that tobacco was as easily grown as a crop of tomatoes and predicted that if the orange grower combined the two industries, "he will make this [Florida] one of the wealthiest agricultural sections in the Union."[30] At Hastings, New Smyrna, Rockledge, and Titusville, people were given tobacco seed. Many of them raised the weed with some degree of success, but all of the growers lacked experience. Before long, the production of this crop was abandoned for fruits and vegetables. They were considered more promising and entailed less risk. Flagler himself undertook farming on a large scale in Florida at various points. He established a model farm at Hastings. As a result, the little town had a good lead in the production of potatoes. In 1909 the products of Hastings' farms realized nearly $1,000,000 to their owners, chiefly from Irish potatoes. At San Mateo Flagler owned a large orange grove in which he took much pride and interest. Just south of West Palm Beach he had a large plantation on which he raised pineapples. Flagler was not an expert farmer, but he employed men who were; hence his achievements in this endeavor were significant. Through Flagler's and Ingraham's efforts the Model Land Company probably contributed as much to the building of Florida's East Coast as the railroad or the hotel corporations.

*F*lagler's interests in Florida expanded into many other fields, but none of them ever rivaled the organizations of the railroads, the hotels, and the land. The other corporations in the Flagler System were: the Miami Electric Light Company, the West Palm Beach Water Company, the Fort Dallas Land Company, the Okeechobee Land Company, the Perrine Land Company, and later the Florida East Coast Car Ferry Company. Flagler did not live to see this last corporation come into existence. It was put into operation soon after the overseas extension was completed in 1913, operating three ferries each day from Key West to Havana.[31] Flagler also purchased controlling interests in various Florida newspapers during his lifetime, including the *Miami Herald*, the *St. Augustine Record*, and the (Jacksonville) *Florida Times-Union*.

*T*he results of Flagler's efforts in East Florida showed great returns for that state over a period of years. The gross valuation of the seven East Coast counties in which Flagler's developments were centered tripled between 1884 and 1908.[32] Florida's East Coast had definitely taken the leadership in growth and development. His hotels accommodated 40,000 guests and his railroads served a wide range of persons and places. Towns sprang up all along the Atlantic Coast line in Florida. The towns were not mere villages and backwoods hamlets. They were places that were a credit to the state. Flagler's System left a great imprint on the state of Florida.

14. *A Full Life*

*F*lagler's last years were quiet ones. They were spent in Palm Beach among his faithful friends, some of whom were his employees. His personal valet, George Conway, an English lad in his early 20s, was his constant companion.[1] Conway read to him many hours each day. He rolled him along the lake front in his wheel chair and over the grounds at Whitehall to inspect his flower beds of Marèchal Niel roses. The children in the neighborhood learned to watch for Flagler and Conway each afternoon as they wheeled down the lake front at the same hour. It was a common scene to see several children walking alongside his wheel chair. Usually Delos, a little white spitz dog belonging to Mrs. Flagler, followed close behind. Flagler also occasionally traveled into Palm Beach with Conway.

*I*n addition to Conway, others employed at Whitehall at the time included George Cooper, George Holland, Jim Weeks, Lila Cooper, Bernard O'Brien, Sidney Capon, Ida Schieffer, Carl Fremd, and William Fremd.[2] Some of these were persons whom Flagler brought from New York with him and they remained lifelong friends. Such was the case of William Fremd, a German immigrant, who came to America in 1879. He first lived at Rye, New York, later moving to Mamaroneck, where he worked as keeper of the grounds and gardens. After Flagler transferred his interests to Florida, Fremd moved to St. Augustine

George Conway, Henry Flagler, and Delos

where he helped to lay out the grounds for the Ponce de Leon Hotel. Fremd was next made superintendent of the grounds at the Royal Poinciana and the Breakers hotels.[3] He loved Flagler perhaps as much as anyone, yet worked most of his life as a humble servant.[4]

*F*lagler's personal secretary was J. C. Salter. He lived at Whitehall and shouldered many of the responsibilities which otherwise would have fallen heavily on the aging capitalist.

*H*is pastor, George Morgan Ward, paid regular visits to Whitehall where he and Flagler enjoyed long chats. Ward, who was ordained a Congregational minister in 1896, was the President of Rollins College in Winter Park, Florida, for a time. He did not go into the active ministry until Flagler invited him to Palm Beach in 1903 to become pastor of the Royal Poinciana Chapel. The chapel of the Royal Poinciana was nonsectarian, having been built for the guests of the Flagler hotels in Palm Beach. Although Flagler and Ward seldom agreed on anything, there was much understanding and friendship between them.[5]

Mary Lily and Henry Flagler

*W*hitehall remained his home and he and Mary Lily continued to live there quietly. For Flagler, a man who had been so mentally and physically active, it was extremely difficult for him to accept his declining physical abilities. On January 15, 1913, as he was slowly descending a flight of white marble stairs, his leg gave way. Flagler fell. He was badly bruised and shaken up and his right hip was broken. He suffered much pain but seemed to rally after several days. Improvement thereafter was slight and his friends realized that he would never again leave his bed. By early April, many expected his death. His condition grew much worse at that time and J. R. Parrott and J. E. Ingraham of the Florida East Coast Railway were summoned.[6] Warm weather came early that spring and Flagler showed signs of suffering from the heat. He was moved to his beachside Nautilus cottage which was about two miles from Whitehall. Although he rested more easily there, his condition grew more and more serious.

𝓑y May 10, he was taking so little nourishment that his immediate family, friends, and business associates were called again.[7] His only son, Harry Flagler, who had not seen his father since his marriage to Mary Lily Kenan in 1901, was informed of Flagler's critical illness. Harry was invited to Whitehall for the first time and came promptly to his father's bedside. By the time he got there, the dying man had lapsed into a state of unconsciousness and did not recognize his son. George M. Ward; Dr. Owen Kenan, his physician; George Conway and Jim Weeks, personal servants; and Mrs. Flagler were the only persons who saw Flagler frequently after he became critically ill.

𝓗enry Morrison Flagler died at 10 o'clock on the morning of May 20, 1913. He was 83 years old. His end came peacefully, as though he were sinking into slumber.[8] His death was attributed to old age and sheer exhaustion.

𝐼t was his wish to be buried in St. Augustine where his Florida developments had started. Henry Flagler had always loved the ancient city and had spent many happy hours there. His body was carried from Palm Beach to St. Augustine, on May 23, where it lay in state at the Ponce de Leon Hotel for several hours before the funeral services. At three o'clock in the afternoon the funeral procession made its way from the Ponce de Leon Hotel to the Memorial Presbyterian Church, where the funeral rites were conducted. The church overflowed with friends and admirers. Among the active pallbearers were his close personal friends, including J. R. Parrott, J. E. Ingraham, J. A. McGuire, J. A. McDonald, J. C. Salter, T. V. Pomar, Leland Sterry, and W. J. Krome. Honorary pallbearers numbered 50 or 60. A large group of people from Jacksonville attended the funeral, including members of the Board of Trade. The Reverend J. N. MacGonigle, former pastor of Memorial Presbyterian Church, and close friend of Flagler, read selections of which his deceased friend was especially fond. His tribute to Flagler was brief but sincere. Others who assisted Reverend MacGonigle were Dr. George M. Ward, Flagler's old friend from Palm Beach, and the Reverend Alfred S. Badger, pastor of the Memorial Presbyterian Church. The services were simple, in keeping with Flagler's wishes.

$\mathcal{T}$he committal service, which followed the funeral, was private; only the members of the family and immediate friends remained for it. Flagler's body was placed in the mausoleum adjoining the church, very near the vault containing his daughter, Jennie Louise, and her infant daughter.[9] This service was conducted by Dr. Ward and the Reverend Peyton Hoge, of Louisville, Kentucky. Organ music and the reading of a poem completed the last rites for Henry M. Flagler.[10]

$\mathcal{N}$o period of mourning was declared in Florida for its benefactor. Mrs. Flagler requested that it not be done, despite the fact that several towns expressed a wish to so honor him. She thought that Flagler would not have approved of it.[11] Thousands of telegrams of sympathy were sent to his widow and hundreds of floral wreaths were placed around his vault in the mausoleum. Flagler was admired and loved by many people throughout the state and the nation.

$\mathcal{F}$our days after his burial, on May 27, 1913, Flagler's will was made public for the first time. It brought to light an estate worth nearly $100,000,000. The will spoke in endearing terms of his wife and the bulk of his fortune was left to her under a trusteeship. J. R. Parrott of Jacksonville, W. H. Beardsley of New York, and William R. Kenan, Jr. of Lockport, New York, were named as trustees.[12] The trusteeship was to continue for five years from Flagler's death. At the end of that time if the condition of the Florida East Coast Railway and the hotel companies called for financial assistance, then the trusteeship would continue. It was stipulated, however, that the trusteeships should terminate after two five–year periods.[13] Under the trusteeship, Mrs. Flagler received $100,000 a year, the residence Whitehall at Palm Beach, and Flagler's New York City realty. After the trust expired and all other bequests were made, she was to inherit the balance of the vast estate.

$\mathcal{H}$arry Flagler, his only son, received 5,000 shares of stock of the Standard Oil Company and his children received 8,000 shares each. Horace Flagler, a cousin, was left $2,000 a year until the trusteeship ended. The Memorial Presbyterian Church, where Flagler was buried, received $3,000 during the trusteeship and $75,000 as an endowment.[14] The following bequests were to be made at the expiration of the trusteeship: J. R. Parrott, $100,000; Hamilton College, $100,000; W. H. Beardsley, $50,000; J. E. Ingraham, $20,000; J. A. McGuire, the contractor who built the Ponce de Leon Hotel, $10,000; J. C. Salter, his private secretary, $10,000; Robert Murray, manager of the Ponce de Leon Hotel, $10,000; J. G. Greaves, manager of the Royal Palm Hotel, $10,000; Leland Sterry, $10,000; J. P. Beckwith, vice–president of the Florida East Coast Railway, and Mrs. Ella Green of Palm Beach, $5,000 each.[15] The will did not list the properties which included the entire East Coast Railway system, the hotels Ponce de Leon, Alcazar, Cordova, Continental, Royal Palm, and other stock in the Peninsula and Occidental Steamship Company, Standard Oil, and other corporations, vast tracts of valuable Florida lands, many small manufacturing plants, and other enterprises.[16]

*F*lagler, like many people with money, power, and ability was a controversial figure. His critics at the time of his death might be classified into several groups. People opposed to big corporations naturally thought of him as one of the leaders of the Standard Oil Company. But his enemies did not stop there.

*M*any Floridians were opposed to his efforts in that state. During his life, he had been made aware of that fact on every turn. Every move he made was closely watched by the public and certain antagonistic groups soon formed. One group disliked and distrusted him because of his divorce from Ida Alice and his subsequent marriage to Mary Lily. He never quite lived it down, although people who understood sympathized with him in his predicament. Persons who knew Flagler only through reputation remembered the divorce and ignored or discounted everything else he did.

*A*nother group which opposed Flagler was made up of those who kept fresh the memory of the Civil War and Reconstruction in Florida. To them Flagler was a carpetbagger from the North and nothing more. They believed his purpose in coming to Florida was to choke from them what profits he could.[17] They belittled him whenever possible and made his work in the state extremely difficult at times by not extending ordinary courtesies he was due. It is believed that in several cases citizens refused to sell him land on which to construct certain buildings because they thought his motive was not for their best interest.[18]

*S*till another group opposed to Flagler were those who were jealous of his money. These citizens made Flagler the target of their condemnation and persistently persecuted him.[19] They were would–be developers themselves, but never had the ability, ingenuity, aggressiveness, or money to put into operation any large program of improvement. Because of their clamor the state was placed in a position which, in the end, wrought much damage. Over the years, as Flagler's program of development was pushed toward completion, there was a subsidence of this malicious agitation, and he was finally permitted to work out his plans in comparative peace. Concerning these critics, Flagler had said to his friend T. T. Reese, President of the Farmers Bank and Trust Company, Palm Beach,

> *I have lived too long and have been a target too often to allow myself to be disturbed by the jealousy of others who have been less fortunate. I don't know of anyone who has been successful, but that he has been compelled to pay some price for success. Some get it at the loss of their health; others forego the pleasures of home and spend their years in the forests or mines; some acquire success at the loss of their reputation; others at the loss of character, and so it goes; many prices paid, but there is one universal price that I have never known any successful man to escape, and that is the jealousy of many of the community in which he moves.[20]*

Though the hostility to Flagler centered in Palm Beach, men like Reese upheld him and encouraged him to go forward with his plans.

$\mathcal{M}$ost of Flagler's employees liked him, but those who were not ambitious were never given much consideration. They saw him at his worst, for he had no patience with workers who loafed or wasted his time. On one occasion while the Ponce de Leon was under construction, Flagler was inspecting the work in the lower part of the structure. In one remote portion of the building he came upon four or five employees who were idle, with seemingly nothing to do. "Well," said Flagler, "can't you men find something to do?" Not recognizing his employer, and certainly not expecting to find him supervising the details of construction, one of them answered, "Yes, we've got plenty to do, but old man Flagler will never miss the money he is paying us just to do a little loafing." Indignant but collected, Flagler replied, "Go straight to the office; get the portion of 'old man Flagler's money' that is due you and don't ever come back to me for employment." Embarrassed and subdued the men went hastily for their last pay envelope.[21] Other employees who were not punctual and efficient found very little about Flagler which they liked.

*I*n the South, Flagler was generally well received except in extreme anti–corporation circles. At one time, Governor Hogg of Texas, desiring to keep himself before the public, became active in a crusade to uphold the Sherman Anti–Trust law. Since Flagler had received much acclaim in Florida, Hogg centered his Standard Oil attack upon the railroad builder. Expressing a desire to arrest every official of the Standard Oil Company, the Texas Governor sent requisition papers to Governor Mitchell of Florida for the arrest of Flagler on the grounds of violation of the antitrust law. Hogg had particular reason to dislike railroad builders, for the railroad interests in Texas had fought him in a recent election.[22]

*G*overnor Mitchell honored Governor Hogg's request since it was sent through regular channels. It appeared for a time as if Hogg might take Flagler to Texas for trial. Florida's Governor was besieged by Flagler's friends to revoke his decision. Letters and telegrams flooded the Governor's office, each asking for mercy in Flagler's behalf. Governor Mitchell was a stubborn man. He held out for several days and declared that he knew no difference in a pauper and a millionaire where the law was concerned. However, he quickly changed his decision when he was reminded that his political life in Florida would last considerably longer if he were not so hard on Flagler. It was too much public pressure for the Governor. He explained his action to the press by declaring that Governor Hogg could not establish his claim to Flagler as a fugitive from Texas.[23]

*F*rom time to time, Flagler's foes tried to drag him into politics. He consistently refused to become involved, either in local or national affairs. Nationally, he was a Republican, but he never manifested much zeal or enthusiasm over any of the big issues. He followed with considerable interest each national campaign, but when he was in Florida he said little about it because he knew how solidly Democratic the South had been since the Civil War. In one or two campaigns he manifested a little more interest than usual. For instance, in the campaign of 1884 he was particularly anxious for the Republicans to win because their candidate, James G. Blaine, represented the capitalist element of the nation. Flagler supported Blaine with a substantial contribution, and was disappointed when Grover Cleveland was elected.[24] Another election in which Flagler became concerned was the McKinley–Bryan campaign in 1896. The Republicans, more than ever before, espoused the cause of men like Flagler. A victory for McKinley meant a victory for the moneyed class. Mark Hanna, McKinley's campaign manager, called on Flagler to exert his influence in Florida on the party's behalf. Flagler knew there was almost nothing a Republican could do in St. Augustine for his party. He knew that Florida would vote a Democratic ticket, but he expressed faith in an overwhelming victory for McKinley in the East.[25]

*F*lagler was acquainted with many of the Republican leaders, but he probably knew Theodore Roosevelt better than any of the others. Flagler was Roosevelt's guest at a White House dinner on one occasion, but the affair was purely social.[26] The railroad builder never received patronage of any sort from President Roosevelt and received very little from any of his other Republican connections. To him, politics was for the politician and not for the business person. However, in the summer of 1901 he was proposed by several newspapers in Florida for a post in the United States Senate. At this particular time, Flagler was already in the limelight. The state legislature had just passed the much discussed Flagler divorce law. He was accused of having encouraged the legislative body to create the law by making liberal gifts of money. Persistent rumors connected him with the senatorial job for a time. Many doubted if he would ever be appointed by a Democratic legislature.[27] The *Ocala Banner* argued that it would not be a breach in party policy for him to be selected. The editor reminded his readers that "under the very flexible definition given to democracy it is a very easy matter for Mr. Flagler to be styled a Democrat, though, really if at heart he be not one."[28] The *Pensacola Journal* voiced an opinion that Flagler would be a good choice for the Senate, "as the senate has many rich men in it, and could at this time be called a convocation of millionaires."[29]

*D*espite the backing Flagler got for the high post, he refused to give any thought to a political career. He had never entertained political ambitions and when he became a citizen of Florida he specifically said so. He reminded the people that:

As far as political ambitions are concerned, I do not now, nor have I ever entertained them. There is no office in the gift of the American people that I could be induced to accept, and I hope my Florida friends will not fall into the error of thinking otherwise.[30]

He perhaps could have held any of the better political jobs in Florida had he desired to do so. One of his contemporaries, William Dudley Chipley, builder of the Pensacola and Atlantic Railroad in western Florida, became prominent in the public life of the state and threw his influence behind the forces opposing Wilkinson Call, United States Senator from Florida. Chipley fought Call, a progressive Democrat, to a finish because the latter had given much opposition to the railroads. Chipley came out of the fray with political scars and a defeat in the senatorial race of 1897.[31] It is safe to say Flagler was the wiser of the two.

*A*lthough Flagler refused to become involved in state politics, there was nevertheless a faction which organized within the state to oppose him. It was short–lived, however, since it had only one objective. It was appropriately called the anti–corporation party and was headed by Guy Metcalf, editor of the West Palm Beach *Tropical Sun*. The faction spread throughout east Florida, but was strongest in the Palm Beach area. Metcalf and Flagler had not always been enemies; in fact, at one time the two men had been very friendly. The break came when Metcalf defaulted in the payment of a debt amounting to $3,750, which Flagler felt he was fully able to pay. After the break with Metcalf over the debt, Flagler made it a rule never to lend money to a friend, though often he made money gifts to people close to him. Several years later, the people of West Palm Beach elected Judge William Metcalf, father of Guy Metcalf, to the mayorship of the city. Flagler was much opposed to the selection and ceased to take any interest in the public affairs of West Palm Beach. Until this time, Flagler had always expressed a love for West Palm Beach, but after the Metcalf episode, he requested that he not be buried there.[32]

*N*o one, not even his enemies, doubted his modesty and his sincerity. He was known generally for kindness and his slow elaborate manner. He never had a flair for words, but the statements he made were sound. He neither swore nor used indecent language. "Thunder" was his strongest word. When he became provoked with anyone, he usually stamped his cane on the floor, frowned, and exclaimed, "Now wouldn't you think a man would have more sense than that!"[33] Flagler was careful to control his feelings concerning his work, accepting the bitter with the sweet. His business affairs were taken in stride. However, his domestic affairs preyed on his mind and kept him upset for a long while. On one occasion in Palm Beach an associate broke the news to him that the Standard Oil Company had just been fined over $20,000,000 by the federal court. Flagler felt strongly about the matter because he was a part of that organization, although he was inactive. For a moment he looked as if he were going to say something but merely nodded and said casually, "Do you happen to have those Whitehall plumbing bills handy?"[34]

*M*any stories were told concerning his kindness. It was not uncommon for Flagler to give a faithful helper a home, a sum of money, or a farm. There was one case of an employee who had done his best to hamper the building operation at Palm Beach. Later, the disgruntled worker was incapacitated by a serious accident. During his period of forced inactivity his wife and children suffered from insufficient care. When approached about the need of the man's family, Flagler paid all their expenses until the wage earner was able to take his place again on the road.

*A*s to his views on intoxicating liquors, Flagler reflected his strict Presbyterian training. He made it a condition in his land contracts and deeds at Miami that no intoxicating liquors should ever be manufactured or sold on the premises, under penalty of forfeiture. The liquor dealers of the state combined and bought a lot, erected a store, and commenced selling liquor. They proposed to test the legality of the restriction and engaged Major Alexander Abrams to represent them. Determined not to be outdone, Flagler obtained an injunction and closed the store.[35] As long as he lived, he did his best to discourage the use of liquor by his friends and employees.

*O*utwardly, he was faithful to his church and to all for which it stood. His enemies contended that he had no deep religious convictions, but after a careful study of his private life, one finds that he had definite religious beliefs.[36] He was reared in a Puritan home by Presbyterian parents and he never forgot his early training. He was active in religious circles wherever he lived. In New York, St. Augustine, Palm Beach, and Miami he took a keen interest in the church. He was never narrow in his denominational beliefs. During his lifetime he subsidized several churches, either by endowment, physical plants, or donating lots on which to build new structures.[37]

*D*espite the enemies he made in getting ahead, Henry Flagler was a man who was genuinely admired by a majority of the people. Measured by the importance to humanity of his achievements, he may justly be regarded as an important historical figure. The evil to which his critics liked to point was so far outweighed by his virtues that it would be unfair to designate him as other than a good man. If he took advantage of the conditions which made it possible for him to accumulate great wealth, it should be remembered that he employed that wealth to far greater advantage to his fellow men than have some of our much-vaunted philanthropists. When men asked for bread he did not give them a promise. His great enterprises opened the way for thousands to secure support while maintaining their self-respect.

*H*is influence upon the development of Florida cannot be overstated. It is not only in the immediate portion of the state where his activities took shape that this influence was operative. The East Coast of Florida owes to him its transformation from a barren, desolate, relatively unpopulated wilderness. In addition, the effect of the Flagler enterprises turned the eyes of the nation upon a state which before had been but slightly regarded. The impetus to immigration thus given affected every portion of Florida then and for many years to come.

*H*enry Morrison Flagler lived a long life, a full life, and a successful life. He had very little else for which to wish. He drank the sweetest draught from the cup of undertaking—the joy of accomplishment. It was given to him to finish the great task of remaking Florida which had so long been his dream, to look upon his completed work and to pronounce it abundant and successful.

REMEMBERING

Did you actually vision to yourself the whole thing? I mean, did you, or could you, really close your eyes and see it all? The derricks? The pipelines? The refineries? Did you see the men working? The tracks? The trains running? And hear the whistles blowing? Did you go as far as that?

Yes.
How clearly?
Very clearly.

From an interview with Henry Flagler at age 76

Nearing the end of the line. With Henry Flagler on board, first train pulls into Key West, January 12, 1912

Footnotes

Chapter 1. Heritage and Youth

[1]*New York Times*, December 23, 1906

[2]Edwin Lefèvre, "Flagler in Florida," *Everybody's Magazine,* (February, 1910), 181

[3]Flagler Family Records, File 1, Flagler Collection.

[4]*Ibid.*

[5]*Ibid.*, also in collected data, Kenan Collection

[6]W. W. Williams, *History of the Firelands*, 416

[7]Flagler Family Records, File II, Flagler Collection

[8]*Western Reserve Historical Society Publication* (October, 1920), 26

[9]W. W. Williams, *History of the Firelands*, 416

[10]*New York Times*, May 21, 1913

[11]Samuel E. Moffett, "Henry Morrison Flagler," *The Cosmopolitan* (August, 1902), 417

Chapter 2. Early Career

[1]*New York Times*, May 21, 1913

[2]*New York Tribune*, December 23, 1906

[3]H. L. Pieke, *History of Erie County, Ohio*, I, 67

[4]Flagler kept the French coin the rest of his life as a good luck piece, and also as an imitation of the character in the Bible who had but one talent. *New York Tribune*, December 23, 1906.

[5]W. W. Williams, *History of the Firelands*, 415

[6]Flagler Family Records, File II, Flagler Collection

[7]*New York Tribune*, December 23, 1906

[8]C. W. Butterfield, *History of Seneca County, Ohio*, 181

[9]C. S. Van Tassil, *Book of Ohio*, II, 754

[10]"He Made Florida," *Literary Digest*, XLVI (May 31, 1913), 1241

[11]*New York Tribune*, December 23, 1906

[12]W. W. Williams, *History of the Firelands*, 416

[13]*Western Reserve Historical Society Publication* (October, 1920), 26

[14]W. W. Williams, *History of Huron County, Ohio*, I, 184

[15]Isabella died on July 5, 1864, at the age of 35. Daniel M. Harkness remarried on June 22, 1897, to Edith Hale, who survived him. See Flagler Family Records, File II, Flagler Collection

[16]Flagler Family Records, File II, Flagler Collection

[17]They had three children: Georgia Harkness York, born March 18, 1865; Robert Hamlin York, born October 29, 1866; and Roy Follett York, born February 4, 1871. See *Ibid.*

[18]J. H. Kennedy, "Stephen Vanderburg Harkness," *Magazine of Western History*, IX (November, 1888), 188-189

[19]W. W. Williams, *History of the Firelands*, 414

[20]"Sketch of Henry M. Flagler," *The Outlook*, CIV (May 31, 1913), 231

[21]"He Made Florida," *loc. cit.*, 1242

[22]W. W. Williams, *History of the Firelands*, 400

[23]T. E. Burton, *John Sherman*, 123

[24]T. W. Latham, "Revelations of an Old Account Book," *Firelands Pioneer*, XXII (January, 1921), 135

[25]At his death his estate was estimated to be worth $30,000,000. See *Ibid.*, 138; also Kennedy, "Stephen Vanderburg Harkness," *loc. cit.*

Chapter 3. Success and Failure

[1]W. W. Williams, *History of the Firelands*, 417

[2]Allan Nevins, *John D. Rockefeller*, I, 140

[3]*New York Tribune*, December 23, 1906

[4]Flagler Family Records, File II, Flagler Collection

[5]Carrie Flagler died on December 7, 1861. Harry Harkness Flagler was born in Cleveland, December 2, 1870. *Ibid.*

[6]Harry Harkness Flagler to the author, October 25, 1945

[7]Harriett T. Upton, *History of the Western Reserve*, I, 441

[8]Harry Harkness Flagler to the author, November 26, 1945

[9]Flagler Family Records, File II, Flagler

collection

[10]Thomas W. Latham, "Revelations of an Old Account Book," *Firelands Pioneer*, XXII (January, 1921), 133

[11]Charles R. Tuttle, *History of Michigan*, 580

[12]James C. Mills, *History of Saginaw County, Michigan*, I, 430

[13]*Ibid.*, 336

[14]*Ibid.*, 436

[15]"He Made Florida," *Literary Digest*, XLVI (May 31, 1913), 1241

[16]*New York Tribune*, December 23, 1906

[17]*Savannah* (Georgia) *Morning News*, May 21, 1913

[18]Allan Nevins, *John D. Rockefeller*, I, 115

[19]Edwin Lefèvre, "Flagler and Florida," *Everybody's Magazine*, XXII (February, 1940), 182

[20]Both Flagler's mother and father were buried in Bellevue. Flagler Family Records, File II, Flagler Collection

[21]Conversation with Harry Harkness Flagler

[22]*Cleveland Leader*, December 27, 1867

[23]Allan Nevins, *John D. Rockefeller*, I, 22

[24]*Ibid.*, 28 ff.

[25]*New York Herald*, November 29, 1908

Chapter 4. *Flagler Strikes Black Gold*

[1]Paul H. Giddens, *The Birth of the Oil Industry*, 3-4

[2]Allan Nevins, *John D. Rockefeller*, I, 149

[3]P. H. Giddens, *The Birth of the Oil Industry*, 7

[4]*Ibid.*, 18-19

[5]Ida M. Tarbell, *History of the Standard Oil Company*, I, 5

[6]Frank A. Taylor, "George H. Bissell," *Dictionary of American Biography*, II, 301-302

[7]I. M. Tarbell, *History of the Standard Oil Company*, I, 7

[8]P. H. Giddens, *The Birth of the Oil Industry*, 40

[9]I. M. Tarbell, *History of the Standard Oil Company*, I, 9

[10]*Ibid.*, 14-15

[11]*Ibid.*, 24 ff.

[12]Gilbert H. Montague, *The Rise and Progress of the Standard Oil Company*, 6-7

[13]Ida M. Tarbell, "The Rise of the Standard Oil Company," in *McClure's Magazine*, XX (December, 1902), 116

[14]Allan Nevins, *John D. Rockefeller*, I, 192

[15]*Cleveland Leader*, January 3-25, 1866

[16]Matthew Josephson, *The Robber Barons*, 111-112

[17]Thomas W. Latham, "Revelations of an Old Account Book," in *Firelands Pioneer*, XXII (January, 1921), 136

[18]*Firelands Pioneer*, XIII (June, 1916), 137-138

[19]G. H. Montague, "The Rise and Supremacy of the Standard Oil Company," *The Quarterly Journal of Economics*, XVI (February, 1902), 267

[20]*Cleveland Leader*, March 5, 1867

[21]John D. Rockefeller, "Random Reminiscences of Men and Events," *World's Work*, XVII (November, 1908), 10881

[22]John K. Winkler, *John D., A Portrait in Oils*, 74

[23]John D. Rockefeller, "Random Reminiscences of Men and Events," *loc. cit.*, 10882

[24]Ella G. Wilson, *Famous Old Euclid Avenue*, 2-15

[25]*Cleveland Leader*, 1865-1880

[26]*Ibid.*, May 7, 1867

[27]*Ibid.*, December 3, 1867

[28]J. K. Winkler, *John D., A Portrait in Oils*, 85

[29]J. D. Rockefeller, "Random Reminiscences of Men and Events," *loc cit.*, 10881

[30]Allan Nevins, *John D. Rockefeller*, I, 275

[31]Matthew Josephson, *The Robber Barons*, 112

[32]Allan Nevins, *John D. Rockefeller*, I, 254-255

[33]C. M. Destler, "The Standard Oil, Child of the Erie Ring, 1808-1872. Six Contracts and a Letter," *Mississippi Valley Historical Review*, XXXIII (June, 1946), 93. Professor Destler differs with Professor Nevins on this point concerning the first rebate re-

ceived by the firm of Rockefeller, Andrews and Flagler. Destler maintains that this early connection between the Erie System and Rockefeller, Andrews and Flagler was very significant, and helped materially in the later development of the Standard Oil Company, *Ibid.*, 96

[34]John T. Flynn, *God's Gold, The Story of Rockefeller and His Times*, 145

[35]*New York Tribune*, December 23, 1906

[36]I. M. Tarbell, "Rise of the Standard Oil Company," *loc. cit.*, XX (December, 1902), 117

[37]J. K. Winkler, *John D., A Portrait in Oils*, 78

[38]*Ibid.*, 80-84

[39]J. D. Rockefeller, "Random Reminiscences of Men and Events," *loc. cit.*, 10885

[40]Rockefeller to Allan Nevins, quoted in Nevins, *John D. Rockefeller*, I, 274

[41]Allan Nevins, *John D. Rockefeller*, I, 274

[42]J. T. Flynn, *God's Gold, The Story of Rockefeller and His Times*, 172.

[43]J. K. Winkler, *John D., A Portrait in Oils*, 74

[44]I. M. Tarbell, *Rise of the Standard Oil Company*, I, 50

Chapter 5. The Standard Oil Company

[1]G. H. Montague, "The Rise and Supremacy of the Standard Oil Company," *loc. cit.*, 272-273

[2]John Moody, *Truth About the Trusts*, 112

[3]Edwin Lefèvre, "Flagler and Florida," in *Everybody's Magazine*, XXII (February, 1910), 183

[4]William H. Allen, *Rockefeller, Giant, Dwarf, Symbol*, 188

[5]The act of incorporation was signed on January 10, 1870; however, the *Cleveland Leader* claims January 11, 1870, as the day for incorporation.

[6]*Cleveland Leader*, January 19, 1870

[7]Allan Nevins, *John D. Rockefeller*, I, 292

[8]Ida M. Tarbell, "The Rise of the Standard Oil Company," in *McClure's Magazine*, XX (December, 1902), 121

[9]John T. Flynn, *God's Gold, The Story of Rockefeller and His Times*, 160

[10]"He Made Florida," *Literary Digest*, XLVI (May 31, 1913), 1241

[11]*New York Tribune*, December 23, 1906

[12]Conversation with Harris Gillespie

[13]*New York Tribune*, December 23, 1906

[14]Gilbert H. Montague, *The Rise and Progress of the Standard Oil Company*, 11

[15]Allan Nevins, *John D. Rockefeller*, I, 296-297

[16]G. H. Montague, *op. cit.*, 269-271

[17]J. T. Flynn, *God's Gold, The Story of Rockefeller and His Times*, 151

[18]Herbert Asbury, *The Golden Flood*, 300

[19]G. H. Montague, *op. cit.*, 272

[20]*Cleveland Leader*, April 11, 1872

[21]I. M. Tarbell, "The Oil War of 1872," *loc. cit.*, XX (January, 1903), 248

[22]*Ibid.*, 252

[23]*Ibid.*, 249

[24]*Cleveland Herald*, March 2, 1872

[25]*Cleveland Leader*, February 27-April 10, 1872

[26]*Ibid.*, April 11, 1872

[27]Henry D. Lloyd, *Wealth Against Commonwealth*, 59

[28]I. M. Tarbell, "An Unholy Alliance," *loc. cit.*, XX (February, 1903), 390-391

[29]*Ibid.*, 495-496

[30]*Ibid.*, 496

[31]Allan Nevins, *John D. Rockefeller*, I, 478

[32]I. M. Tarbell, "Death of the Pennsylvania," *loc. cit.*, XX (April, 1903), 612-621

[33]G. H. Montague, *The Rise and Progress of the Standard Oil Company*, 66

[34]Festus P. Summers, *James N. Camden*, 185

[35]James N. Camden to Henry M. Flagler, December 13, 1878

[36]*Ibid.*, May 20, 1878

[37]Telegram, James N. Camden to Henry M. Flagler, May 26, 1878

[38]*Ibid.*, May 25, 1879

[39]James N. Camden to Henry M. Flagler, January 29, 1879

[40]John K. Winkler, *John D., A Portrait in Oils*, 124

[41]James N. Camden to Henry M. Flagler, February 6, 1879

Chapter 6. Retirement from Oil

[1]Allan Nevins, *Emergence of Modern America*, 93

[2]*Ibid.*, 91

[3]Conversation with Harry Harkness Flagler

[4]L. M. Hacker and B. J. Kendrick, *The United States Since 1865*, 54-55

[5]This was the only home in New York City that Flagler ever owned. He did not sell it until after he moved his residence to Florida in the 1890s. Conversation with Harry Harkness Flagler

[6]Flagler Family Records, File II, Flagler Collection

[7]Conversation with Harry Harkness Flagler

[8]From Flagler ledger on Mamaroneck property, Kenan Collection

[9]*New York Times*, February 10, 1924

[10]William B. Shaw, "John Dustin Archbold," in *Dictionary of American Biography*, I, 337

[11]*New York Times*, May 21, 1913

[12]John Moody and George K. Turner, "The Masters of Capital in America," in *McClure's Magazine*, XXXVI (March, 1911), 565

[13]*House Reports*, IX, 308

[14]John Moody, *Truth About the Trusts*, 119. See also C. M. Destler, "The Standard Oil, Child of the Erie Ring, 1868-1872," *Mississippi Valley Historical Review*, XXXIII (June, 1946), 100. Professor Destler maintains that the Standard Oil Trust was nothing but a gigantic offspring of the Erie ring, 1868-1872. Five of the nine trustees appointed had been connected with Jay Gould in the old Erie oil ring.

[15]Matthew Josephson, *The Robber Barons*, 277

[16]*House Reports*, IX, 311

[17]Allan Nevins, *John D. Rockefeller*, II, 60-61

[18]Harold U. Faulkner, *American Economic History*, 446-447

[19]*House Reports*, IX, 287

[20]*Ibid.*, 289

[21]*Ibid.*, 302-303

[22]Ida M. Tarbell, *History of the Standard Oil Company*, II, 139

[23]*House Reports*, IX, 298

[24]Allan Nevins, *John D. Rockefeller*, II, 131

[25]*House Reports*, IX, 768-790

[26]I. M. Tarbell, *History of the Standard Oil Company*, II, 139

[27]This decision was rendered in the case of State *ex rel.* Attorney General *vs.* Standard Oil of Ohio. See Ryan, *History of Ohio*, IV, 398

[28]Carl Wilkins, *History of the State of Ohio*, 212

[29]I. M. Tarbell, *History of the Standard Oil Company*, II, 151-152

[30]*Ibid.*, II, 356

[31]*Ibid.*, II, 266

[32]"The Standard Oil Melons," *The Literary Digest*, LXXV (October 28, 1922), 6. This has a good description of the "melon-cutting," as breaking up of Standard Oil Company was called.

Chapter 7. A Florida Honeymoon

[1]*New York Herald-Tribune*, June 6, 1883

[2]Conversations with Theodore Pomar, Anna Fremd Hadley, and Belle Dimick Enos

[3]*New York Times*, May 21, 1913

[4]*Ibid.*

[5]Conversation with Harry Harkness Flagler

[6]*Ibid.*

[7]G. W. Nichols, "Six Weeks in Florida," *Harper's Magazine*, XLI (October, 1870), 655

[8]*Ibid.*

[9]*Florida Dispatch* (Live Oak), July 3, 1878

[10]T. Frederick Davis, *History of Jacksonville*, 82

[11]*Ibid.*, 487

[12]Conversation with Harry Harkness Flagler

[13]Harry G. Cutler, *History of Florida*, I, 61

[14]*New York Herald-Tribune*, January 6, 1884

[15]*Ibid.*, February 24, 1884

[16]Clarissa Anderson Dimick to author, February 28, 1946

[17]St. Augustine, Florida, the first permanent settlement in the United States, was reached by Pedro Menéndez de Avilés in 1565. See Kathryn T. Abbey, *Florida, Land of Change*, 33-34

[18]Many Spanish explorers had visited Florida before Menéndez made his settlement at St. Augustine, the first being Ponce de León, who landed in Florida in April, 1513, and named the peninsula *Pascua Florida*, because it was discovered "in the time of the Feast of Flowers." See *Ibid.*, 6

[19]Sidney Walter Martin, *Florida During the Territorial Days*, 44

[20]Dorothy Dodd, ed., *Florida Becomes a State*, 426

[21]Rembert W. Patrick, *Florida Under Five Flags*, 79

[22]J. E. Ingraham, "The Story of the East Coast," *Picturesque Florida*, I (January, 1910), 3

[23]Edward King, "The Great South," *Scribner's Monthly*, IX (November, 1874), 3

[24]G. W. Nichols, "Six Weeks in Florida," *loc. cit.*, 661

[25]Branch Cabell and A. J. Hanna, *The St. Johns, A Parade of Diversities*, 239, 242

[26]*A Brief History of the Florida East Coast Railway*, 4

[27]*Florida Dispatch* (Live Oak), September 26, 1877

[28]J. T. Van Campen to author, March 2, 1946

[29]*A Brief History of the Florida East Coast Railway*, 5

[30]Rowland H. Rerick, *Memoirs of Florida*, II, 167

[31]*Ibid.*, 180

[32]R. H. Rerick, *Memoirs of Florida*, II, 187

[33]W. B. Hesseltine, *The South in American History*, 560-564

Chapter 8. Permanent Stakes in Florida

[1]Henry M. Flagler Diary, February 19, 1885, St. Augustine Historical Society Library.

[2]*Ibid.*, February 25, 1885

[3]J. T. Van Campen to author, March 2, 1946

[4]*Ibid.*

[5]Seavey later became manager of Flagler's hotels in St. Augustine, remaining in that position until March, 1894, when he resigned. *The Tatler of Society in Florida (St. Augustine)*, February 17, 1894

[6]*Florida Times-Union* (Jacksonville), January 13, 1888

[7]After Franklin W. Smith finished his Casa Monica in 1888, he operated it for only a short time. Flagler purchased this hotel in 1889, and for several years operated it independently from his others. He renamed it the Cordova. In 1894 he built a connection between this hotel and the Alcazar, and operated it in connection with the latter. William R. Kenan to author, March 8, 1946.

[8]R. H. Rerick, *Memoirs of Florida*, II, 201

[9]The *Observer* (Daytona Beach), January 4, 1936

[10]Henry M. Flagler Diary, March 27, 1885

[11]Clarissa Anderson Dimick to author, February 28, 1946. Dr. Anderson died in St. Augustine, December 1, 1924.

[12]Sworn statement to court by Andrew Anderson, 1923

[13]Flagler Diary, April 1, 1885

[14]Sworn statement to court by Andrew Anderson, 1923. Flagler visited in the Anderson home from time to time thereafter.

[15]Flagler Diary, April 22, 1885

[16]Henry M. Flagler to G. T. Atwood, June 9, 1885

[17]Henry M. Flagler to Andrew Anderson, June 18, 1885, Dimick Collection. The story is told that later Flagler tried to buy some property in Palatka in connection with his railroad which ran through East Palatka, but the Palatkans involved refused to sell it to him, because of their earlier treatment.

This story is perhaps true, though the author has not been able to authenticate it.

[18]Henry M. Flagler to Andrew Anderson, June 27, 1885

[19]*Ibid.*, June 30, 1885

[20]*Ibid.*, July 29, 1885

[21]*Ibid.*, July 16, 1885

[22]*Ibid.*, August 5, 1885

[23]Some sources state that Flagler sent Hastings and Carrère to Spain to study the architecture of that country, but this is untrue. They studied Spanish architecture, it is true, but from secondary sources. *Ibid.*, June-August, 1885

[24]Clarissa Anderson Dimick to author, February 28, 1946

[25]Sworn statement to court by Andrew Anderson, 1923

[26]*Ibid.*

[27]Diary of Henry M. Flagler, October 22-31, 1885

[28]*Ibid.*, December 2-17, 1885

[29]L. C. Frohman, "From the Florida East Coast Files," MS., 3

[30]Magnolia Springs later became Green Cove Springs

[31]*The Tatler*, January 21, 1893

[32]Louis Larson to Barron Bridges, undated letter in Florida Historical Society Files

[33]Printed Menu, January 10, 1888, St. Augustine Historical Society Library. The *Times-Union* gives the impression that the opening did not take place until January 12, but that was perhaps the day the newspaper reporter arrived on the scene. Several souvenir menus, dated January 10, 1888, for the formal opening dinner are in existence.

[34]Charles B. Reynolds, *Architecture of the Hotel Ponce de Leon*, 3-4. The Ponce de Leon set a new standard in American architecture. It gave Carrère and Hastings a place in the forefront of the profession. From that time the firm exercised a preeminent influence in its field. Among its works were the interior of the original Metropolitan Opera House, the New York Public Library, the Senate and House office buildings in Washington, D.C., the home of the Carnegie Institution of Washington, D.C. and the Memorial Ampitheater at Arlington, Virginia.

[35]*Ibid.*

[36]*Ibid.*, 5-6

[37]*Ibid.*

[38]*Florida Times-Union*, January 13, 1888

[39]Conversation with William R. Kenan, Jr.

[40]*Florida Times-Union*, January 28, 1893. The casino was destroyed by fire on January 24, 1893, but was rebuilt immediately, and was used until the hotel closed. The Alcazar stood idle for a long time, but was ultimately converted into town offices and the Lightner Museum. The Ponce de Leon Hotel became the main building of Flagler College.

[41]*Florida Times-Union*, January 16, 1893

[42]*The Tatler*, December 15, 1894. This building is no longer a hotel, and the connection between it and the Alcazar was removed.

[43]*The Tatler*, March 4, 1893

[44]Conversation with Amy McMillan

[45]*The Tatler*, February 6, 1892

[46]*Ibid.*, February 27, 1892

[47]*Ibid.*, March 25, 1893

[48]Conversation with T. V. Pomar

[49]Harry Harkness Flagler gave much time and money to the Symphony Society of New York, and later became its president. Leopold Damrosch organized the society, and was its first conductor; later his son, Walter Damrosch, succeeded him. Harry Flagler was also president of the Philharmonic Symphony Society of New York. Conversation with Harry Harkness Flagler.

[50]Henry M. Flagler to Andrew Anderson, August 19, 1896

[51]Conversation with William R. Kenan, Jr.

[52]Harry Harkness Flagler to author, November 26, 1945

[53]*Florida Times-Union*, March 17, 1890

[54]*St. Augustine Evening Record*, May 20,

1913

[55]*The Tatler*, February 3, 1900. About ten years before Flagler's death, the name was changed to Flagler Hospital; later a large sum of money was promised by the third Mrs. Flagler for a new plant, but she died in June 1916, before the new building became a reality; so the trustees of the estate gave $175,000 for the new hospital which bore his name. Conversation with William R. Kenan, Jr.

[56]J. E. Ingraham, "The Story of the East Coast," loc. cit., 4

Chapter 9.
Penetrating the Florida Frontier

[1]Speech by Scott Loftin, July 8, 1935, Florida East Coast Files

[2]Thirty pound rails weigh 30 pounds per yard

[3]E. S. Luther, "The Transformation of the Florida East Coast," *Banker's Magazine* (February, 1909), 259

[4]George M. Chapin, *Official Program, Key West Extension of the Florida East Coast Railway*, 5

[5]Edwin Lefèvre, "Flagler and Florida," in *Everybody's Magazine*, XXII (February, 1910), 176

[6]Conversation with the late Sims W. Rowley

[7]*Florida Times-Union*, March 1, 1892

[8]*A Brief History of the Florida East Coast and Associated Enterprises*, 12

[9]*Ibid.*, 10

[10]*Florida Times-Union*, April 22, 1888

[11]J. T. Van Campen to author, March 2, 1946

[12]*Florida Times-Union*, April 15, 1887

[13]Edwin Lefèvre, "Flagler and Florida," loc. cit., 171

[14]*The Tatler*, December 23, 1889

[15]*A Brief History of the Florida East Coast and Associated Enterprises*, 13

[16]*Weekly Floridian* (Tallahassee), June 4, 1890

[17]J. E. Ingraham, "The Story of the East Coast," in *Picturesque Florida*, I (January, 1910), 4

[18]*Weekly Floridian*, June 25, 1892

[19]*Florida Times-Union*, April 24, 1893

[20]J. T. Van Campen to author, March 2, 1946

[21]*Ibid.*

[22]Unidentified clipping, Welsh Scrapbook, Vol. 48, 6

[23]W. T. Travers, *History of Palm Beach*, 4

[24]*Palm Beach News* (Souvenir Edition), 1903. Lake Worth later became the name of a community several miles down the coast.

[25]*Palm Beach Post-Times*, November 17, 1940

[26]*A Brief History of the Florida East Coast and Associated Enterprises*, 4

[27]Conversations with J. Borman and T. V. Pomar

[28]*Florida Times-Union*, April 10, 1893

[29]*Miami Herald*, August 5, 1944

[30]*Ibid.*

[31]*Palm Beach Tropical Sun*, March 5, 1937

[32]Conversation with J. Borman

[33]*Miami Herald*, August 5, 1944

[34]*Florida Times-Union*, April 10, 1893

[35]*Florida East Coast Homeseeker*, June, 1916, 10

[36]J. W. Travers, *History of Palm Beach*, 6

[37]Conversation with Lillian Bradstreet

[38]It was condemned in 1928 and the frame structure was torn down soon thereafter. Conversation with J. Borman

[39]*Palm Beach News* (Souvenir Edition), 1936

[40]This building burned in 1925 but was rebuilt soon thereafter and made into one of the finest hotels in the world. The 'new' Breakers, located on the ocean shore in Palm Beach, remains an outstanding resort hotel. See William R. Kenan, Jr., *Incidents By the Way*, 81

Chapter 10. The City that Flagler Built

[1]Florida Press Association, *Bulletin*, March 22, 1901

[2]Harry Hargis, *Miami in Your Pocket*, 14

[3]Florida Press Association, *Bulletin*, March 22, 1901

[4]E. V. Blackman, *Miami and Dade County, Florida*, 59

[5]Harry G. Cutler, *History of Florida*, I, 396

[6]*Florida Times-Union*, December 29, 1894

[7]*Ibid.*, February 8, 1895

[8]*In Memoriam, Henry Morrison Flagler*, 12

[9]Harry G. Cutler, *History of Florida*, I, 396

[10]J. D. Ingraham to author, February 14, 1946

[11]Charles E. Nash, *The Magic City of Miami Beach*, 82

[12]*The Florida East Coast Homeseeker*, 9

[13]Conversation with William R. Kenan, Jr.

[14]Charter of Florida East Coast Railway, Florida East Coast Files, Jacksonville. The charter was amended on September 14, 1899, June 12, 1909, July 23, 1909, June 28, 1911, February 10, 1914, September 12, 1920, and September 10, 1924.

[15]*Orlando Sentinel-Star*, November 26, 1933

[16]Conversation with William R. Kenan, Jr. In 1915 the coal burners were changed to oil burners, and in 1939 the first Diesel-electric locomotive was acquired.

[17]John Sewell, *Memoirs and History of Miami, Florida*, 10. John and George Sewell were born in Hartwell, Georgia, and went to Florida in 1886.

[18]E. V. Blackman, *Miami and Dade County, Florida*, 21

[19]*The Florida East Coast Homeseeker*, 11

[20]E. V. Blackman, *Miami and Dade County, Florida*, 55. James E. Summers succeeded Reilly as mayor in 1900, and served until 1903. The other mayors of Miami during the Flagler era were John Sewell, Frank Wharton, and R. B. Smith

[21]Conversation with William R. Kenan, Jr.

[22]John Sewell, *Memoirs*, 8

[23]*Miami Metropolis*, January 22, 1897

[24]Agnew Welsh Scrapbook, #2, 26

[25]*Miami Metropolis*, January 15, 1897

[26]J. E. Ingraham, "The Story of the East Coast," *Picturesque Florida*, I (January, 1910), 5

[27]Agnew Welsh Scrapbook, #35, 59

[28]E. V. Blackman, *Miami*, 27

[29]First Presbyterian Church, Miami, 2.

Pamphlet in Kenan Collection

[30]*Miami Metropolis*, September 5, 1902

[31]*Miami Daily News*, May 12, 1946

[32]E. V. Blackman, *Miami*, 85

[33]John Sewell, *Memoirs*, 165. In 1912 Flagler offered to expend $300,000 in port improvements, if the government would appropriate a like amount. The offer was promptly accepted. *Florida Times-Union*, January 23, 1912.

[34]John Sewell, *Memoirs*, 156-157

[35]Agnew Welsh Scrapbook, #8, 24; #6, 26; also see *Miami Herald*, July 8, 1945

[36]George M. Chapin, *Official Program, Key West Extension of the Florida East Coast Railway*, 55. By 1948 Miami had grown to be Florida's largest city.

Chapter 11. Turbulent Years

[1]William R. Kenan, Jr. to author, July 10, 1946

[2]Flagler Yacht Ledger, Kenan Collection

[3]Henry M. Flagler to Andrew Anderson, August 21, 1896

[4]*Ibid.*, August 4, 1885

[5]A divorce case which involved two socially prominent New Yorkers.

[6]Shelton Testimony, Flagler Diorce Proceedings, August 12, 1901, Seventh Judicial Circuit, Miami, Florida

[7]*Ibid.*

[8]George G. Shelton to Andrew Anderson, October 25, 1895

[9]*Ibid.*

[10]Peterson Testimony, Flagler Divorce Proceedings, August 12, 1901, Seventh Judicial Circuit, Miami, Florida

[11]*Ibid.*

[12]George G. Shelton to Andrew Anderson, October 25, 1895

[13]Shelton Testimony, Flagler Divorce Proceedings, August 12, 1901, Seventh Judicial Circuit, Miami, Florida

[14]Henry M. Flagler to Andrew Anderson, May 20, 1896

[15]*Ibid.*

[16]*Ibid.*, May 30, 1896

[17]*Ibid.*, June 8, 1896

[18]Conversation with Harry Harkness Flagler

[19]Henry M. Flagler to Andrew Anderson, July 5, 1896

[20]*Ibid.*, June 17, 1896

[21]*Ibid.*, July 5, 1896

[22]Conversation with Harry Harkness Flagler

[23]Henry M. Flagler to Andrew Anderson, July 5, 1896

[24]Flagler always ended his letters to Dr. Anderson with this phrase, "With love to you and your good wife, I am, Affectionately yours, H. M. Flagler." See Dimick Collection for Flagler's correspondence with Dr. Anderson.

[25]Henry M. Flagler to Andrew Anderson, July 9, 1896

[26]*Ibid.*

[27]*Ibid.*, August 18, 1896

[28]*Ibid.*, August 28, 1896

[29]J. C. Salter to Andrew Anderson, October 24, 1896

[30]Henry M. Flagler to Andrew Anderson, November 3, 1896

[31]*Ibid.*, November 13, 1896

[32]Shelton Testimony, *Ibid.*

[33]Peterson Testimony, Flagler Divorce Proceedings, August 12, 1901, Seventh Judicial Circuit, Miami, Florida

[34]MacDonald Testimony, *Ibid.*

[35]*Ibid.*

[36]*Ibid.*

[37]Records from the Files of the New York Supreme Court, enclosed in Flagler Divorce Proceedings, August 12, 1901, Seventh Judicial Circuit, Miami, Florida

[38]Exhibit No. I, Divorce Proceedings, Flagler Divorce Proceedings, August 12, 1901, Seventh Judicial Circuit, Miami, Florida

[39]*Acts of Florida*, 119-120. The law was repealed in 1905.

[40]Conversation with Amy McMillan and A. B. Otwell

[41]*Ocala Banner*, May 31, 1901

[42]*Palmetto News*, May 27, 1901

[43]*Pensacola Journal*, May 28, 1901

[44]Florida Agricultural College was set up in 1884 in Lake City. The name was changed to the University of Florida in 1903, and it was moved to Gainesville, its present location, in the summer of 1906. See Bristol, MS., "The Buckman Act: Before and After," 2-25

[45]J. R. Parrott was also one of the trustees of the college, so it could have been that the gift came as a result of his friendship with Flagler. Flagler no doubt would have given $50,000 if the gymnasium had cost that much. See *Ibid.*

[46]Bill of Divorce, Flagler Divorce Proceedings, August 12, 1901, Seventh Judicial Circuit, Miami, Florida

[47]Flagler Divorce Proceedings, August 12, 1901, Seventh Judicial Circuit, Miami, Florida

[48]MacDonald Testimony, Flagler Divorce Proceedings, August 12, 1901, Seventh Judicial Circuit, Miami, Florida

[49]Flagler Testimony, *Ibid.*

[50]Ashley Testimony, *Ibid.*

[51]Final Decree, *Ibid.*

[52]*New York Times*, July 13, 1930.

Ida Alice Flagler's wealth had increased rapidly from 1901 to 1930, largely because of Standard Oil securities. She had no will and it was known that the money was to be divided among her relatives. This fact attracted the attention of persons, some of whom had an actual claim upon the money by their relationship, while the kinship of others was so remote as sometimes to be invisible to the eye of the law. A few of her distant cousins won awards from her estate before her death. The legal expense of defending the estate against the relatives was out of proportion to the actual expense of paying the claims allowed. A hearing in one case in which an annuity of $1,500 was recommended cost the estate

$17,000. The fees of those who were administering the estate also were large. In 1925 Cornelius Sullivan and the Guaranty Trust Company, who had acted for years as the committee of Mrs. Flagler's estate, received allowances of $7,000 each as commissioners and a special allowance of $30,000 each for the year. In the same year the care of dependent relatives came to $61,000, while Mrs. Flagler's maintenance had increased to $132,211.

The exact amount of Ida Alice Flagler's estate at the time of her death was $15,247,925. This sum was divided equally among her nearest of kin—two nephews and a grand niece.

This was a report made by Guaranty Trust Company as of March 16, 1930. See *New York Times*, March 17, 1930. A few weeks later the *New York Herald-Tribune* said the tax appraisers had filed a report showing her net estate to be worth $13,277,814.

[53] *Atlanta Journal*, August 22, 1901

[54] Her father was William Rand Kenan, and her mother Mary Hargrave, formerly of Chapel Hill, North Carolina. See W. R. Kenan, Jr., *Incidents by the Way*, 9-12

[55] Jessie Hargrave Kenan married Clisby Wise; Sarah Graham Kenan married Graham Kenan (a cousin); and William Rand Kenan, Jr., married Alice Pomroy. See *Ibid.*, 10

[56] *New York Tribune*, August 25, 1901

[57] *St. Augustine News*, March 22, 1891

[58] *New York Tribune*, August 25, 1901

[59] *Ibid.*

[60] *Palatka Times-Herald*, August 30, 1901

[61] Henry M. Flagler to Andrew Anderson, August 29, 1901

[62] Conversation with Katherine S. Lawson

[63] Conversation with Anna Fremd Hadley

[64] *New York Herald*, March 30, 1902

[65] *The Tatler*, March 21, 1903

[66] *New York Herald*, March 30, 1902

[67] *The Tatler*, March 21, 1903

[68] "Whitehall, Mr. Flagler's Residence at Palm Beach," *International Studio* (March, 1919), 11

[69] *Palm Beach Daily News* (Annual Historical Number), 1903, 6

[70] *Ibid.*

[71] *Palm Beach Daily News*, March 21, 1902

[72] *The Tatler*, March 20, 1897

[73] *Ibid.*, February 1, 1902

[74] Flagler was generous to Hamilton College in his will, perhaps because of the influence of Root, who was a loyal benefactor of that institution. Conversation with William R. Kenan, Jr.

[75] Conversation with Anna Fremd Hadley and Belle Dimick Enos

[76] *Ibid.*

[77] *Palm Beach Daily News*, February 3, 1909

Chapter 12. Flagler's Folly

[1] H. G. Cutler, *History of Florida*, I, 60

[2] Minutes of Trustees of the Internal Improvement Fund, Vol. IX, 295

[3] *Bartow Courier-Informant*, April 3, 1895

[4] *Daily* (Key West) *Florida Citizen*, September 11, 1895

[5] *San Mateo Item*, June 12, 1909

[6] Philip Jessup, *Elihu Root*, I, 47

[7] *St. Augustine Record*, October 13, 1904

[8] *Miami Metropolis*, February 2, 1905

[9] *Ibid.*, July 31, 1905

[10] *St. Augustine Record*, May 30, 1913

[11] *Florida Times-Union*, January 23, 1913

[12] J. W. Travers, *History of Palm Beach*, 7

[13] J. M. Rockwell, "Opening of the Over Sea Railway," *Collier's*, January 20, 1912

[14] E. V. Blackman, *Miami and Dade County*, 54

[15] J. M. Rockwell, "Opening of the Over Sea Railway," *loc. cit.*

[16] G. M. Chapin, *Official Program Key West Extension*, 13

[17] *St. Augustine Record*, January 22, 1912

[18] *Miami Metropolis*, March 9, 1906

[19] *Palm Beach News*, May 17, 1907

[20] G. M. Chapin, *Official Program Key West Extension*, 17

[21]*Announcement of Key West Extension*, 3

[22]Conversation with William R. Kenan, Jr.

[23]*Announcement of Key West Extension*, 2

[24]*Florida Times-Union*, January 23, 1912

[25]H. G. Cutler, *History of Florida*, I, 69

[26]*Palm Beach Daily News*, May 17, 1907

[27]*St. Augustine Record*, January 22, 1912

[28]S. W. Martin, "The Second Discovery of Florida," (Master's Thesis, University of Georgia, 1935), 45

[29]Pan-American *Bulletin* (February, 1912), 216

[30]E. S. Luther, "The Transformation of the Florida East Coast," *Banker's Magazine* (February, 1909), 262

[31]J. M. Rockwell, "Opening of the Over Sea Railway," *loc. cit.*

[32]G. M. Chapin, *Official Program Key West Extension*, 15

[33]*Ibid.*, 15

[34]Unidentified clipping, Kenan Collection

[35]G. M. Chapin, *Official Key West Extension*, 12

[36]*Palm Beach Daily News*, February 4, 1909

[37]*Savannah* (Georgia) *Morning News*, January 22, 1912

[38]Unidentified clipping, Kenan Collection

[39]*Florida Times-Union*, January 23, 1912

[40]*Miami Herald*, January 26, 1912

[41]*Florida Times-Union*, January 23, 1912

[42]*Miami Herald*, January 22, 1912

[43]*Florida Times-Union*, January 23, 1912

[44]*Miami Daily News*, March 6, 1938

Chapter 13. The Flagler System

[1]S. Price Gilbert to author, October 2, 1945

[2]*Florida Times-Union*, January 23, 1912

[3]Conversation with William R. Kenan, Jr.

[4]*St. Augustine Record*, May 30, 1913

[5]William R. Kenan, *Incidents By the Way*, 30-50

[6]He served as President of the Florida East Coast Railway and Hotel Companies

[7]E. S. Luther, "The Transformation of the Florida East Coast," *Banker's Magazine (February, 1909)*, 263

[8]*Miami Metropolis*, February 11, 1898

[9]*The Tatler*, January 14, 1899

[10]*Miami Metropolis*, February 11, 1898

[11]Conversation with William R. Kenan, Jr.

[12]*Ibid.* The steamship line was run by the Atlantic Coast Line Railroad, which bought out the Plant System

[13]*St. Augustine Record*, May 30, 1913

[14]*Florida Times-Union*, April 24, 1893

[15]H. G. Cutler, *History of Florida*, I, 67

[16]Conversation with William R. Kenan, Jr.

[17]*History of the Florida East Coast*, 25. The Florida East Coast Railway had plans for the construction of a cutoff to connect the main line at Fort Pierce with the Okeechobee division at a point ten miles north of Port Mayaca. The distance was only 30 miles and the cost was over $1,000,000, but it would shorten the distance considerably from the Everglades area to Jacksonville. Conversation with William R. Kenan, Jr.

[18]Conversation with E. D. Anthony

[19]Milton S. Heath, "Analysis of the Florida East Coast Railway," MS., 2

[20]R. H. Rerick, *Memoirs of Florida*, II, 188

[21]*Minutes of the Trustees of the Internal Improvement Fund*, V, 265

[22]*Twenty-seventh Biennial Report of the Department of Agriculture of the State of Florida, Land and Field Note Divisions*, July 1, 1942, 21

[23]Conversation with E. D. Anthony

[24]*The Tatler*, January 18, 1896

[25]H. G. Cutler, *History of Florida*, III, 370

[26]*The Tatler*, January 18, 1896

[27]*Florida East Coast Homeseeker*, 1897, 12

[28]*Miami Herald*, November 16, 1941

[29]H. G. Cutler, *History of Florida*, I, 67

[30]*Florida East Coast Homeseeker*, 1895, 6

[31]After the storm in 1935 the overseas extension was badly wrecked, and the Key West base was moved to Port Everglades on the Florida mainland, from which point the same schedule was operated to Havana. With the coming of World War II the Navy Department took over the ferries as mine sweepers for the duration.

Conversation with William R. Kenan, Jr.
[32]Florida East Coast Files, St. Augustine
[33]Henry Morrison Flagler Museum Collection

Chapter 14. A Full Life

[1]Conversation with George Conway
[2]Conversation with the Carl Fremds and the George Conways, all of whom were personal servants of the Flaglers
[3]Fremd died in 1943. Conversation with Anna Fremd Hadley
[4]J. W. Tavers, *History of Palm Beach*, 6
[5]Conversation with George Conway
[6]*New York Times*, April 2, 1913
[7]*Savannah Morning News*, May 10, 1913
[8]*St. Augustine Record*, May 30, 1913
[9]The body of Flagler's first wife, Mary Harkness Flagler, has since been placed in the mausoleum
[10]*St. Augustine Record*, May 23, 1913
[11]*Atlanta Journal*, May 23, 1913
[12]"Last Will and Testament of Henry M. Flagler," Florida Historical Society Collections
[13]The trusteeship ended after Mrs. Flagler's death
[14]The will stated that Stetson University was to receive $60,000 and Florida Agricultural College (later the University of Florida) was to receive $20,000 at Flagler's death, unless it was paid prior to that time. The University of Florida got Mary Lily Flagler's $20,000 in 1903, and Stetson received her grant several years later.
[15]*New York Times*, May 28, 1913
[16]Mary Lily Flagler did not live long to enjoy the vast fortune which was left her. She died suddenly on July 27, 1917, after having married, during the preceding December, Robert Worth Bingham, Louisville, Kentucky, publisher, an acquaintance of long standing. Only six weeks before her death, she added a codicil to her will leaving $5,000,000 to her husband. The bulk of her fortune, however, went back into a trust fund from which payments were made

to the various enterprises. Bingham contributed a great deal of money to the Democratic campaign in 1918, and was later sent to England as ambassador. Conversation with William R. Kenan, Jr.
[17]Unidentified clipping, June 23, 1893, Marcotte Scrapbook
[18]Conversation with the late Sims W. Rowley
[19]*St. Augustine Record*, May 30, 1913
[20]Henry M. Flagler to T. T. Reese, April 19, 1906, Kenan Collection
[21]Conversation with T. V. Pomar
[22]*Florida Times-Union*, December 26, 1894
[23]*Ibid.*, January 4, 1895
[24]Conversation with Harry Harkness Flagler
[25]Henry M. Flagler to Andrew Anderson, August 18, 1896, Dimick Collection
[26]Henry M. Flagler Diary, December 12, 1904
[27]At the time United States senators were elected by the various state legislatures
[28]*Ocala Banner*, June 7, 1901
[29]*Pensacola Journal*, June 1, 1901
[30]*Miami Metropolis*, June 16, 1899
[31]Edward C. Williamson, MS., Wilkinson Call, A Pioneer in Progressive Democracy, 191
[32]Conversation with E. D. Anthony
[33]Edwin Lefèvre, "Flagler in Florida," *Everybody's Magazine* (February, 1910), 178
[34]*Ibid.*, 179
[35]*Bartow Courier-Informant*, December 16, 1896
[37]Conversation with E. D. Anthony
[38]Conversation with Harry Harkness Flagler
[38]Edwin Lefèvre, "Flagler in Florida," *Everybody's Magazine* (February, 1910)

Bibliography
Books

Abbey, Kathryn Trimmer, *Florida, Land of Change*. Chapel Hill: The University of North Carolina Press, 1941

Aldrick, Lewis Cass, *History of Erie County*. Syracuse, New York: D. Mason and Company, 1889

Allen, William H., *Rockefeller, Giant, Dwarf, Symbol*. New York: Institute for Public Service, 1930

Asbury, Herbert, *The Golden Flood*, New York: Alfred A. Knopf, 1942

Blackman, E. V., *Miami and Dade County, Florida*. Washington: Victor Rainbolt Publisher, 1921

Browne, Jefferson B., *Key West, the Old and the New*. St. Augustine: The Record Company, 1912

Burns, Arthur Robert, *Trusts and Economic Control*. New York: McGraw-Hill Company, 1936

Burton, Thomas E., *John Sherman*. New York: Houghton, Mifflin and Company, 1906

Butterfield, C. W., *History of Seneca County*. Sandusky: D. Campbell and Sons, 1848

Cabell, Branch, and Hanna, A. J., *The St. Johns, A Parade of Diversities*. New York: Farrar and Rinehart, Incorporated, 1943

Cutler, Harry Gardiner, *History of Florida, Past and Present*. Three vols. Chicago: Lewis Publishing Company, 1923

Dau, Frederick W., *Florida, Old and New*. New York: G. P. Putnam's Sons, 1934

Davis, Thomas Frederick, *History of Jacksonville, Florida and Vicinity, 1513 to 1924*. Jacksonville: Florida Historical Society, 1925

Dodd, Dorothy, ed., *Florida Becomes a State*. Tallahassee: Florida Centennial Commission, 1945

Faris, W. W., *First Presbyterian Church, Miami: Some Memorials of Early Days*, 1918

Faulkner, Harold Underwood, *American Economic History*, Fifth Edition. New York: Harper and Brothers, 1943

Flynn, John T., *God's Gold, The Story of Rockefeller and His Times*. New York: Harcourt, Brace and Company, 1932

Giddens, Paul H., *The Birth of the Oil Industry*. New York: The Macmillan Company, 1938

Gilbert, S. Price, *A Georgia Lawyer, His Observations and Public Service*. Athens: University of Georgia Press, 1946

Hacker, Louis M., and Kendrick, Benjamin B., *The United States Since 1865*. Third Edition. New York: F. S. Crofts and Co., 1939

Hargis, Harry, *Miami in Your Pocket*. Miami: Pan American Printing Corporation, 1945

Jessup, Philip C., *Elihu Root*. Two vols. New York: Dodd, Mead, and Company, 1938

Johnson, Allen, and Malone, Dumas, editors, *Dictionary of American Biography*. I, New York: Charles Scribner's Sons, 1928-1937. Twenty vols.

Josephson, Matthew, *The Robber Barons, The Great American Capitalists, 1861-1901*. New York: Harcourt, Brace and Company, 1934

Kenan, William R., Jr., *Incidents by the Way, Lifetime Recollections and Reflections*. Lockport, New York: Privately Printed, 1946

Lawson, Thomas W., *Frenzied Finance*, Vol. I. New York: Ridgeway-Thayer Company, 1906

Leonard, John W., ed., *Men of America*. A Biographical Dictionary of Contemporaries. New York: Lewis R. Hamersly and Company, 1908

Lloyd, Henry Demarest, *Wealth Against Commonwealth*. New York: Harper and Brothers Publishers, 1894

Martin, Frederick T., *The Passing of the Idle Rich*. Doubleday, Page and Company, 1912

Martin, Sidney Walter, *Florida During the Territorial Days*. Athens: The University of Georgia Press, 1944

Mills, James Cooke, *History of Saginaw County, Michigan*, Vol. I. Saginaw: Seemann and Peters, 1918

Montague, Gilbert Holland, *The Rise and Progress of the Standard Oil Company*. New York and London: Harper and Brothers, 1903

Moody, John, *Truth About Trusts*. New York: Moody Publishing Company, 1904

Nash, Charles Edgar, *The Magic of Miami Beach*. Philadelphia: David McKay Company, 1938

Nevins, Allan, *The Emergence of Modern America*. New York: The Macmillan Company, 1927

_____, *John D. Rockefeller: the Heroic Age of American Enterprise*. Two vols. New York: Charles Scribner's Sons, 1940

Patrick, Rembert W., *Florida Under Five Flags*. Gainesville: University of Florida Press, 1945

Pieke, H. L., *History of Erie County, Ohio*, Two vols. Cleveland: Penton Press Company, 1925

Post, Charles Asa, *Doans Corners and the City Four Miles West. With a Glance at Cuyohoga County and the Western Reserve*. Cleveland: Caxton Company, 1930

Randall and Ryans, *History of Ohio*, Four vols. New York: Century History Company, 1912

Rerick, Rowland H., *Memoirs of Florida*, Two vols. Atlanta, Georgia: Southern Historical Association, 1902

Ryan, Daniel J., *History of Ohio*, Four vols. New York: Century History Company, 1912

Sewell, John, *Memoirs and History of Miami, Florida*. Miami: The Franklin Press, 1933

Tarbell, Ida M., *The History of the Standard Oil Company*, Two vols. New York: McClure, Phillips and Company, 1904

Travers, J. Wadsworth, *History of Palm Beach*. Palm Beach: Privately Printed, 1927

Tuttle, Charles Richard, *General History of the State of Michigan*. Detroit: Tyler and Company, 1873

Upton, Harriet Taylor, *History of the Western Reserve*, Three vols. New York: Lewis Publishing Company, 1910

Van Tassil, C. S., *Book of Ohio*, Two vols. Toledo, Ohio: B. F. Wade Printing Company, 1901

Wilkins, Carl, *History of the State of Ohio*, Five vols. Ohio State Archeological Society, 1843

Williams, W. W., *History of the Firelands*, comprising Huron and Erie counties, Ohio. Cleveland: Leader Printing Company, 1879

_____, *History of Huron County*, Two vols. Chicago: S. J. Clarke Publishing Company, 1909

Wilson, Ella Grant, *Famous Old Euclid Avenue*, Two vols. Privately Printed, 1937

Winkleman, B. F., *John D. Rockefeller*. Philadelphia: Universal Book and Bible House, 1937

Winkler, John K. *John D., A Portrait in Oils*. New York: The Vanguard Press, 1929

Documents

Acts and Resolutions Adopted by the Legislature of Florida at its Fourth Regular Session Under the Constitution of A.D. 1885. Tallahassee, Florida: Privately Printed, 1893

Acts and Resolutions Adopted by the Legislature of Florida at its Eighth Regular Session, April 2 to May 31, 1901, Under the Constitution of A.D. 1885. Tallahassee, Florida: Privately Printed, 1901

Divorce Proceedings of the Henry M. Flagler Complaintant vs. Ida A. Flagler Defendant, Divorce Case. In the Circuit Court, 7th Judicial Circuit of Florida, in and for Dade County. At Titusville, Florida, August 12, 1901 (unpublished)

House Journal. Florida, 1901

Minutes of the Board of Trustees Internal Improvement Fund of the State of Florida. Twenty-four vols. Tallahassee, Florida: Privately Printed, 1904. IV, V, VI

Poor's Manual, Railroads of the United States. New York, New York: Privately Printed, Vol. 22, 1889; Vol. 23, 1890; Vol. 25, 1892; Vol. 28, 1895; Vol. 33, 1900; Vol. 46, 1913

Senate Journal. Florida, 1901

The Reports of Committees of the House of Representatives for the First Session of the Fiftieth Congress. 1887-1888. Eleven volumes. Washington, D.C.: Government Printing Office, 1888. IX

Twenty-seventh Biennial Report of the Department of Agriculture of the State of Florida, Land and Field Note Division. Tallahassee, Florida: July 1, 1942

Manuscript Collections

Note that primary materials noted above may no longer be housed in their original depositories.

Anderson Collection. Contains nearly a hundred letters, mostly personal; Henry M. Flagler to Andrew Anderson; J. C. Salter to Andrew Anderson; George G. Shelton to Andrew Anderson. Sworn statement about facts concerning Henry M. Flagler by Andrew Anderson in 1923. Owned by St. Augustine Historical Society, Restricted Collection.

Florida Historical Society Library Collection, St. Augustine, Contains: Letters, clippings, manuscripts, and last will and testament of Henry M. Flagler.

Flagler Collection. Consists chiefly of family records and newspaper clippings. Biographical collection, St. Augustine Historical Society.

Florida East Coast Railway Collection, Jacksonville, Florida. Includes: corporate history, Florida East Coast Railway; Charter of the Florida East Coast; and newspaper clippings, pamphlets, etc.

Kenan Collection. Includes: Newspapers, magazines, pictures, two ledgers (one on Yacht *Alicia* and one on Mamaroneck property)

St. Augustine Historical Society Library Collection. Scrapbook kept by Captain Henry Marcotte, *Florida Times-Union* correspondence, 1884-1893

Camden Collection. Contains several dozen letters from J. N. Camden to Henry M. Flagler; in library of West Virginia University, Morgantown, West Virginia.

Martin Collection. Private correspondence of the author from the following persons: Philip C. Jessup, S. Price Gilbert, Harry Harkness Flagler, James P. Martin, Mrs. Katherine S. Lawson, William R. Kenan, Jr., James D. Ingraham, Paul H. Giddens, and Mrs. Clarissa Anderson Dimick

Smith Collection, Duke University, Durham, North Carolina. Several letters written by Flagler to E. C. Smith in Raleigh, North Carolina

Henry Morrison Flagler Museum Collection

Newspapers

The *Atlanta Journal.* Scattered copies of 1901, 1913, and 1914

Bellevue Gazette, May 22, 1913

The *Cleveland Herald.* Scattered copies of 1872 and 1873

Cleveland Leader. Complete files 1866 through 1913

Cleveland Plain Dealer. Broken files of 1913

The *Courier-Informant* (Bartow, Florida). Files 1893 through 1912

Daily (Key West) *Florida Citizen,* September 11, 1895

The *Everglades News* (Canal Point, Florida), June 1, 1945

Florida Times-Union (Jacksonville, Florida). Complete files of 1885 through 1896. Also broken files of 1906, 1910, 1912, and 1941

Fostoria (Ohio) *Daily News.* Scattered copies of 1913 and 1941

Lake Worth News. Broken files of 1896-1898, 1900-1903

Marine Journal. December 26, 1914

Miami Daily News. Scattered copies of 1938 and 1945

Miami Herald. Scattered copies of 1911-1912, 1944-1945

The *Miami Metropolis.* Complete files from 1896 through 1906, 1913

New York Herald-Tribune. Broken files of 1872, 1884-1885, 1894, 1901-1902, 1906, 1913, and 1930

New York Times. Scattered copies of 1883, 1913, 1924, and 1930

The *Observer* (Daytona Beach, Florida*),* January 4, 1936

Ocala Banner, 1901, 1913

Oil City Daily Derrick. Complete files of 1877-1879

Orlando Sentinel-Star. January 2, 1938

Palatka Times-Herald. Broken files of 1901-1902, 1904

Palm Beach Daily News. This was a seasonal newspaper. Files of 1898-1910. Also the Historical Edition for 1936 and a souvenir number for 1903

Palm Beach Post-Times, November 17, 1940

Pensacola Journal, 1901-1902

Pittsburgh Daily Post, 1879

San Mateo Item, June 12, 1909

Savannah (Georgia) *Morning News.* Scattered copies of 1912-1913

St. Augustine Evening Record. Scattered copies of 1899-1900 and 1913. The *Daily Herald* became the *Evening Record* on September 1, 1899. Later became the *Record*

St. Augustine Record, March 17, 1940

St. Augustine Weekly News. Scattered copies of 1889-1890

The Tatler of Society in Florida (St. Augustine, Florida), January 9, 1892 through March 30, 1901. This publication, edited by Anna M. Marcotte, was a society sheet published 12 weeks during each winter season.

Tropical Sun (West Palm Beach, Florida). Scattered copies of 1896, March 5, 1937

Weekly Floridian (Tallahassee, Florida). Broken files of 1888, 1891-1893

Pamphlets and Booklets

A Brief History of the Florida East Coast Railway and Associated Enterprises. St. Augustine: The Record Company, 1936

Announcement of Key West Extension, opened January 22, 1912. Privately printed pamphlet, 1912

Chaplin, George M., *Official Program, Key West Extension of the Florida East Coast Railway.* St. Augustine: The Record Company, 1912

Cleveland City Directory (Privately printed), 1880-1881

Florida East Coast Homeseeker, St. Augustine: January, 1897

Florida Press Association Bulletin. Miami: March 22, 1901

In Memorium Henry Morrison Flagler. The Matthews-Northrop Works: New York, 1914

Official Program, Centennial of Fostoria. (Privately printed), 1941

Reynolds, Charles B., *Architecture of the Hotel Ponce de Leon.* (Privately printed), no date

Western Reserve Historical Society Publication. Cleveland, Ohio. October, 1920. (No. 102)

Periodicals

Destler, Chester McArthur, "The Standard Oil, Child of the Erie Ring, 1868-1872. Six Contracts and a Letter," in *Mississippi Valley Historical Review.* XXXIII, No. 1 (June, 1946), 89-114

Firelands Pioneer, Firelands Historical Society, Norwalk: American Publishing Co., Vol. XIII, June, 1916; XXII, June, 1921; Vol. XX, Jan., 1920

"Florida East Coast," *Locomotive Engineers Journal*, Vol. 69 (October, 1935), 726-727

"He Made Florida," *Literary Digest*, XLVI (May 31, 1913), 1240-1242

Ingraham, J. E., "The Story of the East Coast," *Picturesque Florida*, I (January, 1910), 3-7

Kellogg, Frank B., "Results of the Standard Oil Decision," *Review of Reviews*, XLV (June, 1912), 728-730

Kennedy, James H., "Stephen Vanderburg Harkness," *Magazine of Western History*, IX (November, 1888), 288-292

"Key West and Cuba," *Bulletin of the Pan American Union*, XXXIV (February, 1912), 212-222

King, Edward, "The Great South," *Scribner's Monthly*, IX (November, 1874), 1-31

Latham, Thomas W., "Revelations of an Old Account Book," *Firelands Pioneer*, XXII (January, 1921), 133-138

Lefèvre, Edwin, "Flagler and Florida," *Everybody's Magazine*, XXII (February, (1910), 168-186

Luther, E. S., "The Transformation of the Florida East Coast," *Banker's Magazine* (February, 1909), 259-264

Moffett, Samuel E., "Henry Morrison Flagler," *The Cosmopolitan*, XXXIII (August, 1902), 416-419

Montague, Gilbert H., "The Rise and Supremacy of the Standard Oil Company," *The Quarterly Journal of Economics*, XVI (February, 1902), 265-292

_____, "The Later History of the Standard Oil Company," *The Quarterly Journal of Economics*, XVII (February, 1903), 291-325

Moody, John and Turner, George K., "The Masters of Capital in America," *McClure's Magazine*, XXXVI (March, 1911), 564-577

Nichols, George Ward, "Six Weeks in Florida," in *Harper's Magazine*, XLI (October, 1870), 655-667

"No One-man Ownership in Standard Oil," *The Literary Digest*, LXXVI (January 13, 1923), 73

Rockefeller, John D., "Some Random Reminiscences of Men and Events," *The World's Work*, XVII (November, 1908), 10878-10894. (March, 1909), 11340-11355

Rockwell, J. M., "Opening of the Over Sea Railway to Key West," *Collier's*, XLVIII (January 20, 1912), 16-17

"Sketch of Henry M. Flagler," *The Outlook*, (May 31, 1913), 231-232

Tarbell, Ida M., "The Rise of the Standard Oil Company," *McClure's Magazine*, XX (December, 1902), 115-128

_____, "The Oil War of 1872," *loc. cit.*, (January, 1903) 248-260

_____, "An Unholy Alliance," *loc. cit.*, (February, 1903) 390-403

_____, "The Price of Trust Building," *loc. cit.*, (March, 1903), 493-508

_____, "Defeat of the Pennsylvania," *loc cit.*, (April, 1903), 606-621

"The Standard Oil Decision," *The Nation*, Vol. 89 (November 25, 1909), 502-503

"The Standard Oil Melons," *The Literary Digest*, LXXV (October 28, 1922), 5-6

"Whitehall, Mr. Flagler's Residence at Palm Beach," *International Studio*, XL (March, 1919), 11-12

Unpublished Works

Anonymous, "Life of Stephen V. Harkness." (A short manuscript in Western Reserve Historical Society Library, Cleveland, Ohio)

Bristol, L. M., "The Buckman Act: Before and After." (Unpublished manuscript: University of Florida), 1946

Frohman, L. C., "From the Florida East Coast Files." (Unpublished manuscript: St. Augustine), 1928

Heath, Milton S., "Analysis of the Florida East Coast Railway." (Unpublished manuscript: privately owned), 1933

McGuire, Robert E., "My Family." (Unpublished manuscript: Florida Historical Society Library), 1940

Martin, S. Walter, "The Second Discovery of Florida." (Unpublished thesis, University of Georgia), 1935

Williamson, Edward C., "Wilkinson Call: A Pioneer in Progressive Democracy." Gainesville, Florida. (Unpublished thesis: University of Florida), 1946

Index

*Photographic
Credits*

Henry Flagler, Visionary of the Gilded Age

Author's Acknowledgements

To
Clare Philips Martin

Many persons made contributions to this study for which the author was deeply indebted. They included William R. Kenan, Jr., Flagler's brother-in-law; Harry Harkness Flagler, Henry Morrison Flagler's only son; and Mrs. Clarissa Anderson Dimick, close friend of the family.

In addition, Professors E. Merton Coulter, University of Georgia; Allan Nevins, Columbia University; and Robert S. Cotterill, Florida State University, gave their critical and constructive criticism. Special acknowledgement was also made to Julien C. Yonge, University of Florida; Mrs. Jessie D. Wynn; and Mrs. Katherine S. Lawson, for their help in locating much of the material on Flagler. Also assisting in the undertaking were: Mrs. Jean Adams, E. D. Anthony, Joseph Borman, Mrs. Lillian Bradstreet, Louis Clarke, George Conway, Mrs. Ida Cross, Dorothy Dodd, Mrs. Bell Enos, Clyde E. Feuchter, Carl Fremd, Paul H. Giddens, Harris Gillespie, Mrs. Anna Hadley, Nina Hawkins, Fred M. Hopkins, J. D. Ingraham, Mrs. Alberta Johnson, Mrs. Virginia Jordan, C. J. King, Scott Loftin, Harvey Lopez, Amy McMillan, James P. Martin, Horace Montgomery, Joanne Newman, James M. Owens, Ruby Pierce, Theodore Pomar, Theodore Pratt, Mrs. Isabel Rath, Sims W. Rowley, Donna L. Root, Mrs. Ruth Tebeau, J. Chal Vinson, and Agnew Welsh.

Financial assistance for the study which led to the book was received through the office of George H. Boyd, then Director of Research at the University of Georgia, from funds made available jointly by the Carnegie Foundation and the University; and also through the office of William M. Crane, then University of Georgia Alumni Secretary, from the M. G. Michael Memorial Fund.

Lastly, to the friends and associates who gave encouragement all along the way, the author expressed his indebtedness.

Sidney Walter Martin

Other Books in the Southern Pioneer Series include:

An Uncommon Guide to Florida, A Resident's Guide to the Real Florida. Travel the byways of a remarkable state to learn about Florida's unusual, exceptional, and uncommon people and places.
ISBN 0-9631241-9-6 $16.95

Review Comments

"This study of Henry M. Flagler should receive widespread popular approval. It is written in a lively and engaging style; it is scholarly and unbiased; it gives the complete story of this colorful businessman's life, and naturally his empire-building in Florida stands out most boldly. Dr. Martin has written an important book."
— E. M. Coulter

"A much needed study, Flagler and his Florida activities are here rescued from the legend and folklore already enveloping them.... Well written for general reading as well as documented for serious students..."
— Charlton W. Tebeau

"Mr. Martin's portrait of the Florida empire builder illuminates a gaudy phase of Southern history..."
— C. Vann Woodward

America's First City, St. Augustine's Historic Neighborhoods. Learn about the history and architecture of one of America's most interesting cities.
ISBN 0-9631241-8-8 $16.95
Especially for younger readers
Henry Flagler, Builder of Florida
ISBN 0-9631241-3-7 $9.95
Marjorie Kinnan Rawlings and the Florida Crackers
ISBN 0-9631241-5-3 $14.95
Jacqueline Cochran, America's Fearless Aviator
ISBN 0-9631241-6-1 $14.95